GATHERING ISRAEL
THE JOURNEY OF TWO CONVERTS

BY MICHAEL MORTON & JOHN WUDEL

CHRISTMAS 2016

DEAR NICK,

THANK YOU FOR TAKING SUCH
GOOD CARE OF NANCE. SHE
THINKS A GREAT DEAL OF YOU.
HAVE A JOYOUS CHRISTMAS

YOUR FRIEND

Michael

Critical Acclaim For Gathering Israel

"Gathering Israel is loaded with interesting stories and experiences that are full of heart and reveal lovely stories of conversion."

T.C. Christensen
Writer, Director, Producer
The Cokeville Miracle, Ephraim's Rescue, 17 Miracles

"Thanks, John and Michael! I pray for your message to reach those who have ears to hear."

Billy Dean
Award Winning Country Music Singer & Songwriter
Billy The Kid, Somewhere In My Broken Heart, Let Them Be Little

What Readers Are Saying........

"I laughed, I cried, I felt the Spirit throughout....I love this book!"
Anne R. - Mother of 3

"Readers of Gathering Israel will be delighted to read this well-written narrative about Michael and John. Their separate and unrelated journeys eventually lead each to embrace membership in the Church of Jesus Christ of Latter-day Saints, and then come together to form a strong friendship. I found this to be a wonderful and honest account of two remarkable individuals."
Craig Linford - Father of 7, Grandfather of 12

What Readers Are Saying Continued........

"This book is a mesmerizing story of hope and faith. It is a journey that people of all faiths will want to read. I want to give this to my kids."

Mary D. - Mother of 4, Grandmother of 6

"Gathering Israel is an insight into the details of how The Church of Jesus Christ of Latter-day Saints is designed to exalt the human family. The experiences of these two men brought to mind the importance of the revelation from God that I have received in my own life. It is their testimony that God our Father loves us. He will do all that we can accept to give us joy and happiness in this life and the life to come."

Wayne Budge - Father of 7, Grandfather of 23

"I have attended several of Michael's firesides and each is a unique experience where I learned something new and felt the Spirit of the Lord."

Amos Abplanalp - Father of 5

"We are all on our own journey through life, each struggling to find our way. Reading about John and Michael's journey and seeing God's hand in their lives, helped me to recognize God's hand in my life. Their story about faith in God and friendship is heartwarming and inspiring."

Kristy F. - Mother of 4

"In the Gathering Israel book, I see Moroni's prophesy being fulfilled that the Book of Mormon shall come forth to convince the Jews and the Gentiles that Jesus is the Christ."

Ron Mann - Father of 9, Grandfather of 43

GATHERING ISRAEL
THE JOURNEY OF TWO CONVERTS

BY MICHAEL MORTON & JOHN WUDEL

Dedication

We dedicate this book to all those who recognize the value of faith, and who love and treasure the truth as to the purpose of this life......

Acknowledgements

Special thanks to...............

(From Michael)

I wish to express how grateful I am to my wonderful mother and father, my daughters Sarah and Rachel, my brothers, aunts, uncles, nephews, nieces, cousins, friends, my Thunder Mountain Ward family, the ward missionaries who taught me, my Gospel Doctrine teachers, my fellow workers in the Mesa Arizona Temple Baptistery and to all those who have been an inspiration to me throughout my life.

(From John)

I'm deeply grateful for my wonderful parents, my big brother Jim, my amazing eternal one and only Nanci, my faithful children, Tricia, Robyn, David, and Johny and their wonderful spouses: Bret, Jason, Amy, Corinne and my 16 remarkable grandchildren, Brayden, Rebekah, Gavin, Emily, Brinkley, Blake, Summer, Jenna, Kate, Nichole, Sam, Thomas, Alexa, Jane, Will, and Josh.

Acknowledgements Continued

(From Michael and John)
Thank you to all those who are mentioned in this book and have helped make this book possible. We are deeply grateful for your contributions. We wish to especially thank: Evelyn (Evie Clair) for her wonderful voice and musical ability that has added so much to Michael's firesides; Hillary Abplanalp, for creating our website and helping us to publish this book; Rebekah Baird, (John and Nanci's granddaughter), for her excellent photography skills and creative help in assisting us in collecting the pictures that appear in this book.

The following people have encouraged, inspired and contributed valuable insights to help bring this book to print:

Amos and Hillary Abplanalp, Sarah Baxter, Wayne Budge, T.C. and Katy Christensen, Billy Dean, Dean and Sheila Dutton, Lareme and Dawn Fessler, Kristy and Clint Fincher, Dan Gilchrist, Cory and Mindy Holman, Eric and Susan Jensen, Craig and Tina Linford, David and Paige Reeb, Jason Rencher, Joanne Russell, Ken Russell, Lee and Martha Watkins, Jack and Jeannie Welch, Sam and Cherri Woodruff, David Wudel, Nanci Wudel, and Cathy Zufelt.

GATHERING ISRAEL
TABLE OF CONTENTS

GATHERING ISRAEL
TABLE OF CONTENTS
CONTINUED

<u>Introduction</u>

The cover of this book, **Gathering Israel**, is symbolic of the present condition of this world.

The darkness represents the spiritual darkness that covers the earth.

The burst of light represents the restoration of the Gospel of Jesus Christ, the coming of living prophets, modern day apostles, and the full truth being restored to the earth. Jesus Christ is the light, the truth, and the life of this world.

The heavenly swirls depict God working His miracles to gather back covenant Israel in preparation for the return of the Messiah in these last days.

We have a God that is a perfect Father. He loves all of His children the same, no matter who they are: Jew, Hindu, Muslim, Christian, Buddhist, Agnostic or Atheist. He has a plan that if we follow it, will bring us all back home from where we came. It is our choice, as God will force no man to Heaven.

The gathering of Israel is God working His miracles among all of His children. It includes the Jews returning to their promised land to form the State of Israel as well as the tens of thousands of missionaries searching for those who desire the truth. It is both a literal and a spiritual gathering.

This book, **Gathering Israel,** captures a small part of a global religious movement. From its perspective, we gain an appreciation for the miracle that is the gathering of God's people, in this Last Dispensation.

12 And he shall set up an ensign for the nations, and shall assemble the outcasts of Israel, and gather together the dispersed of Judah from the four corners of the earth.

13 The envy also of Ephraim shall depart, and the adversaries of Judah shall be cut off: Ephraim shall not envy Judah, and Judah shall not vex Ephraim.   Isaiah 11:12-13

This is the story of two individuals, Michael Morton and John Wudel, who come from two very different spiritual backgrounds. Michael grew up as a Jew, while John grew up as a Methodist. Both men loved the religions of their youth, but they both felt something was missing.

As time goes on, they end up searching for the same answers. They sense that what is absent from their lives is a fuller truth that can lead them to their own spiritual salvation.

Their search takes them along two very different paths, but eventually they meet and find that both have come to the same conclusions. Both have discovered that the complete truth of God's plan is on the earth, and if you want to find it badly enough, God will show you His truths when you are ready to accept them.

Michael and John will tell their stories separately. Then when they meet each other, their discovery process will continue to happen.

They enjoy each other's company and love good food. As often as possible they meet in Booth One in a special unnamed fast food restaurant. It is in this unusual setting where both physical and spiritual nourishment is dished up as "Fine Dining." Michael and John hope you'll enjoy their compelling journey.

Chapter 1
Rock Bottom
(Michael)

I woke up in a sweaty haze. My head was pounding. I opened one eye and looked around and knew instantly that something wasn't right. I was lying half on and half off my bed, fully clothed. The night before, I decided that I had had enough, the type of enough that comes from constantly being beaten down for years. A troubled marriage and a contemptuous divorce had taken its toll. Then the economic crash of 2008 took me down financially. I was a real estate agent and had lost everything. I couldn't seem to recover. It was like a tsunami had gone through my life destroying everything. I had raised my fist to the sky and denounced God. I yelled, "If there really is a God, then how could he let all these horrible things happen to me? I don't deserve this."

As I had gotten older, I cared less and less for the taste of alcohol. Maybe I had gotten my fill, after working in restaurants and bars in my 20's and 30's. Nevertheless, I had easily downed several drinks and a half-full bottle of prescription pain pills that I had found in my medicine cabinet. I didn't think that there was any reason to go on.

As I started to regain consciousness, I rolled over onto the floor and on top of the prescription pill bottle. It should have hurt, but I could barely feel it. I dug it out from underneath my back and with one eye closed, I tried to focus one eye on the label. It said the prescription in the bottle had expired in 2004. It was 2012 and the pill bottle was empty. Had I taken them all? I groped around on the floor and tried to find the rest of them. I couldn't find any more pills. Could I have taken all of them? Had I finally had enough to try and take my own life? Maybe so or maybe not, but my head hurt so much, that I really didn't care.

Over the years, it seemed that some of those who were the closest to me were the most abusive. Anti-Semitic slurs by the ones who would say they loved me was devastating. Being Jewish and growing up in a Christian world was confusing to say the least. Anti-Semitism was real. At different points in my life, I seemed to be surrounded by so-called Christians who hated me for what I believed in. I felt that the cross they wore around their necks was a symbol of thousands of years of hate and persecution towards Jews.

In those situations, I couldn't help but internalize some of that hate myself. Then without even knowing it, I would take it out on others. The hate that others had shown me over the years was the hate that I was mirroring back. In reality, I was a broken soul and life wasn't something to be happy about. I was freefalling down a dark well that seemed to have no bottom. I felt like life held nothing more than another day of drudgery. As I continued to regain consciousness, I tried to touch my forehead, but I couldn't even feel my head.

I had put together enough money for a plane flight and was supposed to go on a business trip the following week. I thought it would do me good to get away for a while, but the night before I had changed my mind. I had thought, *"Why go? I'm played out."*

Someone once said, "The truth will set you free." Free from what? Who said that anyway? I always thought, *"Money is the only thing that will actually set me free."* My mantra was as follows: "The more money I make, the more freedom I have." Good words to live by, or so I thought. So, I chose business as my career and turned all my time and talents to making money. My father had taught me to do my best no matter what I chose to do in life. So I set out to be the best "natural man" that I could be. At the time, I had no idea that the "natural man" was an enemy to God, and also to myself.

I wanted to create a better reality for myself. The only problem was that money wasn't flowing in like it used to. My talent to earn money had seemed to hit a long downturn. Something big was missing in my life. Something important was missing inside of me. I couldn't figure out what was missing. I didn't think I had any purpose in life, except to keep working until I died and went to my grave.

That wasn't much to look forward to. So why continue? Why go on this trip? Would this be the glimmer of hope that I needed to continue on? The only thing that sounded like a good reason to go was the opportunity to make more money. So, I decided to go on the business trip, to see if there were any chance of turning my finances around.

At this point in my life, God had every reason to turn his back on me. After all, I had denounced Him. I hadn't discovered it yet, but God never gives up on any of us. He has a plan for all of us, whether we realize it or not.

I Am Home

November 5, 2012, was a cold, sunny day in Denver, Colorado. I boarded a plane with a business associate for a flight to Mesa, Arizona, for a week long business trip. I immediately became apprehensive as I entered the cramped cabin of the plane and looked for my seat. I have always had quite a bit of anxiety when I fly. I wanted to have a drink to calm myself down. I decided not to, because I was still apprehensive about drinking, after waking up with a pill bottle imbedded in my back from the week before.

The phrase "cattle car" came to mind. I thought, *"Am I just overweight or are the seats getting smaller?"* The seats seemed to be shrinking and placed closer together every year. They seemed to pack more people into an already cramped space. Oh well, I guess it's just good business, and I'm all about good business.

We arrived in Phoenix without any mishaps and proceeded to get our bags. I was a real estate broker in Denver, but this business trip was concerning a side project I was working on with a couple of business associates who were friends. Our host, Ken, lived in Mesa and was going to meet us at the baggage claim. Ken had invited us to spend the week at his house. Ken was a Mormon.

While working at an open house the week before, I had questioned Mike, a fellow real estate agent, about Mormons.

I said, "I am staying at a Mormon's house on my trip. Don't they have special customs in their homes? Do they have multiple wives?" One of the last questions I asked was: "Do you know any Mormons?"

He answered "Yes, I do and you do too."

I replied, "Really......who?" (I was sure that I had never met a Mormon.)

He stated, "I'm a Mormon."

I said, "Really, are you kidding?" We had never talked about religion during our open houses, or in any of the conversations that we had each week. I enjoyed working with Mike, but now I secretly thought, *"Does he have more than one wife?"* After all, that's how Mormons were depicted on TV and in any movies that I had seen.

He then proceeded to tell me about a normal Mormon household. He said, "You can't drink alcohol or smoke in their house. They don't drink coffee, and you should watch your cursing."

I exclaimed, "I don't curse!"

He shook his head and said, "Yes, you do."

I replied, "What the hell are you talking about? I never curse."

Mike pointed out that I had a lot of curse words in my vocabulary. Swearing was a sign of the times, and some people seemed to curse to make a point when they were passionate about something. So, I kept myself occupied on the plane, by practicing replacements for different cursing phrases, like "gosh darn", "poo happens" or "gee whiz." I thought, *"I sound stupid."* This mental exercise occupied me during the flight and I didn't feel so anxious about being crammed into the small seats on the airplane.

We met Ken at the baggage claim. First up was a meeting with a potential investor, before we went to his home. I thought, *"It's always about the money, isn't it?"* Our initial meeting went well and our potential investor wanted to meet with us again. I remember sitting at the meeting and wondering all sorts of outlandish things. I wondered if anyone knew that I was Jewish, and how well that would go over. Was I paranoid or just cautious? I seemed to have that question in my mind everywhere I went, and especially when it dealt with business.

Being Jewish all my life, I had gotten used to keeping my religion under wraps. There are many people in the world who don't care for Jews and still practice anti-Semitism.

We went to Ken's home after the meeting where his wife, Joanne, had prepared a very nice dinner. I didn't see any evidence of any additional wives, so I quickly dropped that idea.

At dinner, they mentioned that they would like to take us to the Visitors' Center that was next to the Mesa Latter-day Saints (LDS) Temple on Wednesday night. In Judaism, many temples or synagogues have a gift shop that is run by the sisterhood to raise money for their charity projects. In a Jewish temple gift shop, you could purchase prayer books, menorahs, games and other gifts for different holidays or events. So I thought: *"I get it, the Visitors' Center must be a gift shop!"* I thought maybe they sell postcards with pictures of the Latter-day Saints (LDS) Temple on it. I had also seen a picture online of a Book of Mormon. I didn't know what it was about, but maybe they sold the Book of Mormon on CD's. I was clueless when it came to Mormons.

Joanne was off on Wednesday, so we spent the day driving around looking at the sights, which included a lake, called Canyon Lake, just a few minutes from their house. We were driving in a van that had seats for nine passengers, with several family members and the two of us that had flown in from Denver. As we came over the crest of a hill, a large canyon wall appeared in front of us. The canyon wall formed the far side of the lake. As I looked out the window of the van, I saw an amazing sight. Written on the rock face of the canyon wall, were huge capital letters spelling, "I AM HOME." The letters appeared to be 50 feet high.

I thought to myself, *"Who would put that there?"* As we drove down the other side of the hill to the picnic area, I remember saying, "Is that a prank by some crazy teenagers?""

I Am Home
Photo by Rebekah Baird

Everyone was chattering about different subjects and seemed to ignore what I was saying.

I said, "Why would someone write 'I AM HOME' on the canyon wall? Does it have any special meaning?"

Someone in the van replied, "What are you talking about?"

I looked again, and there it was, written clearly on the canyon wall, "I AM HOME." No one else seemed to see what I was seeing. I thought, *"Could I be imagining this?"*

For a moment, I reflected back on my home as a child. My mother had converted to Judaism from Christian Science when I was born. She wanted to respect my father's wishes, so she agreed to raise my younger brother and me as Jews. She provided such a happy home to grow up in, rich in Jewish traditions. I never realized it then, but our home had a Christ-like atmosphere, even though I was being raised Jewish, and we never spoke of Christ.

My mother loved everyone and always accepted everyone into our home. The part of a Jewish mother came in when she would feed everyone until they were ready to explode. Relatives, friends and strangers were all treated with the same love and care. She would then say, "Have you eaten enough? Please take something with you for a snack later. I don't want you to get hungry."

At Christmas and Hanukkah time, she would always decorate our modest home so that both sides of the family were comfortable. Mom would always decorate a beautiful Christmas tree. Even though there were both Jewish and Christian relatives filling our little home, all of my relatives got along. The Christian relatives would say, "What a beautiful Christmas tree!," and the Jewish relatives would say, "What a beautiful Hanukkah bush!" They were all talking about the same tree. Our love of family bonded us. The outside world would prove to be a different place.

Back in the van, I was picturing in my mind that wonderful feeling that you get when you are home with your family. Was I being shown signs that my home was now in Arizona? Is that what "I AM HOME" means? It wouldn't be until a couple of years later that I would understand what "I AM HOME" really meant.

The conversation had changed and everyone decided that they were hungry and we should go grab a quick dinner before going to the Visitors' Center. I looked around at this desolate desert scenery and thought, *"I AM HOME? I don't think so!"* Maybe it was a mirage, and I just needed to drink some extra water. I was in the desert after all.

Visitors' Center

I was about to experience the old Mormon trick "Take them to the Visitors' Center, and they will feel the Spirit." This really isn't a trick, but Mormons understand that the Holy Spirit can change hearts in an instant. In other words, if they take a nonmember to the

Visitors' Center, they will feel the Spirit and want to learn more. My experience was a slight variation of that possibility.

Mesa Arizona Temple Visitors' Center
The Church of Jesus Christ of Latter-day Saints
Photo by Rebekah Baird

So we went to the Visitors' Center and just for the record, it was not a gift shop. It was a wonderful information center that had a magnificent, ten-foot-high statue of Jesus Christ as the centerpiece in the lobby as you walked in. Being a Jew, walking by a gigantic statue of Jesus Christ was a little intimidating to me.

In a different room, there was a display showing the ancient city of Jerusalem in miniature that highlighted all of the important places during the last days that Jesus was on the earth.

There was also a display showing all of the languages in which the Book of Mormon had been translated. There were also computers to enable you to look up your family history. In addition, a couple of small movie theaters played different movies that were sponsored by the Church.

My hosts asked if we could see the movie about Joseph Smith. I didn't know much about the Mormons, nor did I know anything about their prophet, Joseph Smith.

Joseph Smith   1805-1844

The movie was very well done and showed the life of Joseph Smith. It showed him receiving the golden plates to translate the Book of Mormon and the forming of the Church of Jesus Christ of Latter Day Saints. It also included the persecution that the early Mormons suffered, until Joseph's untimely death in his 30s. I was told that people came out of the movie with a better understanding of the origins of the Mormons and an appreciation for their prophet.

Some people watched the movie and were inspired. I watched the movie and became angry. That's right; I came out of the movie very angry! My emotions were confusing to me at first, but as I thought about it, it brought up memories that were buried deep inside my mind.

The Joseph Smith movie reminded me of some of the persecution that I had suffered during my life for being a Jew. I identified very strongly with the persecution that I saw on the screen. An angry mob dragged Joseph out of bed, tried to force poison down his throat and then tarred and feathered him. I thought, *"Why should they hate him so much for his beliefs?"* Just because Joseph Smith chose to believe something different from what others believed?

This sounded like a tragic Jewish story of persecution, instead of a Mormon story of persecution. It was a profound moment for me.

I have rarely talked about the following incident that happened earlier in my life, because I have had filed it away, deep inside my mind. It wasn't the first time I had been persecuted for being Jewish, nor would it be the last. Sometimes there are things or events that are just too painful to remember. These are things that we hide deep down inside of us, hoping to never remember them again. This was one of those events. Watching the Joseph Smith movie seemed to bring everything back to the surface.

I was in high school and about 16 years old. My family didn't live in an area of town where any other Jews lived. My father had bought a new home that was about a 30-minute drive from our synagogue. I think the reason we lived where we did, was that my mother had gone to the same high school that I was attending. It was a very large school, and there were well over 500 in my graduating class.

I was one of only two Jews in the whole school. I learned quickly to hide the fact that I was Jewish because of the snide remarks, bullying, and outright hatred for Jews from kids that said they were Christians.

I had been playing different musical instruments since I was five years old. My mother had been a music teacher, so you can imagine the important part that music played in my life. In fact, I played in every band that the school offered: orchestra, marching band, stage band and pep band. I loved playing music and anytime I could get out of a study hall or even a class, I would go to the band room and practice. Music was a big part of my life, and I loved it.

One day, I didn't put my books in my locker as usual and was hurrying to the band room. The band room was in one of the farthest wings of the school. I rushed into a bathroom on the way and immediately realized that I had made a big mistake. All the kids knew that during the afternoon, this particular bathroom was the one that a few of the tougher seniors smoked in. We all knew not to disturb those guys, but I guess I forgot that day. Usually, if you went into the bathroom where they were smoking, they would just yell at you and make fun of you until you left.

Not on this day; this day was different. I'm sure that the teachers knew about their smoking, but they were usually in the teachers' lounge during that period, smoking also. Smoking was accepted in society back then, but students' smoking on school grounds wasn't allowed.

There were four older kids smoking in the bathroom that day. The bathroom reeked of smoke from the minute I burst through the door. From the looks on their faces, I had intruded on sacred ground. I was immediately grabbed and spun around several times. My books flew out of my arms, and my glasses flew off my head. I was thrown to the floor, and one of the boys sat on me. The other boys held me down. A lit cigarette was produced and held very close to my right eye. Time seemed to stop.

The guy sitting on me, holding the cigarette said "You're that Jew." He said it as if he was saying something vile and disgusting. "The Jews killed Jesus and now you are going to pay for it."

I don't remember if I was yelling or not, but I'm pretty sure that I was, because an adult man came in right before they had a chance to complete their plans. I don't know if the man was someone's dad or a teacher I had never seen before. As the man was yelling at them, they let go of me. I somehow grabbed my glasses and a couple of my books and ran out of the bathroom.

I never saw that man again, and I was never called into the office to explain what happened that day. The incident did make a lasting impression on me. I never told my parents, even though I had to get my glasses repaired. I just made up some excuse as to why they were bent. I couldn't understand why someone hated me so much for an event I had nothing to do with. Growing up Jewish, we didn't learn about Jesus, and I certainly didn't have any reason to rejoice over him being put to death.

It was the same feeling of disgust and anger that struck me when I came out of the Joseph Smith movie. Why do people hate others, just because you believe something different than what they believe?

Michael Morton - College Sophomore Picture

The slander and persecution directed at me in my youth, for being Jewish, continued throughout my life. It was the reason I didn't finish scouting, and why I was passed over for advancement in several jobs. It was even present in my closest relationships.

After the Visitors' Center movie, I went over to a pictorial display of ancient Hebrew Temples. The display, encased in thick glass stands, covered the area in front of a giant glass wall that spanned the length of that side of the Visitors' Center. Looking out of that glass wall, I could see a reflecting pool, a courtyard and beyond that, the Mesa Arizona Temple.

The display included pictures of Moses' portable Tabernacle in the wilderness, King Solomon's Temple, and Herod's Temple. The last of the great temples, Herod's Temple, operated during the time of Jesus. I wondered why Heavenly Father had stopped inspiring his people to build temples. I looked up and realized that there was a temple right in front of me. The Mesa Arizona Temple! I thought, *"Why had Heavenly Father inspired the Mormons to build Temples? What were they being used for?"*

As I was looking at the temple, I couldn't help but notice the people that were walking out of the building and along the sidewalk. Some of them were carrying garment bags. I thought, *"Why were they carrying small suitcases? Did they stay overnight in the Temple?"*

On that same Wednesday night, John and his wife Nanci, a faithful Mormon couple, were two of the people carrying their garment bags out of the Mesa Arizona Temple. I hadn't met John yet, but I was later to learn that he too was a convert to Mormonism in 1961. Little did I know that our paths were to cross in a rather profound way.

Chapter 2
Is The Full Truth On The Earth?
(John)

Walking down the Temple sidewalk that same night, John thought, *"I've come a long way since my first experience with Mormonism. Just now coming out of the light of the temple, into the darkness of the night, reminds me that fifty years ago, I had come out of the darkness of misunderstanding into the light of the truth that was revealed to me."*

When I was 14 years old, I came home one Sunday from Methodist Sunday school. I had the feeling that although I enjoyed it very much, it seemed as if something was missing.

Mesa Arizona Temple
The Church of Jesus Christ of Latter-day Saints
Photo by Rebekah Baird

Since I was a little boy, my mother had always taught me to pray and ask God when I had a question. So I went into my bedroom, got down on my knees and prayed for an answer. It was a simple prayer. "Heavenly Father, if the truth is on the earth, please show me where it is. If someone has the full truth, please show me who they are and where they are."

At that tender age, I seemed to sense that all the religions that I was familiar with had some of the truth as to the purpose of this life, but what was missing was the complete truth. After praying for that at 14 years old, I went on about being a teenager and basically forgot about my prayer.

After graduating from Long Beach Polytechnic High School, my parents and I went on a trip to visit all of the major universities in the western part of the United States. We wanted to see where I might attend college. One of places we visited was Brigham Young University (BYU) in Provo, Utah. When we stopped there, I filled out an application applying for acceptance to begin school in my sophomore year.

I had plans to attend Long Beach City College for my freshman year because I didn't know where else I should go. When we returned home from our trip, an acceptance letter had come from BYU, but strangely it had a clerical error. The letter accepted me for my freshman year instead of my sophomore year. The freshman year would start in two weeks! I was blown away. What should I do?

I remember looking at the acceptance letter in total amazement. I had actually been accepted for my freshman year at Brigham Young University. I turned to my parents and said, "What do you think?" I was surprised at their response. They had such total faith and confidence in me to say, "If that's what you would like to do, John, you have our full support." At that point, I couldn't believe my mom and dad. What parents would have total faith in an 18-year-old to make this kind of a decision on his own?

I then contacted BYU and accepted their offer. The next Sunday, as I normally did, I went to church, the United Methodist Church in Long Beach. I loved going to church. I also appreciated the Reverend that presided there. I asked for an appointment with him after the services.

As I sat in his office, I said to him, "Reverend, I'm going off to college and when I get back, I want to become even more active than I have been." I had been about 70% active and wanted to improve my attendance and participation.

Photo Courtesy of California Heights United Methodist Church
Long Beach California

The Reverend asked me, "John, where are you going to college?"

I answered, "Brigham Young University."

He paused and as an unusual expression came to his face, he said something that I'll never forget, "John, I'm afraid this is the last I'll ever see of you."

I said, "No, no Reverend, I'll be back and be even more active than I've been in the past." He smiled, shook my hand, and bid me farewell.

I sensed that the good Minister understood something that I didn't. I didn't know then, but I was later to find out what he meant. The prayer that I had asked four years earlier was a simple prayer asking, "Which church had the complete answers to life's most important questions?" including questions like, "Why are we here on earth?", "What's the purpose of this life?", "Where did we come from before we were born?", "Where are we going after we die?" The other thing I didn't realize at the time was the prayer that I had offered at 14 years of age was about to be answered.

Once again, to my total amazement, the next week, my parents put me on a bus to Provo, Utah, to attend BYU. I knew nothing about where I was going, and there would be no one waiting for me when I got off the bus. I felt totally alone, but I felt that somehow Heavenly Father was watching over me. I only went because I could feel in my heart that it was the right thing to do.

Brigham Young University Provo, Utah
Photo Courtesy of BYU TV

I did it because years before, when I was just a little boy, my mom had taught me the importance of prayer. Among the first words that I remember my mother saying to me were these: "John, you have two fathers, one on earth and one in heaven. They both love you very much and they both want you to succeed. Talk to both of them. Tell them your desires, your fears, your hopes and dreams. Tell them all that you are doing, and let them help you in your life decisions."

Deciding to go to BYU was one of those important decisions. I had prayed and felt that it was right to get on that bus. I still didn't know why, but I remembered the quote by Yogi Berra, "When you come to a crossroads in life, take it." I smiled at that thought and stepped on the bus.

What Church?

Hours later, I arrived in Provo, Utah. Landing in a city with no friends and no place to live, my first concern was to find a place that had room and board. I walked to the Abraham O. Smoot Administration Building and found the off-campus housing office. I asked the secretary a simple question. "Is there anyone that offers a room that also provides meals and is a good cook? I don't think that it is safe to eat my own cooking." She smiled and said, "Interesting that you would ask that. There is one, but they are always filled up in advance. They take in six male college students. They provide breakfast and dinner each day. It's a family residence, and the mom is a great cook. It's a long shot, but let me go check to see if there are any openings."

She came back with an even bigger smile on her face and said, "You're in luck. One of the young men who was scheduled to stay there just joined the Army. Now there is an opening, and here's the address."

When I arrived at the address that was on the piece of paper she had given me, I was shocked. I had to do a double take. The address that I held in my hand was correct, but I was standing in front of a funeral home. It was named Our Chapel of Memories. I stood there and paused for a moment, thinking, *"No way am I going to live in a mortuary. I'm not about to make my memories of college about dead bodies."* I'd never seen one before, and I wasn't about to start now.

The building was a two-story, and I could see that the living quarters were on the top floor, with the funeral home on the first floor. I stood there for a moment and thought again, *"There is absolutely no way, that I'm going to live in a funeral home."*

However, my curiosity got the best of me. I wondered what kind of college students would live in a funeral home. Were they all pre-med? I had to find out. I walked up and knocked on the door.

Former Aura C. Hatch Mortuary
Photo Courtesy of Walker Sanderson
Tribute Center and Crematory Provo, Utah

I was greeted by a nice, older woman who invited me in. She asked who I was and then proceeded to explain to me how her family had been taking in college students for years. Her family loved these students dearly. She took me on a tour of both the funeral home and the upstairs living quarters. Even though I had planned to say, "No", I was so taken with her kindness and radiant goodness that I had to say "Yes."

The college students lived in a group of rooms adjacent to where the family lived. The family consisted of a father, mother and their oldest daughter. The oldest daughter also attended BYU. My room contained three beds, a set of bunk beds and a single bed. I was given the top bunk. I moved my few belongings into my room and put them away. School orientation was going to start the next day.

On the next morning, I smelled breakfast cooking in the kitchen. I got dressed and followed my roommates into a dining room that contained a large dining room table. The family sat at the table with all of my roommates. That morning, they invited me to sit at the foot of the table; the father of the family was at the head. His wife began bringing out all kinds of food. She brought out plates of bacon, eggs, pancakes, toast, homemade jams and jellies. There were also pitchers full of fresh orange juice and milk. I thought, *"Wow, I hit the jackpot!"* The food just kept coming, and I started to fill my plate. I then noticed that nobody else was touching the food. Their plates were empty.

Then they all slid off of their chairs onto the floor. I thought, *"Did I miss something? Did one of them drop a contact lens, and now they're all looking for it?"* There I sat, with my plate full of food, wondering what to do next. One of my roommates, on his knees, looked up at me and said, "We're going to have family prayer, would you like to join us?"

So I slid down onto my knees and listened, for the first time in my life, to a beautiful family prayer, given by the head of this family. He asked for God's blessings on the food, to give us the nourishment we needed. He asked for blessings on his own family first and then on each one of us students. He asked for blessings for us to do well in school and to be happy in our educational pursuits. I was amazed. I thought, *"How could I go for 18 years and never experience a family prayer?"* I had two wonderful Christ-like parents, but we had never knelt in family prayer. Getting back up into my chair, I glanced up to notice that everyone around the table was now looking at me. They had strange expressions on their faces.

One of them said, "Are you a member of the Church?"

I replied, "What church?" How clueless would you have to be to attend Brigham Young University and not know who Brigham Young was, and what church they were talking about?

They looked startled and answered, "The Mormon Church."

I responded, "No, I'm a Methodist."

Embarrassed, I looked down at my food and started to eat. Looking back on this, I can only imagine what must have happened among this group, the looks that must have gone on between the two returned missionaries, the two future missionaries, and the father who was the local stake president. They must have thought, *"Is this guy for real?"*

My oldest roommate was a southern boy from Louisville, Kentucky. He was a rebel fanatic and even had a Confederate flag hanging over his bed. As we were leaving the table, after breakfast was over, I turned to him and asked "What's the difference between the Methodist Church and the Mormon Church?"

Without hesitating, he said, "We believe in a living prophet of God."

I stammered, "You what…a living prophet? You mean to tell me that you think you have someone in your church who talks for God? You have a real prophet of God, just like they did in the Old Testament?" (I remembered my Methodist Sunday school lessons. The prophets were old, had long white hair, beards and sometimes lived in caves.)

He said, "That's right."

I countered, "Really? Who is he, and where does he live?"

He answered, "He lives in Salt Lake City."

I continued probing, "Do you have a picture of him that you can show me?"

He then proceeded to go into his room and get out a current LDS Church magazine that had a picture on the cover of President David O. McKay. He handed it to me, and I will never forget the feeling I had when I looked at it. I was holding an incredible portrait of a white-haired man dressed in a black tux, getting ready to go to the theatre.

President David O. McKay
Portrait by Alvin Gittins

I turned to my roommate and asked, "Do you really believe that this man is a prophet of God?"

He stated simply, "Yes I do. He is a prophet of God."

I thought, *"Wow. If I could ever imagine what a modern day prophet might look like, this is that man."*

This started a barrage of relentless questions to my roommates that would go on for several nights, often until 2 a.m. I had so worn them out with questions that one night, they finally said, "Please

John, just go to sleep." They had had enough of my interrogations, so the next morning, they called in the missionaries for relief.

The Challenge

The stake missionaries came the following Sunday. A stake usually consists of eight wards. Wards are individual congregations of about four hundred members each. These missionaries were different from the returned missionaries that I lived with. I learned that stake missionaries were active members of the stake who had served full-time missions and then been called to voluntarily teach investigators part-time. These particular missionaries happened to be BYU students who were in their senior year. One of them would later go on to become the attorney general for the state of Utah. These were two very impressive young men who came to answer my questions.

Every Sunday afternoon at 2 p.m., they would show up at the mortuary. We would sit in a lovely living room on the second floor and have an opening prayer. They would then give a brief lesson and then have me read scriptures that pertained to the topic at hand. I loved these sessions because I had so many questions. The missionaries were very skilled at answering my questions with an appropriate scripture. I was amazed that these young men had such knowledge. One of them had a set of scriptures that was so worn that the pages were loose and literally falling out of the book. Every time I asked him a question, he would open those worn-out scriptures, turn to a page, and say, "Here, read this." It was always the perfect answer to my question. I thought, *"How can he be so young and have read the scriptures to the point where his book is literally falling apart from use?"*

When I asked him about it later, he said, "No, my dog got hold of these scriptures and chewed them up. That's why they're falling apart!" Still, returned missionaries are so impressive in their ability to immediately find answers to important questions in the scriptures.

My missionary discussions went on every Sunday for about two months, until they had run out of lessons. They then began to assign topics to me, so that I could be the one giving the lessons. One of the first topics they gave me was about the "Aaronic Priesthood." It was a great learning experience.

In addition to the lesson assignments, they gave me a Book of Mormon. They told me that if I would read it and pray about it, I would come to know that it was true. They also told me that if the Book of Mormon was true, then Joseph Smith was a true prophet of God and that the church that he started was also true.

The first time that the missionaries told me about Joseph Smith, I was amazed at the simplicity of his beautiful story. It was a story of a young farm boy living in upstate New York, who had a very minimal education. He was concerned about his personal salvation and wondered which church he should join. He went into a grove of trees, knelt down and asked a simple question in prayer. "Which church is true?" Then the heavens opened before him, and he was visited by the Father and the Son. They told him not to join any of the other churches.

Concerning those churches, Joseph Smith quoted Jesus who said;

"They draw near to me with their lips, but their hearts are far from me, they teach for doctrines the commandments of men, having a form of Godliness, but they deny the power there of."
Joseph Smith History (JS-H1:19)

In time, Jesus would restore the true church of Jesus Christ once again to the earth. When the missionaries told me this remarkable story, I immediately thought, *"Wow, I hope this is true."* Of course, I did not know enough to know whether it was true, but I hoped that it was. Joseph Smith had asked God, "Which church is true?" I had asked God, "Is the full truth on the earth, and if so, who has it?" I was amazed at how similar our questions to God were.

As time went on and my hope grew, I began to believe. I realized that there is a process to conversion and it starts with hope. When you first hear the truth about your personal salvation, whether you believe it or not, you must hope that it is true. If you don't hope that the full truth is available here on earth, then your journey to find it is over. I did have hope, so my journey to the truth was just beginning.

The missionaries kept asking me if I was reading the Book of Mormon and praying about it. To be honest, I was not. At this point I was conflicted. On the one hand, I hoped that what they were telling me was true. On the other hand, I was afraid that it was.

I realized that if it was true, then all of my plans for the future would need to change. I had laid out a career path and made plans of how my life would go. If what the missionaries were teaching me was really true, this would change everything. I was struggling with my internal conflict and I really didn't want to become a Mormon. I just wanted the truth. Now, I was hesitating with the very thing I had wanted since age 14.

I went home for Christmas break. My good friend Bill, who had been my high school buddy and was attending the Air Force Academy, asked me, "How is it going at BYU?"

I said to him, "The Mormons want me to become one of them. They're trying to get me, but they never will."

I went back to BYU after the break, and the missionaries gave me a challenge. They said, "Our prophet, David O. McKay, is coming to speak to the student body of BYU. You should take the time to go hear him." I thought, *A living prophet of God? Coming here?"*

I circled the date on my calendar and decided that I would arrive 15 minutes early to get a good seat. Little did I know how clueless I still was! When I arrived at the Smith Field House, at BYU, all 10,000 seats had been filled for hours. I had no place to sit, so I stood in the shadows adjacent to the podium and waited.

Chapter 3
A Prophet of God?
(John)

The year was 1961 and BYU's enrollment was about 11,000 students. At this time in BYU's history, the field house was where the major sports events and devotional assemblies were held. So with the President of the Church coming, the building was filled to capacity. The raised basketball floor was converted into a stage area, with the south end being set up with VIP seating and a speaker's podium. I could not find a seat, so I stood off to the side in the shadows, about 20 feet away from the podium area. As I was waiting for the arrival of President McKay, I noticed that the room went completely silent. I looked to the north through the glass doors and saw a black car pull up.

As President McKay entered the building, everyone started to sing the beautiful hymn, "We Thank Thee, O God, For A Prophet." There was no chorister leading the audience, it was just a spontaneous response to his entering the building. President McKay was 87 years old and was walking slowly with a General Authority on either side to help steady him.

As the students were singing, he actually walked past me on his way to the podium. I had only one question in my mind, *"Was this man truly a Prophet of God?"* As he came within 15 feet of me, I closed my eyes and asked God my question. *"Heavenly Father, is this man your prophet?"*

Words cannot describe what immediately happened to me. I can only say that from the top of my head to the tips of my toes, the answer came as a powerful, "Yes." To me in that moment, the heavens opened, and truth was revealed. A Prophet of God was alive on the earth!

President McKay then took his seat directly behind the podium. After the opening song and prayer, he was introduced by one of the

General Authorities accompanying him. As he stood up to approach the stand, he stumbled on an electrical cord on the floor. Here was an 87 year-old Prophet of God starting to fall! Within that singular moment, 10,000 people instantly came out of their seats, reaching out to help him. The sound was like a cannon going off.

As President McKay caught himself on the podium, preventing his fall, a collective sigh of relief filled the building. He straightened himself and as he began his remarks, I thought, *"What kind of a man is it that can have 10,000 people sitting on the edge of their seats like coiled springs, who would instantly jump up and reach out to help him if they could?"* I left the building that day, knowing absolutely that there was a living prophet on the earth. David O. McKay was that prophet.

Now that I had been given that knowledge, I thought, *"What am I going to do about it?"* As I pondered what just happened, the doubts, the confusion and the conflict inside of me had all faded away. I thought, *"The power of truth is amazing in its ability to change your attitude and your direction in life."*

I called the missionaries when I got home and told them that I was ready to be baptized.

Baptism

Joseph Smith taught that before you receive the truth, you are standing on neutral ground. Although once you receive the truth, you have an important decision to make. Are you going to accept the truth that you are given and move forward, or are you going to reject that truth and regress? Joseph taught that once you have been given the truth, you can no longer remain on neutral ground. You are either moving forward, or you are moving backwards. My decision to be baptized was a huge step forward. It happened on April 1, 1961, in a stake center in Provo, Utah.

The small group attending the baptism included my roommates, my host family and the missionaries who taught me. Following my baptism and confirmation, I returned to the mortuary, went upstairs to my room alone and lay on my bed. It was in the afternoon and sunshine was coming through the window onto the bed where I lay.

As I pondered what had just happened to me, I was overcome with joy. I realized that I was now a member of the Kingdom of God on this earth. I felt cleansed of my past mistakes and was starting over to make the most of my life. I reflected on what Joseph Smith taught regarding the purpose of this life. We are here on this earth to progress. There is a process to this progression. It's a process that is not just limited to this mortal life, but can go on for eternity. Therefore, it's called eternal progression.

The key to this process is Jesus Christ. He came to earth to show us the way to progress. He's the pure model of how to live a life of constant improvement. He set the perfect example for us to follow. As these thoughts rested upon me, I formed a motto for the remainder of my life. It was only five words: "Always move forward with love." The joy I now felt at following Christ and being baptized was proof enough to me that my conclusions were correct.

As I pondered this, a scripture came to mind:

> **20** Wherefore, ye must press forward with a steadfastness in Christ, having a perfect brightness of hope, and a love of God and of all men. Wherefore, if ye shall press forward, feasting upon the word of Christ, and endure to the end, behold, thus saith the Father: Ye shall have eternal life.
>
> **21** And now, behold, my beloved brethren, this is the way; and there is none other way nor name given under heaven whereby man can be saved in the kingdom of God. And now, behold, this is the doctrine of Christ, and the only and true doctrine of the Father, and of the Son, and of the Holy Ghost, which is one God, without end. Amen.
>
> 2 Nephi 31:20-21

Something occurred next that was difficult to explain. I could sense the presence of someone near me, but not in my physical world. Without any words being said, I felt that this was a male ancestor that had come from beyond the veil. He was so thrilled that I had chosen to be baptized that he had come to congratulate me. It was almost as if his spiritual hand had come through the veil and was reaching out as a gesture to shake my hand. I didn't move, but felt an amazing joy from his presence. It was as if this ancestor of mine had been waiting for a long time for what had happened that day. I wondered who he was. I would later make the discovery of who this ancestor was in real life and be shocked at my own heritage.

After my baptism and the school semester ended, I returned home to Long Beach to be with my family for the summer. Upon returning home, I announced that I had joined the Mormon Church. My parents were very supportive. When I told my grandmother, she said, "John, I think that your great, great grandfather was a bishop in the Mormon Church. His name was William Preston." I was shocked, *"How could I have a Mormon ancestor when no one in my family is LDS?"* I didn't show my surprise to my Grandmother, but I made a mental note of it, thinking that when I returned to BYU, I would look him up.

I was so excited at what I had discovered concerning God restoring the true church to the earth that I couldn't wait to tell my angel mother. In our kitchen, there was an ironing board that was fastened to the wall and would fold down when needed. My mother was ironing, and I decided to tell her about the exciting news.

I said, "Mom, God has called a living prophet again on the earth."

She smiled as she was ironing and said, "That's nice, dear."

I raised the energy in my voice and said, "No, Mom, God has actually called a living prophet, just like he did in the Old Testament. It's incredible, Mom!"

Still ironing with a sweet smile on her face, she said, "How nice, dear."

I went back to my bedroom deflated and completely frustrated, because I considered my mom to be the most Christ-like person that I had ever known. This was my first experience with the true principle, "There is a time and a season for everyone to have the opportunity to learn the truth." This wasn't the time for my mom. I understood the principle, but it didn't take away the frustration.

Years later, before she passed away, the reality of what I had told her hit home. My mother was in her 80's, very frail and in a wheelchair. I would take her to church where she fully embraced the Gospel of Jesus Christ as taught by the LDS Church. I decided not to have her baptized in mortality because she was so frail, but to baptize her by proxy in the temple after she passed away. I did the temple work for both my mother and father in the Mesa Arizona Temple, where they were baptized and sealed together for all eternity.

Many people that don't have the opportunity to hear the Gospel in this life will have the chance to accept it in the next life. We are told that there is more missionary work going on in the spirit world than here on earth.

My mom and dad are a good example of this wonderfully true doctrine. Every son and daughter of God that did not have the opportunity to understand the full truth and be baptized on earth with the proper authority will have that opportunity presented to them.

God is no respecter of persons which means all of his children will have the same opportunity for salvation and exaltation. Every single person will have the choice to accept or reject the atonement offered by Jesus Christ after they fully understand it.

Chapter 4
Heavenly Tears
(Michael)

Friday morning came. It was the last day of my business trip, and we had to catch a plane back to Denver in the afternoon. The Joseph Smith movie in the Visitors' Center had triggered my curiosity. I hadn't slept very well the night before and I was tired. I was tired and kept remembering my experience of seeing "I AM HOME," written on the canyon wall. I still wasn't sure what that meant. I didn't feel like my home was supposed to be in Arizona, because I was rebuilding my real estate career in Denver, after the economy had crashed. I thought, *"What did it mean? Did it mean that I was supposed to move to Arizona?"*

On that Friday morning, I was eating a late breakfast by myself at the dining room table. Everyone else was getting ready to go to the airport. It was the last day of my trip. As I was finishing my breakfast, drops of water started falling on the table in front of my plate. The drops fell slowly and deliberately, one at a time. I sat there mesmerized as I counted seven drops before they stopped.

I thought, *"There must be someone taking a shower upstairs and it's leaking through the ceiling above me."* I immediately got up on the chair and felt the ceiling. The ceiling was not damp. I looked back down at the table, and sure enough, there was a small puddle of water on the table. I went upstairs, but no one was in the shower, nor had the shower been used for quite some time. I went back downstairs, got up on the chair again and felt around the ceiling. It was dry. I sat down in amazement and wondered, *"How could this happen?"*

In that moment of contemplation, I heard my mother's voice. My mother had been deceased since 2001. Here it was 2012, and I was hearing her voice as if she was sitting next to me at the table.

She said, "Michael, these are heavenly tears for all that you have been through." It was definitely her voice!

It seemed as though her message to me was that Heavenly Father loved me, had sympathy for me and knew all of the trials that I had been through.

I sat there not knowing what to do next. Sure, I had been through a lot in my life. I saw the end of a contemptuous marriage, followed by an equally-trying divorce. My immediate family, which included my two beautiful daughters, was torn apart. Then came the downturn in the economy. With the financial crash, my real estate business also crashed. This quickly became one of the most difficult periods in my life.

I wondered, *"Why had God forsaken me?"* In my infinite wisdom, I had denounced God. I raised my fist and yelled up at the sky, "There is no God, if he would allow all of these horrible things to happen in my life."

At the time, I didn't really get the concept that the trials in my life were happening for a reason and were there to strengthen me. A wise sage once said, "Whatever doesn't kill you, makes you stronger!" I thought, *"Was hearing my mother's voice also meant to make me stronger?"*

This was one of those defining moments in my life. I realized that the trials of my life had been a refiner's fire. The refiner's fire is not a comfortable place to be. It involves intense heat and repeated hammering. It is in the refiner's fire that we are purified and prepared to meet Heavenly Father. My mother's words were a great comfort to my mind that morning.

Some people would say that the "heavenly tears" were a figment of my imagination. My reply is, once you experience a miracle, no matter how big or how small it is, you become a believer and it can change your circumstances in an instant.

I went back upstairs and packed my bags to get ready to go to the airport.

The Book Is True

It was Friday afternoon and the last day of my business trip to Mesa, Arizona. It had been mentioned to me that week that the LDS Church was building a new temple in Gilbert, Arizona. Gilbert and Mesa are both cities in the metro Phoenix area. I asked if on the way to the airport, we could go by the Gilbert Arizona Temple that was under construction. Everyone that I met during the week who was Mormon seemed thrilled that a temple of this size was being built in Arizona. When finished, this temple would be the 13th largest LDS Temple in the world.

As a real estate broker, I loved seeing different structures being built. So, I kept telling myself that I wanted to go see the architecture of the newly-built temple. The truth of the matter is that I felt drawn there. I wasn't sure why, but I knew that I had to see the temple before I left for Denver.

Gilbert Arizona LDS Temple
Picture Courtesy of Ryan's Gilbert Temple Update

Gilbert Temple Construction Trailer
Picture Courtesy of Ryan's Gilbert Temple Update

When we arrived at the Temple site, I realized that this structure was in its last stage of being built. A construction trailer had been set up in the parking lot, to show visitors a short video about LDS Temples. Unfortunately, we were about 30 minutes too late. It was closed. A member of our party, Daniel, knocked on the trailer's door and it partially opened. After a few words were exchanged, the door opened the rest of the way, and we were invited in.

I wasn't sure what had been said, but I thought, *"How cool, the Mormons must have secret passwords!"* I later learned that the secret password was "We have an investigator." Inside the trailer, I was shown a short video about how the LDS Church is building temples around the world. At that time, there were 141 temples.

Growing up Jewish, I had received an early education about Moses' Tabernacle in the wilderness, Solomon's Temple and Herod's Temple. I thought, *"Why are the Mormons building Temples?"* The video related that one of the reasons the LDS Church builds temples is so that their members can unite their families for all eternity. They also showed us samples of the stone and materials used in the building. The presentation was fascinating.

I had received a flood of information during the week, which made me ask a lot of questions about the LDS Church. This was very unusual for me to be interested in a Christian religion, because I am Jewish. Although, I couldn't deny that I had received personal revelations during the week that created an interest in the LDS Church. To put it mildly, I was confused and overwhelmed at the same time.

After the video, one member of our party asked if the couple, who worked in the trailer, had a Book of Mormon for me before I left. We were told that they had given out all of their complimentary copies and didn't have one left for me. Someone asked if there might be another copy anywhere else in the trailer. Both of the hosts went into a back room, we could hear them rustling around in some boxes.

After a minute or two, they came back out and the man said that they had found one last book in the bottom of a box. He handed me a new hard back edition of the Book of Mormon and said, "I didn't think that there were any copies left."

There can be moments in your life when everything changes in an instant. This became one of those moments!

I looked down upon the Book of Mormon as I held it in my hands. Whatever anyone was saying in the trailer seemed to quickly fade. I was transported back to when I was a boy of 13 or 14, sitting in Friday night services in my Jewish Synagogue. As I looked at my hands, they were my hands as a boy.

I was holding a copy of the Jewish Prayer Book, not the Book of Mormon. The Jewish Prayer Book was the book we used all year long for Friday night services and holidays. It had a dark blue cover with gold embossed letters.

As I looked to my right, I could see my mother holding a prayer book and saying a prayer. I could hear her voice. I looked to my left and I could see my father holding a prayer book and saying a prayer also. I could hear his voice. I looked up and saw the Rabbi on the podium; he was leading the congregation in prayer. The prayer that they were saying was one of the most sacred prayers in Judaism. They were reciting the Shema. The first line of the Shema reads:

Shema Yisrael Adonai Elohenu Adonai Echad
Hear, O Israel, The Lord Our God, The Lord Is One.

I heard my mother's voice again, just like I had heard her voice that morning at breakfast. My mother's voice! How sweet it sounded in prayer. I could feel my heart pounding in my chest.

People were talking in the trailer as things came back into focus. A rush of different feelings came over me. What seemed like a long time, had only been a few seconds.

Still gazing at my hands, I was looking down upon the Book of Mormon that I had just received. It had a dark blue cover with gold embossed letters, just like my Jewish prayer book!

Reform Jewish Prayer Book (Left), The Book Of Mormon (Right)
Photography by Rebekah Baird

Then a kind, gentle voice spoke to me. It was a man's voice that I would hear many times in the coming weeks and months.

The voice said "The book is true!"

Even now, I have a hard time explaining all of the feelings that I had as I held that book in my hands. It was the first time that I had ever held a Book of Mormon or read a single word from it. Yet, I knew, with all my heart, that Heavenly Father was telling me that the Book of Mormon was true.

The Angel

A couple of hours after my experience at the Gilbert Arizona Temple construction site, I boarded a plane for Denver. I usually get nervous flying and have an alcoholic drink to calm myself down. A mixed drink, light beer, or something similar, would usually take away my anxiety. This flight home was different. I didn't want a drink. I wanted to be alert and sort out everything that had happened over the last week, because I was still confused, as if I had been in a dream.

I landed at Denver International Airport around 9 p.m., collected my bags, and found my friends for the ride back home. I sat in the back of their car, and my friends sat in the front. It was a cold, clear night with a thousand stars in the sky. The air was cold and crisp.

On the ride home, my two friends in the front seat were discussing all the stars in the sky. I heard them say, "Look at all the stars tonight. Is that the Big Dipper over there?" they asked, pointing through the windshield, looking up into the sky.

I decided to roll down my window, stick my head partially outside, and take a look for myself. When I looked up into the sky, I couldn't believe what I saw. It was a giant angel shimmering in white and outlined by stars. The angel was dressed in a flowing white robe, and its wings were magnificent. I pulled my head back into the car and rolled up the window.

I thought, *"Did I really see an angel in the sky?"* I sat there for a moment listening to them talk about all the stars. They said nothing about seeing an angel.

Can you imagine what it was like to see
a giant angel in this beautiful night sky?

I couldn't resist, so I rolled down the window and stuck my head out again. It was still there. A giant angel dressed in a flowing white robe with magnificent white wings and outlined by the stars. It seemed to look right at me. I couldn't believe it. It was gigantic, and I could see it so clearly. I thought, *"My friends in the front seat must be able to see it too. Why aren't they saying anything about it?"* This caused me to be unsure. So they wouldn't think that I was crazy, I said, "Do you guys see the North star? It is straight up in the sky to the right." I was wondering if my friends could see the same giant angel that I saw. After looking for a moment, they said "No, we don't see the North Star."

I waited a minute and then rolled down the window for the third time. The angel was still there, shimmering white and outlined in stars. It had a kindly face and seemed to be looking directly at me. I decided not to say anything else, so I pulled my head back in the car and rolled up the window.

I felt off balance, almost lightheaded. I didn't know what to do, but I sure wasn't going to look out the window again! I was simply overwhelmed. I thought, *"Was I crazy or was this a sign from God? If so, what did it mean?"*

When we got to my car, I thanked my friends and drove home. There were so many events from the week that were confusing. All I wanted to do was to get home and get to bed. I didn't want to see anything or hear anything else. I was going home, confident that if I got a good night's sleep, everything would go back to normal. I couldn't have been more wrong.

Chapter 5
What Are You Going To Do About It?
(Michael)

I had seen the giant angel in the sky on Friday night after returning from Mesa to Denver. I didn't sleep very well that night after all the events that had happened that week. The next morning, on Saturday, I had an open house scheduled with my friend, Mike, the real estate agent who had revealed that he was a Mormon before I left on my trip. Our routine consisted of showing up at the open house early, and then driving around to make sure that the signs for the open house were put up properly. We got into his car to take a ride around the neighborhood to check our signs.

I suddenly asked Mike, "Have you ever had a vision or heard any voices talking to you inside your head?" I knew that it was a weird question, but I needed some answers about what had happened the previous week. Somehow, I thought that Mike would understand what I had gone through.

He replied, "I have had revelation before. Did something happen on your trip?" I told him that there had been several events that happened on my trip and explained them to him one by one. I finished with the experience that happened the night before, when I saw the giant angel in the sky.

I said, "What's happening to me, Mike? What does all this mean?"

He answered, "You are asking the wrong question."

I said, "What question should I be asking?"

He suggested, "The question that you should be asking yourself is: 'What am I going to do about it?'"

This hit me like a ton of bricks. I thought, *What was I going to do about it?* I said, "What do you mean?"

He explained, "It's obvious to me that Heavenly Father has chosen this time in your life to speak to you through the voice of the

Spirit and in vision. It doesn't happen this way for everyone. You shouldn't be asking, what is happening? The Lord is inviting you to join Him. Will you follow Him and be baptized, or will you ignore the call and go back to what you were doing?"

I thought, *"I just want to go back to what I was doing."* I didn't want to hear another voice or see another vision. I wanted to be left alone, but Heavenly Father had other plans for me.

The Visit

I woke up on Sunday to a bright, sunny, and cold day in Denver. I had gotten a tentative night's sleep and was hoping that today was going to be uneventful. The day started out that way. Sunday was not considered the Sabbath to me. Jews celebrate the Sabbath from sundown on Friday night to sundown on Saturday night, just like it has been done for thousands of years.

As I lay in my bed that morning, I thought about what had happened the previous day. I remembered what Mike had said, *"What am I going to do about it?"* I decided to try to forget about it and lose myself in some work in my home office. I decided to get a little food in my stomach and maybe that would help me sort out my thoughts. As I was eating, a powerful thought, which seemed like an epiphany came to me. The logical answer to my questions seemed to be: *"The events that have happened to me in the last two weeks are preparing me to have the capacity to receive something new."* I took that thought and put it in the back of my mind since I had to catch up on my work.

Since I had been gone the previous week, Sunday turned out to be my "catch-up-on-work day." As a real estate agent, I worked from home and had turned a small bedroom into an office. I had a TV to stay caught up with the news, my computer, file cabinets, and a desk to work at. Often times when I was trying to figure things out, I would pace around the room. Most of the time, it would just give me a break from sitting at the desk.

At around 7 p.m. when I was finishing my work, I remember pacing around the room, contemplating my next business week. All of a sudden, the room started to go dark. I had the TV turned on, all the lights were on, and my computer was on, too. The darkness started in the corners and crept into the center of the room where I was standing. Everything that was turned on went quiet, like someone had hit a mute button. I ended up standing in the center of a pitch black room with no sound from the TV or anything else.

The funny thing about this was that it didn't scare me at all. I thought, *"Shouldn't I be scared?"* I felt completely calm as the darkness was spreading into the center of the room. I realized later that the darkness was preparing me for the light that was to come, just like theatre lights coming down before the curtain raises and the story begins. Then a light suddenly shined down, next to me, as if someone had turned on a soft spotlight to highlight the space immediately to my left. As I looked to my left, a figure appeared, dressed in a brilliant white robe.

The figure was shimmering in white, in the same way as the giant angel that had appeared in the sky, two nights previous. This time the figure did not have wings. It was a male figure in a white robe. He had long white hair and a kind face. He looked directly at me and said, "Michael, I sent you the vision of the angel, because I knew that if I had sent you a vision of Jesus, you would have rejected it. I am here at this time in your life, so that you can see the path that you are to take."

He then proceeded to show me my life, as if we were in a diorama in a museum. I thought back to being a kid on a field trip when our teacher had taken us into a big room in a museum. Then the lights were turned off, and windows were lit up, one at a time around the room. I remember that it showed the evolution of life and how monkeys evolved into modern man. This time it was slightly different.

So, one at a time, my visitor would point to a particular place in the room and it would light up a window showing me a certain time period in my life. After he explained what was happening in each window, that window would go dark and another one would light up next to it. I saw things from my childhood, young adulthood, and finally as an adult. As each new window would light up, he would raise his right arm and point to that window. I could feel the brush of his robe as he raised his arm and pointed each time.

This session of how my life had unfolded over the years didn't seem spectacular at all. I have to admit that there were several painful events that happened in my life. Some were painful events that I had caused, and some were painful events that others had caused.

There were many joyful events. Some events contained the joy that I had experienced, and some contained the joy that I had brought to others. Whether joyful or painful, his voice never changed in tone. He did not condemn me, nor was he judgmental.

Imagine having someone show you your life in that manner. Would you have any regrets, or would you be proud of everything that had happened? It seemed daunting to me to have someone go through my life like that. Joy, love, pain, heartbreak, laughter, it was all there.

Then the figure turned to me and said, "Michael, if you follow what I tell you to do, this is how the rest of your life will turn out."

He raised his arm again and pointed to a new set of windows. As each window lit up, he showed me another future segment in my life. One window showed me standing at a podium speaking before a large crowd. I was in a vast hall, where I couldn't see the back of the auditorium. I had a hard time believing this, because I am deathly afraid of getting up in front of people and speaking. Another window opened up and showed me standing with a silhouette of a family.

He said, "You will have an eternal companion." I thought, *"What does he mean by eternal companion?"*

Many more windows were opened to show me all types of wonderful things that could be possible during the rest of my life. It was hard to believe that he was speaking about me. I had made many mistakes and struggled with many issues in my life so far.

The figure then said, "Your many trials have prepared you for what you will have to deal with in the future."

This statement scared me. Some of my trials in the past had been horrific. I certainly didn't want to deal with those issues again. He then said, "Follow my word, and you will receive the abundance of heaven."

After that final statement, the figure disappeared as quickly as he had come. Normal light and sound started to return to the room. It started from where he had been standing and expanded out to all four corners. The TV and my computer were both back on as I tried to get my bearings.

I stood in the center of the room, exhausted, as if I had just run a marathon. My mind couldn't comprehend what had just happened. I thought, *"Did this really happen or did I just imagine this?"* I tried to gather my thoughts as I sat down at my desk to make notes. Although I was overwhelmed, I tried to remember everything that the figure had said and write it down.

I looked at the clock and it said 11:20 p.m.. I was shocked! I remember looking at the clock right before the figure appeared, and it was about 7 p.m.. What I thought had happened in a few minutes, had gone on for four hours.

I realized that the personage hadn't told me his name. I thought, *"Could it have been Heavenly Father Himself, or was it an angel or some kind of messenger from God?"* I continued writing down all that I could remember and stumbled into bed.

I have since learned that God's pattern is to send angels with messages from him. Sometimes they introduce who they are, and sometimes they don't. In this case I don't have any idea who it was that visited me that night.

In the context of Joseph Smith receiving revelation through word and vision, he said, "If I had not experienced what I have, I would not have believed it myself."

Many times during the first year of my conversion process, I would pray and ask Heavenly Father "Did this really happen? Did I really see and hear these incredible things?" These events were so fantastic that I could hardly believe them myself. The answer from the Holy Spirit was always the same. "You know in your heart what you have heard and seen. Remember the vision of the angel."

Move Right Now

I woke up at 11 a.m. on Monday morning. I had slept almost 12 hours. I lay in bed for a few minutes thinking about the previous night. Surely it was just an incredible dream. I got up and went about my daily routine, but I felt different somehow.

The difference started as I got down on my knees for the first time in many years and said a morning prayer. I decided to put what had happened the previous night in the back of my mind and get my day started. That lasted for a while, but sometime in the late afternoon, I started hearing a voice in my head. It sounded like the same voice as the figure who had appeared in my home office.

The voice said, "Pack your belongings and move now."

I thought, *"Why would I want to move now, and to where?"*

As if the voice had heard me, it said, "Pack your belongings and move to Mesa, Arizona."

I questioned, "Why?"

The voice said, "If you follow my word, you will receive all of the abundance of heaven."

I replied, "I can't move, I am rebuilding my real estate career here in Denver. It is starting to take off again."

The voice repeated, "If you follow my word, you will receive all of the abundance of heaven."

I argued, "I can't do that. This is crazy. I am receiving abundance by selling homes and making money. What will I do in Mesa, Arizona? How will I earn a living?"

The voice did not answer the last statement that I made, but he was far from done with me. I went about the rest of my afternoon and didn't hear the voice again, until that evening after I had dinner.

The voice calmly said, "Pack your belongings and move now."

Again, I replied, "I can't do that. I'm not ready."

The voice repeated, "If you follow my word, you will receive all of the abundance of heaven."

This exchange went on, periodically, for several days. It seemed to happen three or more times a day, the first day. The number of times for this exchange increased every day. I got to the point where I couldn't get it out of my head. It would happen in the shower, in the car, and while I was eating. I couldn't get it to stop. It finally got to the point where I couldn't concentrate on work and started to anticipate when would be the next time that this exchange between me and the voice would happen again.

By the end of the week, I couldn't take it anymore. It was like when you're a little kid, and your mother keeps telling you to tie your shoes, and you finally say, in a loud irritated voice, "ALL RIGHT Mom, I'll tie my shoe!"

It was like something inside me snapped, and I yelled, "ALL RIGHT, I'll move!" I happened to be in the middle of the grocery store when I yelled it!

From that day forward, I started to organize my belongings. I then held a garage sale the following month and sold as many things as I could. I rented a truck with a trailer for towing my car. I did most everything myself, except for one friend, Chris, and his family who helped me with the garage sale and hooking up the car trailer.

As I told my friends that I felt prompted to move, they seemed to turn away from me, one at a time. They thought that I was crazy to leave just as I was rebuilding my real estate business.

It seemed that as long as I was packing or doing something to organize my affairs and move, the voice didn't say anything to me. If I hesitated for a day or two and didn't do anything towards the goal of moving, the exchange between the voice and me would happen again. I never considered myself a slow learner, but I soon thought that the voice thought I was!

The garage sale, packing, moving, and the settling of my affairs all happened within 60 days. I had experienced incredible things of a spiritual nature in Mesa, Arizona, during the first week of November 2012. I followed the directive that had been given to me, and arrived in Mesa in early January 2013.

Where Are The Crosses?

Ken and Joanne agreed to let me stay at their house until I could get settled. Looking back now, I didn't think through my move at all. It was simple; the voice told me to move and I moved. I was confused as to who was behind the voice, but somehow I trusted what the voice was telling me to do. I didn't think about where I would be working or if I would get my real estate license in Arizona. I just felt it was the right thing to do, so I moved.

I hadn't done anything like this before. My nature is to be prepared and plan ahead. I had lived in different cities and states, but I always had a job lined up ahead of time. That wasn't the case this time.

I arrived in Mesa and was invited to join Ken and Joanne for church services the next Sunday. It was unusual that I willingly said yes, without any hesitation at all. I was told that the LDS Church service was actually a "block" that included educational classes that lasted three hours. I would follow Ken around and sit in on the different sessions.

The first thing that I noticed when I entered the church building was that there were no crosses on the building or pictures of Jesus on the cross. It had always felt painful to me when I had gone in a Christian church with friends to see Jesus all bloodied with a crown of thorns and nailed to a cross. It seemed brutal to have those types of pictures on the wall. In the LDS Church, there were no such pictures anywhere within the building.

As we sat down in one of the pews, waiting for the service to start, I asked the question, "Why aren't there any pictures of Jesus on the cross?"

The reply was, "The cross was an instrument of torture. We don't display an instrument of torture; we would rather concentrate on his life. If he had been shot with a gun or stabbed with a knife, would we put a gun or a knife on the top of our church?"

Somehow, this made a lot of sense to me. Why focus on his death and the brutal way that he died, instead of focusing on his life?

Growing up Jewish, we were not allowed to study the New Testament, nor Jesus' life. Jesus was thought of as a High Priest, Rabbi or teacher, not the Messiah. I really wasn't fully aware of all of His life or His teachings.

As the church service started, there was an opening prayer and an opening hymn. I looked through the hymn book and didn't recognize any of the hymns. At the bottom of each page there were the names of the composers of the words and the music, but I did not recognize any of the names. They seemed to all be born in the 1800s.

Then the bishop, the leader of the congregation, went up to the podium, welcomed the congregation, and talked about ward business. I didn't understand what a ward was. I always thought of a ward as part of a prison system!

First, the bishop said that they had released someone from their calling and asked everyone to give a vote of thanks for their service by raising their right hand in the air. That seemed very peculiar to me. It was almost as if they were voting for this person, but the bishop said that it was a show of appreciation for their service.

Next, they sang another hymn, which I didn't recognize. Then there were speakers, youth and adults, talking about spiritual subjects. Each of them ended their talk with, "In the name of Jesus Christ. Amen." I could remember hearing Christian prayers being ended that way, but never a talk. It surprised me, I thought, *"Why did they end a talk that way?"*

As I looked around the chapel, I noticed that there was not one picture of Jesus on the wall. In fact there were no pictures on the wall at all inside the chapel. I thought, *"This chapel could easily have been a synagogue. It just needed an ark behind the podium to hold the Holy Torahs."*

The service lasted about an hour and included the passing of the sacrament. This included bread and water, instead of bread and wine. Everyone then got up and went to the next part of the "block." I thought, *"Isn't that also a prison term?"* The next hour was spent in a religious school class called Gospel Doctrine. It seemed that every year they studied a different holy book. One year they would study the Book of Mormon. The next year they would study the Old Testament, which to a Jew is the Bible. The year after that they would study the New Testament, which to a Jew doesn't really matter. Then the next year they would study the Doctrine and Covenants (modern revelation), which to a Jew really doesn't exist!

This was the year that they were studying the Book of Mormon. I had already read bits and pieces of the Book of Mormon over the last couple of weeks. It seemed like an unusual story, and this class really helped me appreciate the importance of it. I thought, *"Archeologists continue to find ancient scrolls and people seem to be thrilled when these discoveries are made. Maybe the Book of Mormon was one of those discoveries!"*

The next session was called Combined Priesthood. This session had all the young men and adult men of the congregation in it. I wondered, *"Where did all the women go?"* I found out later that the women went to a session called Relief Society. I thought, *"Relief from what? Do the women need relief from being around the men?*

Relief Society meeting turned out to be the same thing as a Sisterhood meeting in a Jewish congregation. The young women and the young men went to their own separate meetings.

The men said a prayer, sang a hymn, and then the bishop asked the different groups, one by one, if there was any news. The adult men seemed to be divided into two groups, Elders and High Priests.

This Combined Priesthood meeting lasted for about 10 minutes, and then they broke into two groups for the men and three groups for the young men. The young men divided into Deacons, Teachers and Priests, 12, 14 and 16 years old respectively.

I followed my friend into the High Priest group. This group consisted of former bishops, high councilmen and other various former leaders of the local church congregations. I wondered, *"Why am I in here?"*

The High Priest group leader asked if there were any visitors. My friend stood up and introduced me by name and said I was a Jew. I got the feeling of apprehension for a moment, because as a Jew, I wasn't always welcomed into new groups, particularly Christian groups. This time nothing happened. No one made a snide remark, nor gave me that look of "you don't belong here" that had become so familiar to me during my life.

The High Priest group leader talked about upcoming activities and then turned over the rest of that hour session to a teacher. There was a lesson that included participation from the group and was very interesting. They talked a lot about service to their fellow man and helping others on their journey through life. This session was the last of the total "block" and concluded the main church activity for the day.

After the third session was choir practice. The choir was made up of volunteers. I had been following my friend all day, so it just seemed natural that I follow him into choir practice. The hymns were still unfamiliar to me, and I realized that I hadn't sung in a choir since ninth grade.

My mother was a music teacher, so from the age of five until the age of 21, I studied music. I was in the choir and the band, but in ninth grade, I decided to just be in the band, since playing an instrument conflicted with being in the choir. I knew the baseline of the music when I played an instrument, so I sat in the bass section.

The bass section consisted of Logan, Sam, Lance and Jim. All of these men would end up having a great influence on me during my conversion process. Who would ever guess that volunteering to sing in a ward choir would have such a profound influence on my future spiritual progression?

I sat in the choir loft, listening to the others singing. In between hymns, one of the men, Lance, whom I had met in the High Priest lesson turned to me and asked, "Michael, have you ever sung any of these hymns before?"

I said, "No, I've never even heard any of these hymns before. Most of the hymns that I know are in Hebrew." I caught myself and wondered if this was going to invite negative comments about being a Jew. No such thing happened.

Lance replied, "Then that means that you can learn some new hymns in your second language, English!" That brought a chuckle between us. As he said it, I looked into his eyes, and there was no malice there. I was pleasantly surprised.

We then went home and had a nice Sunday dinner. It felt unusual, but I looked forward to the next Sunday, and to what I would learn, and who I might meet.

I went to two more Sunday services in January. Each service was more interesting than the last. I kept expecting to hear that familiar voice in my head again. The only time that I would hear it would be when I would suddenly be awakened at 3 or 4 a.m. out of a deep sleep. I had gotten in the habit of having a book of scripture next to my bed.

Before I was fully awake, I would realize that I was reading scripture, either the Book of Mormon, the Bible or the New Testament. The passages were always different, except for one that kept reoccurring. They always seemed relevant to what I was thinking about that week or had heard during the "block" on Sunday. The one reoccurring passage that I would find myself reading was a passage from the Bible,

15 The word of the LORD came again unto me, saying,

16 Moreover, thou son of man, take thee one stick, and write upon it, for Judah, and for the children of Israel his companions: then take another stick, and write upon it, for Joseph, the stick of Ephraim, and for all the house of Israel his companions:
17 And join them one to another into one stick; and they shall become one in thine hand.
18 And when the children of thy people shall speak unto thee, saying, Wilt thou not shew us what thou meanest by these?
19 Say unto them, Thus saith the Lord GOD; Behold, I will take the stick of Joseph, which is in the hand of Ephraim, and the tribes of Israel his fellows, and will put them with him, even with the stick of Judah, and make them one stick, and they shall be one in mine hand.   Ezekiel 37:15-19

Every time that I read that passage, the voice would say, "This passage describes you."

I didn't know exactly what that meant. I thought that I was of the tribe of Judah, because I so strongly identified with my father's ancestry. I seemed to know my identity, from the time that I was a child. I thought, *"What did that passage really have to do with me?"*

I know now that it is Mormon doctrine that explains that the two "sticks" were the Bible and the Book of Mormon. What I didn't know, was that there was an additional meaning that directly related to me that would reaffirm what the voice was telling me about that passage.

On the last Sunday in January, I sat in sacrament meeting for a few minutes after everyone had gone to Gospel Doctrine class, which was the next session in the "block." I remember that I was sitting in the last cushioned pew in the chapel. There were only a few people left in the chapel besides me.

I suddenly heard a voice say, "You will be baptized on your birthday and born again." That thought was so startling, that I quickly looked around to see if there was someone standing behind me and teasing me. I looked around and there was no one, anywhere close to me. This shocked me because I had never thought about being "born again." That wasn't a phrase that would be in a Jew's vocabulary.

I thought, *"Is this the reason that I moved here, to join the Mormon Church?"*

After Gospel Doctrine class, I walked back into the chapel for the High Priest session and walked up the aisle on the side of the pews. I then worked my way into one of the pews towards the middle and saw that someone else was working his way into the middle of that same pew from the other side.

As we approached each other to sit down, the man reached out his hand and said, "My name is Sam Woodruff, and I just moved back into the ward."

I replied, "My name is Michael Morton, and I haven't been baptized yet."

I'm not really sure why I said it that way, but that's how it came out. Both of us chuckled about that and sat down together to listen to the High Priest lesson. Sam and I became good friends from that point forward. I was a real estate agent, and he was an attorney who had spent a good portion of his career negotiating real estate contracts. Sam would tell me later, that when he met me and we shook hands, he thought, *"I really need to get to know this guy."*

He turned out to be exactly the mentor that I needed, to help guide me through my beginning time with the church, as well as the move that I had made to Mesa. We had many discussions about life in general and the gospel. Sam would later help guide me through one of the most valuable experiences of my life.

Later that Sunday, at dinner, I told Joanne about the voice telling me to be baptized. Unbeknownst to me, she went in the other room and called the missionaries.

I learned that there were two missionaries assigned to each ward. These missionaries are between the ages of 18 and 23 years-old and are placed in different cities around the world.

This sneaky move on her part turned out to be the beginning of a new direction in my life. I didn't realize it at the time, but having the missionaries teach me would be the spark that would ignite within me the desire to pursue and teach the truth.

The knowledge that I had gained growing up Jewish would become far more valuable than I imagined once it was combined with the truth of the gospel. These two young sister missionaries were about to provide that spark. That night would be my first missionary lesson.

Chapter 6
My First Talk
(John)

If you have a belief in God, have you ever wondered where it came from? In my case, it was strengthened one day by my aged grandmother. I was in my early teens, and living less than a block from us was my mom's mother. Nana lived in a small apartment on the corner of two very busy streets in North Long Beach, California. She was at a stage in her life where, with the help of two canes, she could still walk. She was suffering from severe arthritis in her joints.

Almost every evening, my mother would prepare a nice meal for her. I would be the one to deliver the meal and have a chance to visit with her while she ate. One night, she told me a story that had a profound effect on my belief that there really was a God. She told me that the previous evening, after I had left; she started to get ready for bed. Before she went to bed, she locked all the doors, took off her dress and went into the bathroom. The floor of the bathroom was tiled, and she slipped on the tile and fell between the bathtub and the toilet. She soon realized that she did not have the strength in her to lift herself back up.

By about 7 o'clock in the evening, the windows of her apartment were still open and the cold night air filled the room. As the sun went down, darkness set in as the lights had not been turned on in her apartment.

She realized that she was in a very precarious situation. She told me that she started to cry out at the top of her lungs for help. Because the windows were open, the noise from the traffic drowned out her cries. After an hour, she realized that no one could hear her and started to cry. She told me that the room was then completely dark and the chill of the night had penetrated her frail body. She felt like she was not going to survive till morning. Nana remembered that she had been taught as a child that she had a loving Father in

Heaven and she started to cry out to Him. She started petitioning Him for help.

Her pleading was answered almost immediately. She said, "John, God sent somebody to help me. I could sense that someone came into the bathroom. It was so dark that I couldn't see who it was. He gently picked me up and carefully helped me into my bedroom. I could feel the strength of his arms and the warmth of his body, but he never said a word. He gently set me on the edge of my bed and left. I was shaking from the cold, so I laid down and pulled the blanket over me. I fell into a deep sleep and awoke the next morning."

She continued, "I don't know if it was Heavenly Father or an angel that was sent from His presence. I do know that there is a loving God in heaven and He answered my prayer." I was riveted to what she was saying, because I knew that she would not make this story up. My Nana was telling me the truth and the truth had penetrated my heart.

That story, from my beloved Nana, had a profound effect on me as a 12-year-old boy. Since my mother had instilled in me the importance of prayer, now both of these women had given me an absolute witness that I have a loving Father in Heaven. Their witness was part of the preparation for me to accept the truth when it was presented to me at BYU. God had called a living prophet and had restored his church to the earth.

In our LDS hymnbook today there is a hymn called "Faith of Our Fathers." The first line says, "Faith of our fathers, living still." Every time I sing that hymn I think, *"The faith of my mothers is living still."* I'll be forever grateful to my wonderful grandmother and mother for their faith and belief in a living God.

New Member

One of the remarkable things about the LDS Church is that young children in Primary are asked to pray, read scriptures and give talks in front of their peers. This is a process of refinement which enables them to learn to communicate clearly. They can express their religious ideas and beliefs without fear. It gives them confidence and poise and the ability to speak in front of groups. This prepares them to be leaders, not only in the church, but in every aspect of life. As I wasn't raised in the Church, I didn't have any of this training. The only time I had spoken in front of a large group was as at my high school graduation where I was the commencement speaker to over 3,000 people.

As a convert, I missed that opportunity of growth. However, as a new member of the Church, I realized that your new peers are anxious to hear from you. So shortly after I was baptized, I was asked to speak in church. You either speak in your ward, which is about 400 people, or you speak to your stake of combined wards, which is about 2000 people. My first opportunity to speak was to a stake at BYU.

The meeting was held in the Ernest L. Wilkinson Center, on the BYU campus. I entered the conference room, was ushered onto the stand, and sat down directly behind the podium. Because of where I was sitting, I could not see who was directly in front of me in the first row. When my turn came to speak, I stepped up to the podium and looked down at those particular seats.

To my total shock, two of the individuals sitting in the front row, were Joseph Fielding Smith and his wife, Jesse Evans Smith. Little did I know, but I was about to speak to a future President of the Church. President Smith was the head of the Quorum of the Twelve Apostles. Can you imagine the feelings that I had when I realized who was sitting in front of me, just a few feet away? In an instant, fear and trembling took on a whole new meaning for me.

As I began to speak and tell my conversion story, a remarkable thing happened. These two wonderful members of the church never took their eyes off of me, but nodded their continual approval and appreciation throughout for my remarks.

The most enthusiastic recipient of my testimony was Jesse Evans Smith. I will never forget the look on her face as she nodded and smiled her total support. I'm sure she sensed the insecurity and sheer fright that was in me. I finished and breathed a sigh of relief. I had just experienced a major growth opportunity that would stay with me to this day. When I am asked to speak now, I often reflect back on the feelings that I had then, and the support that they gave me with their approval and smiles.

There isn't a paid professional clergy in the LDS Church. Isn't it amazing how the Savior set up His church as a lay ministry? If we accept the callings that are given to us in the Church, the opportunities for personal growth will come as a result of serving.

This lay ministry is one of the great tenets of the Church of Jesus Christ of Latter-day Saints. It all started with the Savior calling a group of fishermen to be fishers of men, and it continues to this day.

Poster Boy for Apostasy

I feel very blessed to have been a member of a large extended Christian family. My mother had four sisters, and my father had eight brothers and sisters. All of those aunts and uncles had many children. Out of all those children, many different Christian faiths were represented, except for the LDS faith. I was to be the first practicing Mormon in my current family. I felt a huge responsibility to share the truth that I had gained. So I sat down and filled out missionary referral cards on every one of my relatives. It turned out to be a stack of cards over an inch high.

The way this works is as follows: you fill out a referral card with their name, address and phone number, asking the full time missionaries to make a visit. When the missionaries knock on the recipient's door, they say that they have a special message, and they were sent by whoever referred them. In this case it was me.

Well, you can imagine the phone calls I received, "John, why in the world did you send the Mormon missionaries to my house?" My answer was always the same, "I sent them because I don't want you complaining in the next life that I knew about this and never told you." Some of them laughed at me, but I didn't care, because I felt a sense of relief at having met my responsibility to them, if even in this most minimum way possible.

At BYU, I had enrolled in a church history class. One of the assignments was to do some family genealogy. I was supposed to go back a few generations to discover who my ancestors were. So, to fulfill this assignment, I went to the Harold B. Lee Library, which contained the special historical collections. I remembered the name, William B. Preston, whom my grandmother had told me was a bishop in the Church. When I looked up his name in the card catalog, I saw dozens of cards referencing him!

I took the first reference card and asked the librarian to please let me see the record. She returned with a copy of the Deseret News with the headline, in bold type, "Presiding Bishop William B. Preston Dies." I can't describe the total shock that hit me. My great, great grandfather was not only a member of the Church, but he was a general authority. He was a pioneer and was a founding father of Logan, Utah. He had a beautiful huge home across the street from the Salt Lake Temple. He had many children and was true to the faith until the end of his life. I thought, *"How in the world, does my branch of his posterity have no knowledge of, nor appreciation for, the LDS faith?"*

Reflecting back, one of the first thoughts that I had, as I learned the history of the Mormon Church, was *"I wish that I had a noble pioneer ancestor."* I now realized that my wish had come true. The joy of that thought was mixed with the confusion of what could have caused my ancestors to fall away from the truth. The answer to that question was one that I had to find.

When the opportunity arose, on my next trip home, I asked my grandmother, "Why does no one in our family know anything about the Mormon Church? How could this happen when we had such a famous ancestor who was true to the faith?" With tears in her eyes, my grandmother explained, "My husband passed away when he was in his 40's. When I moved to California from Utah, with my four daughters, I stopped going to the church. Your mother and her sisters were very young and didn't get the benefit of growing up in the LDS faith. Leaving the Mormon Church was the biggest mistake of my life, I can still remember some of the sweet songs that I learned in Primary."

My grandmother was bedridden with arthritic pain and was in the last few years of her life when she told me this. She started singing Primary songs from her bed. She could only remember parts of the songs, but we were both in tears by the time she finished. I think that she realized how different our family would be if she had not let go of the church.

In that moment with my grandmother, I realized how important it is that once you are given the truth, you should treasure it. You must embrace it and hold on to it with all your strength, and never let it go. The words of John Greenleaf Whittier come to mind, "Of all sad words of tongue or pen, the saddest are these: 'It might have been!'"

My grandmother Harriet, whom I lovingly called Nana, passed into the Spirit World, but if I could tell her now what is in my heart, I would say, "You set an example of faith for me, and I'll continue it on for the rest of the family. A family's apostasy can be reversed over time. Most of your posterity has lost the knowledge of their roots in the restored Church of Jesus Christ of Latter-day Saints, but over time, each one of them will have the opportunity to know the full truth. Knowing what good people our relatives are, I have every hope that they will return to the faith of their fathers, to the restored Gospel of Jesus Christ and rejoin the Kingdom of God here on earth. This is going to happen, I'm sure of it. No worries Nana!"

Why Search The Past?

Why study the past? The Mormon Church has always emphasized the importance of searching your family history by doing genealogy. Why? I was now beginning to understand the answer to that question. We search the past to improve our future.

Someone once said those who don't know history and don't study the mistakes of the past are bound to repeat them.

I sensed the positive side of that idea as I came to discover who William B. Preston was. The strength that I gained from learning about my long lost ancestor was beyond belief. His righteous example was empowering to me. I was excited that I would have the opportunity to meet him some day in the next life. I was determined to live in a way that would make him proud to have me as one of his descendants. I was proud of having him as my great, great grandfather. Here are a few reasons why:

William Bowker Preston 1830-1908

1830 Born Franklin County, Virginia

1857 Baptized and ordained an Elder in the Restored Church of Jesus Christ

1858 Married Harriet Thatcher

1859 Among the first settlers of Logan, Utah

1859 November, Made Bishop of Logan, Utah

1862 Member of the Utah Territorial Legislature

1865 - 1868 Missionary to England

1870 - 1882 Mayor of Logan, Utah

1872 - 1882 Member of the Utah Territorial Legislature
Presiding Bishop of Cache County after Peter Maughan, Vice President of Utah and Northern Railway

1879 - 1884 President of the Cache Stake
Director of Logan Cooperative Mercantile Institution, Board of Trustees of Brigham Young College
Chairman of the Executive Committee of Brigham Young College

1884 Called by President John Taylor as the 4th LDS Presiding Bishop

1895 Member of the Utah State Constitutional Convention

1907 December 4, Resigned as Presiding Bishop of the Church due to ill health

1908 August 2, Died of pneumonia (aged 77) Buried Logan City Cemetery

William B. Preston (John's Great, Great, Grandfather)

I thought, *"Wow. This is breathtaking to me. I thought I had a busy life. How could he accomplish so many great achievements in just one lifetime? I am so proud to be his great, great grandson."*

I was now beginning to understand the importance of family history.

Chapter 7
Fast Track
(Michael)

The two missionaries who came over to the house that evening were young women who were about the age of 19 or 20. They were on their 18-month "mission calling" in Mesa. The only thing that I knew about missionaries was that I had politely closed the door on young people like them many times before, because I was not interested in their message.

Ken, Joanne, "Bobby" (Barbara, Ken's mother) and I sat down in the living room with the sister missionaries. This time, I looked at these two young women whose countenances were so full of light and joy, and thought, *"How amazing that these two gave up school, friends, and family to leave home for a year and a half to teach people, like me, what they believe."* I later learned that there are over 90,000 of these young people serving all over the world.

One missionary, Sister Kelsey, was from Georgia, and the other missionary, Sister Christy, was from Hawaii. They carried their "quads" that contained full copies of the Bible, New Testament, Book of Mormon, and Doctrine and Covenants, all bound into one book. Ken and Joanne had recently given me a quad of my own, with my name embossed in gold letters on the cover. I would soon learn how knowledgeable these missionaries were in scripture.

I was still debating as to whether to get baptized or not. I had just packed up everything I owned and moved a thousand miles to Mesa, Arizona. I thought, *"How can I still be undecided about this?"* I moved to Mesa following the prompting of the voice in my head, but I still didn't know if I wanted to convert or not. I was still confused about hearing the voice tell me, "You will be baptized on your birthday and born again."

We all went into the living room and the missionaries introduced themselves. Joanne announced that the missionaries had come over to start giving me lessons. I said, "Lessons in what?"

Sister Kelsey said, "Lessons about the gospel of Jesus Christ."

I thought cautiously to myself, *"Here is another fine mess that I have gotten myself into."* The missionaries then explained that they worked within our ward, teaching members and nonmembers about the LDS church.

This first night seemed to be an introduction into how they taught lessons. They started out by asking me if I had any questions. I said, "Not really" even though I did have many. The lesson continued with the two missionary "Sisters," as they were called, reading different scriptures and explaining the meanings to me. The Sisters ended the session by giving me a pamphlet on Jesus and saying that they would be back in a couple of days for another lesson. We ended with a prayer. They were very nice and seemed quite innocent in their approach.

Two nights later, the same two missionaries came back for another discussion. They sat down and asked me if I had read the pamphlet and did I have any questions about it.

I said, "No, it was self-explanatory." They then asked me if I intended to get baptized. I thought, *"Joanne must have told them what the voice said to me in church."* I was still conflicted about whether or not to get baptized and said "I'm not sure yet."

They discussed this with me for a minute and told me how wonderful it was to receive the gift of the Holy Spirit. Then they said that I should pray about it and ask Heavenly Father for guidance. They set another appointment and left for the evening.

The missionaries came back a couple of days later, but this time Ken had invited a neighbor, Ron, to join our group. Ron was also a member of the ward. Ron was an older gentleman in his eighties. He was a kind, gentle man and very clear in his thoughts and words. I think the word had gotten around the ward that I was something of an anomaly, a Jew who was investigating the LDS faith.

The missionaries started this lesson by telling me that they had prayed about my situation, and that I should be baptized the next Saturday, February 9th. Without thinking, I said, "I would like to be baptized on my birthday, because that is what the Lord has told me to do." I couldn't believe that those words came out of my mouth. The missionaries asked me to pray about the February 9th date and tell them what message I had received about being baptized on their next visit.

They then handed me a pamphlet on tithing and asked me if I knew what it was. I told them that I knew that tithing was a commandment from God which had started in the Old Testament. They looked at me, as if they weren't quite sure what I was talking about. "Tithing is one of our principles that you must follow as a member of the church", they said.

I asked, "Do you know the origin of tithing?" They didn't. So I proceeded to tell them what I had learned years ago in Jewish religious school, that Father Abraham had paid tithing to Melchizedek.

After the missionaries left, Ron just sat there, stared at the floor and shook his head. He chuckled and said, "Those poor girls. They don't have any idea what they're getting into trying to teach you about the gospel."

The missionaries came back a day or so later, and Ron came back too. I guess he was curious to see what would happen next. The missionaries said, "Have you prayed about getting baptized?" I replied that I had. They said, "We prayed about it and think that Saturday, February 16, would be a great day for you to be baptized."

I explained, "I'm sorry, but I would like to be baptized on my birthday, April 8th."

They said that it wasn't necessary to be baptized on my birthday, and that I could be baptized at any time. I told them again that I would be baptized on my birthday, as the voice had told me in sacrament meeting. This exchange went on for a couple minutes. I thought, *"They asked me to get baptized first on February 9th and now on February 16. If they keep coming back, we will soon be in April anyway!"*

The missionaries came back every couple of days to teach me something more about the Church. After they gave me each lesson, they would say, "Please pray about it and you can tell us next time whether you think it is true or not."

My reply was always the same, "I don't have to pray about it, because as you were talking to me, Heavenly Father told me that what you were saying is true." Their response would reflect their amazement.

After a few more lessons, I think that they needed a change of scenery, because they asked me if I wanted to see a couple of the films that were shown at the Visitors' Center. I said yes, and agreed to meet them at the same Visitors' Center that I had been to when I came to Mesa on my business trip the previous November.

The first movie that we saw was about President Monson, the current prophet and President of the LDS Church. It told about how he had served in the Church his whole life. It was humbling to watch a story of such a fine man who had dedicated his whole life to others.

At the end of the movie, the sisters turned to me and remarked, "We would like for you to pray about it and decide if you believe that President Monson is a prophet of God."

I replied, "I don't have to. Heavenly Father already told me that he was a true prophet of God during the movie." They looked at me with a sense of wonderment in their eyes, just as they had at the end of each lesson. I seemed to know that I was being told the truth, even before they asked me to pray about it.

I would see the sisters once or twice every week from then on. I guess they were keeping track of me, so that I didn't flake out and decide not to get baptized. We started talking about my baptism again around the middle of March. The sisters explained to me that they needed to secure a date for my baptism. I explained to them again, that I would be baptized on my birthday, as the voice had told me in Sacrament Meeting. I know I sounded like a broken record as I kept repeating this, but it was just the way it had to be.

They explained to me that April 8 was on a Monday, and baptisms were usually performed on Saturdays. The Saturday before my birthday was April 6th, and that would conflict with the LDS General Conference. So in other words, no baptisms would be performed on that day. I had no idea what a LDS General Conference was, all I knew was that April 6th wasn't my birthday anyway. They explained that I could be baptized on the Saturday after my birthday. I said, "No thank you," and repeated that I wanted to be baptized on my birthday, on April 8th.

The missionaries then told me that they couldn't schedule a baptism on a Monday night, because that was family home evening. Family home evening is every Monday night, and LDS families spend that night teaching their children about the principles of the gospel and building family unity. No church activities are ever scheduled on Monday nights.

I repeated again what the voice had told me, "You will be baptized on your birthday and born again." I explained, "I moved a thousand miles, because the voice told me to do so. I have to follow what I am being told."

The sisters then explained to me that the voice I heard was the Holy Spirit. They explained that the Holy Spirit was the Great Comforter and spoke to everyone in a still small voice. I agreed with what they were saying and what the voice sounded like.

The sisters said that they would have to get permission, from the bishop and the mission president, to be able to baptize me on a Monday. I asked, "Why don't we do it at 4 p.m.? That way people with children will be able to come after they have picked their kids up from school, and then we won't interfere with their family home evening on that Monday night." The sisters said that they would try, but they didn't know if they would get approval.

At that moment the Spirit spoke to me and again said, "You will be baptized on your birthday and born again." I then looked directly at the Sisters and said, "Don't worry, your request will be approved."

Two days later, the sisters came back for another lesson and excitedly said, "Your baptism has been approved for 4 p.m. on Monday, April 8th, your birthday!" I had pushed so hard for this to happen on my birthday and now it had been approved. Even though it had come together in such an amazing way, I still wondered, *"Am I doing the right thing?"* I learned later that it took Brigham Young two years to decide the church was true and then to be baptized. I seemed to be on a faster track. Maybe it was because I was in my late 50's and time was running out!

Looking back, I think that I probably came across as very apprehensive to the sister missionaries about going through this process. I don't think that anyone realized how difficult it was for me to adjust my religious beliefs, after being true to one religion for 56 years.

I had literally fought for my religious freedom to worship as a Jew all of my life. Even though I knew in my heart that I was doing the right thing in accepting the Gospel, I still questioned the change at the same time.

I would like for those two sister missionaries to know that I will be eternally grateful for their efforts. I would like to thank them for their selfless service and for their incredible patience with me during my struggle to understand the restored truth.

Volunteer

I remember sitting in church listening to our bishop at the beginning of sacrament meeting. He was delivering a message to the congregation, of love and gratefulness for the gospel in his life. As I sat there listening to him, I was filled with a wonderful feeling.

At that moment the Holy Spirit spoke to me saying, "You have found one of the lost tribes of Israel." I marveled at that thought and wasn't sure exactly what it meant. I didn't think that there were any recognizable tribes of Israel left on the earth besides the Jews (Tribe of Judah) and the remnants of a few of other tribes. Jews don't believe that the Tribe of Joseph (Ephraim) has been reestablished yet. Somehow, I knew that I had found a very special group of people. Although what did the "lost tribe of Israel" mean?

Each Sunday during the last hour of the block, I would sit with the High Priest group. There I would listen to the lessons, experiences, and testimonies of the High Priests. After one particular lesson, as everyone was getting up to collect their families and go home for Sunday dinner, the High Priest Group Leader, Lynn, took me aside for a moment. "Brother Morton", he said. "Would you give us a lesson?"

I hadn't been baptized yet, so I wasn't fully converted. I said, "There are more knowledgeable men in this group than I am. I don't think I know enough about your scriptures yet to give a lesson."

He explained, "New converts always give the most interesting lessons. Would you do it?"

I countered, "I don't think so, but thanks for asking."

One of the other High Priests overheard our conversation and came up to me in the parking lot, as I was walking to my car. "Michael", he said, putting his arm around my shoulder. "There is something that you should know about the Mormons."

I asked, "What is that?"

He answered, "If they ask you to volunteer for something and you don't accept it, they will assign you something anyway!" We both chuckled about it, but it struck home.

I thought about it for a couple of days and then decided I had better accept his invitation. There was no telling what they would assign me, if I didn't do it.

The next Sunday I went up to Lynn and said, "Ok, I'll give a lesson."

He questioned, "What will your lesson be on?"

I replied, "I don't know." I tried to think quickly of a title because I sure didn't want him to assign me something that I really didn't want to do. As he stood there waiting for my answer, I said, "Every week you say something about gathering Israel. Some of the members don't seem to know much about the Jews, and they are modern-day Israel. So how about if I give a talk on 'How To Gather Israel.' Will that be okay?'"

He said, "That sounds great, I'll talk to the bishop." I later learned that modern day Israel constitutes a large portion of the human family and now includes the Tribe of Ephraim, which is predominantly the LDS Church.

I grew up understanding that the biblical promise in Deuteronomy was given by Moses to the people of Israel prior to their entrance into the Land of Israel.

1 And it shall come to pass, when all these things are come upon thee, the blessing and the curse, which I have set before thee, and thou shalt call them to mind among all the nations, whither the Lord thy God hath driven thee,
2 And shalt return unto the Lord thy God, and shalt obey his voice according to all that I command thee this day, thou and thy children, with all thine heart, and with all thy soul;
3 That then the Lord thy God will turn thy captivity, and have compassion upon thee, and will return and gather thee from all the nations, whither the Lord thy God hath scattered thee.
4 If any of thine be driven out unto the outmost parts of heaven, from thence will the Lord thy God gather thee, and from thence will he fetch thee:
5 And the Lord thy God will bring thee into the land which thy fathers possessed, and thou shalt possess it; and he will do thee good, and multiply thee above the fathers.

Deuteronomy 30:1-5

Writings of the prophets Isaiah and Ezekiel encouraged the people of Israel with a promise of a future gathering of the exiles to the land of Israel has been in the hearts of Jews ever since the destruction of the Second Temple. Maimonides (ancient Jewish sage) connected its materialization with the coming of the Messiah. The gathering of the exiles in the land of Israel, became the core idea of the Zionist movement and the core idea of Israel's Scroll of Independence, embodied by the idea of going up, since the Holy Land is considered to be spiritually higher than all other land. The mass wave of immigration by Jews to the land and the State of Israel has been likened to the Exodus from Egypt.

The part that was amazing to me was finding out that the LDS Church is taking the gathering of Israel seriously. They are sending out tens of thousands of missionaries, their choice young people, on missions with the assignment to find and gather Israel. These missionaries are so dedicated to this goal that they not only give up two years of their youth, but also pay their own way. I feel that this is remarkable that they are sent all over the world. How did I miss this and not even realize that they were doing this incredible project for mankind?

The following Sunday, Lynn told me that the bishop requested that before I gave a lesson that I be baptized. Since I had decided by then to get baptized, I agreed. Then I remembered my fear of getting up in front of people and speaking. This would not be as easy as I thought; maybe I should have let them assign me something else, like cleaning the bathrooms!

Baptism

My birthday, April 8, 2013, was the day of my baptism. I turned 57 years old that day. Joanne helped me organize my baptism and assign duties to different people in the congregation. A baptism usually happens in the following sequence: opening hymn and prayer, special musical number, talk about baptism, the actual baptism, a talk about the Holy Spirit, the bishop's concluding remarks, closing hymn and prayer. The confirmation either follows the baptism or occurs the next Sunday.

The LDS stake buildings each have a baptismal font. The LDS church in Arizona is divided into several stakes (stakes of Zion); each stake typically contains six to eight wards. Each ward is a congregation. There are sometimes three wards that meet in the same church building (chapel), spread throughout the day each Sunday.

I showed up a little early for my baptism, so that I could change into my baptismal jumpsuit. Both the baptizer and baptizee wear a white jumpsuit. As I came back into the baptism room after changing, I was surprised to see about 40 or 50 people waiting to see me baptized. Many members of the congregation and also one of the missionaries that gave me my first lesson, Sister Kelsey, showed up too.

Michael, Kelsey and Ken at Michael's Baptism

Evelyn, an 8-year-old girl from our congregation, the Thunder Mountain Ward in the Salt River Stake, had been chosen to sing a special song. Evelyn sang, "My First Step", a song that her aunt, Phoebe, had written about baptism. Her mother, Hillary, was to play the piano. As they were setting up the microphone, Evelyn's father, Amos said, "My wife, Hillary isn't able to attend and play the piano today. Don't worry about it, Evelyn can both play the piano and sing."

Evelyn (Evie Clair)
Award-Winning Singer & Songwriter

I thought, "Can this little kid pull this off?" Evelyn turned out to be an incredible singer and musician, almost like a child prodigy. A couple of the men pushed a piano up within a few feet of where I was sitting. She sang with the sweetest voice and with such incredible depth for an eight-year-old, that it brought tears to my eyes.

Joanne then gave an inspiring talk on the importance of baptism. Then I went into the font with Ken. Two men are called up to witness the event. They stood on either side of the font to make sure that the person being baptized went completely under the water. I thought I was completely immersed the first time, but as I was taken down into the water my big toe stuck up above the waterline. I had to be baptized a second time!

After being completely immersed in the water a second time, my baptism was approved. I thought, *"I guess I really needed to be cleansed of all my sins, if I needed to be dunked a second time!"*

Then Mike, my real estate friend, gave a talk on the Holy Spirit. I felt grateful that Mike had flown in from Denver just for my baptism. He did something in that talk that I will never forget. When I left Denver, I gave and sold Mike a lot of my belongings that I couldn't take with me in the move. In going through those things, Mike came across a picture that I thought I had lost. It was a picture of me and my two young daughters on an evening when I had taken them to a dinner theatre. It was a treasured picture that I thought I had lost.

During his talk, Mike stepped around the podium in front of me and produced the picture and asked, "Do you remember this?" I sat stunned and looked at my two daughters whom I loved dearly, and my heart ached at the reality that through the divorce, they had been separated from me. In that painful moment, Mike said, "The gift of the Holy Ghost that you are about to receive, will help you to reunite with your two daughters." His talk was very heartfelt, and again I was brought to tears.

After the final prayer, I got up from my chair. As I stood up, I felt lightheaded, almost like I was floating. I felt this amazing feeling of joy inside as I walked around and shook everyone's hand. It seemed like I was walking on marshmallows or pillows. Everyone was then invited back to the house where Joanne and I had made several pans of lasagna for the evening meal.

At dinner, I reflected on how grateful I was to Ken and Joanne for their patience in answering my endless questions and for introducing me to the LDS Church.

I thought that the Mormons were a lot like the Jews in putting their families first and they also loved to gather together to eat. This realization brought back memories of family dinners with my Jewish relatives. I remembered my uncles sitting around the dining room table, joking with each other and playing cards after we had had a large family meal. They would tell me that there were three main elements to every Jewish holiday.

1. We were persecuted and driven from our homes.
2. We rose up and defeated our enemies.
3. Let's eat!!!

Even though we heard the same joke at every holiday, it still didn't stop them from having a good laugh about it. This also seemed to be an inappropriate joke for the festivities of the day, so I kept it to myself. I had an inner feeling of peace and felt grateful that all these people had wanted to show up for my baptism.

After dinner, people lingered around for a while talking. After we finished cleaning up, I was exhausted and went to bed. I lay on my bed and looked at the ceiling thinking about all the events of the day. I realized that I had just embarked on a new way of life.

My story could easily have ended there. I had been taught by the missionaries that the voice I heard was the Holy Spirit. I had followed what the Holy Spirit had told me to do. Now I could just settle in and live a quiet life. I should've known better, because the Lord had other things in mind for me. This was only the beginning of my journey.

Confirmation

Sometime during my missionary lessons, people started to address me as Brother Morton. In the LDS faith, they address each other as Brother and Sister, the reason being that we are all children of God, sons and daughters of our Heavenly Father. So we really are all brothers and sisters on this earth.

The bishop of my congregation, Bishop Holman, had asked me to come into his office before my baptism. Lynn, the High Priest group leader had told him that the High Priests would like for me to give a lesson sometime in April. The bishop talked to me about different things concerning my baptism, as well as what I was going to talk about during the combined priesthood lesson. The bishop then scheduled the lesson I was going to teach for one week after my confirmation.

Bishop Holman was as dedicated and prayerful as any Jewish Rabbi that I have ever known. The only difference is that he wasn't paid for all of the time that he spent, helping everyone in the congregation, since the LDS Church is a lay ministry.

So, first comes your baptism and then comes confirmation. I have learned that there are really two parts to a baptism, the baptism of water and the baptism of fire. The baptism of water is symbolic of the death, burial, and resurrection of the individual. You must be completely immersed to cleanse yourself of all your sins. The idea is that you are burying the old you, the one that had been disobedient to God's laws. Then as you come up out of the water, it is the rebirth of the new you, the one that promises to be obedient from now on. Baptism is the covenant of obedience to God's laws. That is why baptism by immersion is so important.

The baptism of fire is when you receive the gift of the Holy Ghost or Holy Spirit. Once received, it is then your privilege to have the constant companionship of the Holy Spirit. The Holy Spirit is the third member of the Godhead (God, Son and Holy Spirit). God the Father and his Son, Jesus Christ, are not residents of this earth; the Holy Spirit is. The Holy Spirit is here to give you comfort, truth, and to help you make the right choices in your life. I learned that the gift of the Holy Spirit would become the best gift that I could ever receive.

You are born into this life as a "natural man or natural woman." The natural man/woman is self-centered and has a tendency to disobey God. He/she is an enemy to God and God's laws.

Confirmation, receiving the Holy Spirit is called baptism of fire because over your lifetime, the Holy Spirit will help you to burn out the natural man/woman. The natural man's tendencies are replaced with the pure love of God and the selfless love for your fellow man.

> 19 For the natural man is an enemy to God, and has been from the fall of Adam, and will be, forever and ever, unless he yields to the enticing of the Holy Spirit, and putteth off the natural man and becometh a saint through the atonement of Christ the Lord, and becometh as a child, submissive, meek, humble, patient, full of love, willing to submit to all things which the Lord seeth fit to inflict upon him, even as a child doth submit to his father.
>
> Mosiah 3:19

My confirmation was conducted in front of the whole congregation on the Sunday after my baptism. You sit in a chair and priesthood members stand in a circle, putting their right hands on your head and their left hands on the shoulder of the man standing to their left.

One of the brothers in the circle gives the blessing and the rest stand silent until completion, when they all say, "Amen." The most important part of the prayer and blessing is when he says the words, "Receive ye the Holy Ghost." I took it as a commandment to make the Holy Ghost a constant part of my life.

On the day of my confirmation, Bishop Holman called me to the front of the chapel to sit in the chair. The bishop asked anyone who wished to stand in the circle for my blessing come forward. Men started to come forward, and there were a total of thirteen standing in the circle, counting Daniel, who gave the blessing.

As the brothers placed their hands on my head, and the blessing was being given, I felt an incredible amount of power coursing through my body. It was as if a powerful electric current started on the top of my head and worked its way through the rest of my body, all the way down to my toes. It was so powerful that my hands were shaking. They weren't shaking from nervousness; they were shaking from the power of the blessing.

After the blessing, I was congratulated as the newest member of the congregation. Usually, you are baptized around the age of eight years old. I felt a little out of place standing up in front of the congregation next to the bishop, after seeing young children stand in the same place when they were being recognized. However, I felt very calm as I found my way back to my seat, as I now had the Holy Spirit as my constant companion.

Chapter 8
I Believe In You
(John)

The four years (1960-1964) that I spent at BYU were some of the best years of my young life. I thought, at the time, that Brigham Young University was like a Mormon theme park, but it was not a park with a theme of adventure or of the inventions of the future. Instead, imagine a place where becoming more like Jesus Christ is the goal. A place where the themes are to not smoke, not drink alcohol, not do drugs, not swear, and not be immoral... a place where a true code of honor, including honesty and integrity is lived, and the main theme is "Enter to Learn, Go Forth to Serve." It was God's theme park, and it changed my life. For me, it was the happiest place on earth. That was the BYU that I loved; it was pure magic to me.

When you're studying to become a dentist, it requires a tremendous amount of time and effort in the sciences. I decided that I didn't want to continue taking extra money from my dad for my entire four years of college, so I applied for a job in the chemistry department during my freshman year.

I started working part-time as a lab instructor in the chemistry department. By the time my senior year came around, I was the senior lab instructor for qualitative analysis. I had a dozen lab instructors under me and had my own small office cubicle. The class, Qualitative Analysis, that I was in charge of was the final course in chemistry for future doctors and dentists.

During the semester in this class, the students were given three unknown compounds. Applying the chemistry that they had learned in class, they had to report to me exactly what was in those compounds. This is an exercise in reverse engineering. I didn't realize it at the time, but by teaching those students, I was being prepared for a different career path later in my life. This would be a career requiring the ability to replicate existing "secret" formulas of some of the most popular foods available. This is an accepted and legitimate practice in the food industry.

As it turned out, I wasn't going to end up a dentist, but I would become a food formulator. The day would come when I would walk into the largest dairy in three states and proclaim a desire to create a totally new frozen dairy product. The confidence to do that came from my missionary experience and from my experience in college of working with elements and learning how to reverse engineer compounds. That career path was not to happen for another twelve years.

My dad was a successful dentist and wanted to turn over his practice to me. I graduated from Brigham Young University with a Bachelor of Science degree with a double major in zoology and chemistry. I had applied to several schools of dentistry and had been accepted at UCLA and USC. Dental school was to begin in the next school year.

Now, as I reflect back, I realize how amazing it is that God can take us through experiences to prepare us for something in our future, of which we have no understanding at the time.

Graduation

My graduation from BYU was a joyous occasion. My parents came to Provo, Utah, for it. I then returned home to Long Beach and said something to my dad that brought him to tears. Having been accepted at both UCLA and USC dental schools was a huge accomplishment.

However, the Spirit of the Lord had moved on me in such a way that I had to explain to my dad that I would not be attending dental school. The Spirit prompted me to go on an LDS mission. A mission is for two years of service and is paid for by the missionary. Once home, from school, I sat down with my wonderful father and said, "Dad, the Lord wants me to go on a mission."

He responded, "Son, can you go to dental school first, and then go on your mission?"

I said, "No, Dad, I'm supposed to go on a mission now."

My dad continued questioning, "Who will pay for that mission?

I admitted, "I don't know, but I know that I'm supposed to go now."

Dr. Reinhold "Duke" and Kathryn "Kay" Wudel

Then my dad said the most amazing thing to me. He said, "John, I don't know that I understand all the things you've been telling me about your Church, about Joseph Smith finding the Golden plates, or about the angels. I guess I don't know enough about it to believe it. What I do know is that I believe in you. I want to pay for your mission."

I had just given him one of the biggest disappointments of his life. His son had been accepted to two top dental schools and had turned them both down to go on a mission. Even in the pain of that disappointment, he stepped up and did the right thing because he believed in me. He paid for my entire mission, and the Lord blessed him for doing it.

He lived until he was almost 90 and was rarely sick a day in his life. My dad is a hero to me, and I love him for the wonderful quiet example of goodness that he set for me without ever preaching a word.

Why Go On A Mission?

President Gordon B. Hinckley, the previous Prophet and President of the Church, was interviewed by a German reporter at the Winter Olympics in 2002 at Salt Lake City, Utah. He was asked why Mormons go on missions. He said, "I recognize that every church does good. There isn't any question in my mind about that. They all do good. Do we have something to offer? Yes. I say to people of other churches, you bring all of the good that you have and then let us see if we can add to that. Now that's our whole purpose. That's our mission. That's the way we operate."

After being interviewed by my bishop and stake president, I turned in my application papers. With a LDS mission, the missionary does not determine where they are to serve. The Missionary Department of the Church decides which mission area you are going to, and the President of the Church signs the call. The President of the Church at that time was David O. McKay, the same President that had spoken in the field house that day at BYU and provided the catalyst for my testimony of a living prophet.

When I left for my mission in 1964, I had graduated from BYU. I was still a fairly recent convert with no knowledge of how missionary work was really done. I received my mission call to the North Central States Mission, with the mission home on Pillsbury Avenue in Minneapolis, Minnesota. I remembered thinking at the time, *"That's the same address where I sent my cereal box tops to get my Glow-In-The-Dark Decoder Ring."*

Elder John Wudel - North Central States Mission 1964 - 1966

I was disappointed with my mission assignment, not understanding how the Lord works. He will send you to the mission where, hopefully, you can do the most good. He will send you exactly where you need to be, and where you can grow the most. In the mission field, fellow missionaries call new missionaries "Greenies", because they are new and growing into the calling. I needed the growth, because I was as clueless and as "green" as a missionary can be.

Let me put this missionary experience in a historical perspective. The 1960's in the U.S. was the Age of Aquarius. This was the hippie movement of our national history. This was a time when the youth of our country were told, "Be cool and don't worry about tomorrow, just have fun today. Go with the flow." Flowers have all the power, remember, "Flower Power," and of course, "If you want to find the truth, take a drug called LSD."

LSD was a strong hallucinogenic substance. If you took it, your brain would short circuit and make up crazy images. In the end, this caused much damage both psychologically and in some cases physically. There were suicides from using LSD.

The area that I was assigned to do missionary work included the campus of the University of Minnesota. My companion and I went to the campus newspaper and placed an ad. The headline of the ad read, "LDS...Man's Search for Happiness. Come to a free movie." The ad also referenced a large campus classroom where we could meet.

Apparently, someone on the school newspaper staff wanted to have some fun with the Mormon missionaries, because the printed headline read, "LSD...Man's Search for Happiness." When we arrived at the classroom, it was filled to overflowing with over one hundred people with standing room only. I've never seen so many grubby, long-haired hippies in one place. I had to stand up before this group, tell them that we were Mormon missionaries and that a misprint had been made in the paper.

I said to the crowd, "Our film is L-D-S Man's Search for Happiness, not L-S-D. LDS stands for Latter-day Saints." The room evacuated immediately amid some grumbling and cursing. When the dust settled from the exiting stampede, there were six normal-looking people left in the room.

To our surprise, they indicated that they wanted to see our movie. After the movie, one of the six, a university grad student named Willis, gave us his address. He invited us to come by his apartment. Willis was hearing impaired, but only partially deaf. He had been investigating the Church for over two years. My companion and I were the fourth set of missionaries to teach him. After re-teaching him all of the lessons, we asked him if he would be baptized, and he declined.

Knife Trick

I set one last appointment to see him. We wanted to try to convince him to let us baptize him. That appointment became one of those experiences in life that remains so vivid, like it happened yesterday. We were sitting around his yellow kitchen table, my junior companion, Willis and me. There happened to be a large serrated kitchen knife on the table. As I started to give Willis a completely different message than what I had prepared for him, I inadvertently picked up the knife. Without even thinking about it, I began running my thumb along the sharp edge of the knife.

While doing this with the knife, I said to him, "Willis, I've had it with you. The Lord has sent four sets of His missionaries to you. They taught you the pure truth four times. For over two years, you have been investigating the Church."

At this point, Willis' eyes were fixed on my finger running along the edge of the knife. "I believe that you know it's true. You haven't had the courage to do anything about it. I'm done with you, Willis. We have more important things to do than waste any more time teaching you over and over. We are not coming back."

I stood up with my companion, who was in shock, and we left. Outside my companion said, "Elder Wudel, I can't believe that you just did that."

I answered, "I can't believe that I did that either, what's the matter with me?"

When we returned to our apartment later that day, there was a phone message on our recorder from Willis. He simply said, "Elders, this is Willis. I want to be baptized. Please call me back as soon as possible."

What I didn't know at the time was that Willis was an heir to a famous food manufacturing empire. When he first started investigating the Church, his family told him that if he decided to join the Mormons, he would lose his part of a large inheritance.

What I had judged as a lack of courage on his part was something much more complex. Willis was faced with a decision that few of us could handle. Even the young rich man in the New Testament, in the very presence of Christ, failed when it came to giving up his wealth to follow Christ. Willis, on the other hand, had made the right choice.

22 Now when Jesus heard these things, he said unto him, Yet lackest thou one thing: sell all that thou hast, and distribute unto the poor, and thou shalt have treasure in heaven: and come, follow me.

23 And when he heard this, he was very sorrowful: for he was very rich.

24 And when Jesus saw that he was very sorrowful, he said, How hardly shall they that have riches enter into the kingdom of God! Luke 18:22-24

23 And Jesus looked round about, and saith unto his disciples, How hardly shall they that have riches enter into the kingdom of God!

24 And the disciples were astonished at his words. But Jesus answereth again, and saith unto them, Children, how hard is it for them that trust in riches to enter into the kingdom of God! Mark 10:23-24

At Willis's baptism, I asked him, "What caused you to finally make up your mind to be baptized?"

He answered, "That knife trick really caught my attention."

I want to make it clear that this is not how missionary work is done in the LDS Church. We really don't threaten folks to be baptized at knife point. Luckily, my mission president never heard about the "knife trick."

Willis went on to graduate with honors and went on a mission for the Church. As providence would have it, he was called to the hearing-impaired mission in Long Beach, California, my home town.

While on his mission one day, Willis was tracking door to door in North Long Beach. He knocked on the door of my boyhood home. My mom answered the door and, as she always did, invited the missionaries in for cookies and milk. In the course of their conversation, Willis came to realize who he was talking to. He was filled with amazement and joy at his discovery. Here he was, sitting at the kitchen table with my mother as she listened to this humble missionary tell how her son had been instrumental in bringing him into the Church. He told her how grateful he was for her son, who had taught him the gospel and had motivated him to step up and be baptized.

This story would be beyond belief if this Elder had taught my parents and brought them into the Church. That was not to be. My dad was not ready yet, and my angel mother would not go forward without him. I believe that the visit from Willis to my mom was no accident. I also believe that from this kitchen table visit, both my mom and dad came that much closer to the truth.

This experience reminds me that God loves us so much. He knows us so well that He desires to see us improve and progress. He gives us exactly what we need, precisely when we need it. He does this to help us move forward, on one condition, that condition being threefold:

1. We acknowledge His help.
2. We humbly accept His help.
3. We act upon His help.

To me, Willis was an unusual example of this principle. It took a knife trick to get him baptized and a mission call to point him in the right direction.

After my mission, I had no contact with Willis for over 30 years. On the same weekend that I was being called to the stake mission presidency, I received a call from Willis. He had gone on to get a PhD from the University of Minnesota. He had many health problems and was unable to work. He was a faithful High Priest and married to a wonderful woman, Nan, who adored him, even though they were living in relative poverty.

He asked, "Elder Wudel was it worth it?

I questioned, "Was what worth it, Willis?"

He said, "Was going on a mission worth it?"

I choked up at the sound of his voice when he asked that question. I tried to tell him just how worth it, it was. I could have asked him the same question. "Willis was it worth it, giving up a fortune for your membership in the church? You could have been a multi-millionaire." I didn't ask because I already knew his answer. I think he would have answered it with another question, as he often did, "Elder Wudel, what is membership in the Kingdom of God really worth?"

Over the years, I have reflected on the "knife trick" in Willis's kitchen. I've come to see that life has a way of periodically throwing all of us "knife tricks." They come to us in various forms. They come suddenly as a serious illness, a financial reversal, or even as the premature death of a loved one. Their purpose is to refocus our attention onto what is really important in life.

On first blush, trials will shock us and always seem so negative. However, over time, the end result of their influence is often positive. They tend to wake us up and cause us to rethink our priorities. They refocus our energies, and many times, as in Willis' case, they help us make the right decisions at critical forks on our road of life. Often, these decisions are so critical, that if made correctly, they will redirect our lives back to that straight and narrow path that leads us home to God.

The "knife trick" didn't come from me; it came through me and was heaven sent. The hardships, trials, and tribulations in this life can be a blessing. They are the antidote to worldliness, arrogance, self-centeredness, and pride that robs us of our own godly potential.

Why do we do missionary work? We go on missions because we love our fellow man. We want to share the pure joy that only comes from knowing and following the restored Gospel of Jesus Christ.

Why do I do missionary work? I believe the answers to the problems that plague this tired world are found in strong, Christ-centered families. The end result of the Lord's missionary work is ultimately found in the creation and strengthening of the family unit. The family unit is the strength of America and of the entire world. The best help we can give, to help heal this sin-sick world is to be a missionary for the Lord and help bring people to an understanding of the full truth that has been restored.

"You Are Not Going To Be a Dentist"

I returned from my mission in the fall of 1966. My father was very excited for me to start dental school. Both UCLA and USC had accepted me, and both had postponed my entrance until I had finished my mission. I decided to attend the UCLA Dental School.

On the orientation day, when I was to pay my tuition, my father gave me a checkbook and told me to write a check for the initial admission fee. I drove from Long Beach to the campus at UCLA and entered the building for the School of Dentistry. After an introduction by the assistant dean of the school, we were then asked to pay our fees. I opened my dad's checkbook to a blank check that he had signed, and started to write out a check for $2500. As I was about to put pen to paper, the Spirit spoke to me.

In a very clear voice in my head the Spirit said, "John, you're not going to be a dentist!"

I was stunned and in shock as I said to myself, *"I'm not going to be a dentist?"* An indescribable feeling confirmed that new reality. It strengthened me for what I was about to do next. I closed the checkbook and proceeded with the difficult task of telling those in charge, that I would not be attending dental school. It was a huge financial blow to a school that carefully selected, and only accepted, a small percentage of students who applied. It made no sense to put in all the effort to be accepted and then drop out at the last minute.

When the word got to the Dean of the school, he invited me into his office. He asked me, "Why did you come this far, and today decide that you are not going to attend dental school?"

I didn't feel good about telling him that the Spirit of God had just told me that I would not be a dentist. Instead, I told him that my desire for a career was such that I wanted more time to serve my church. He said that dentistry was the perfect career for that. He said many successful dentists work only a partial week. They usually work only four days a week, leaving Friday, Saturday and Sunday to do whatever they choose. He said there are very few careers that can provide enough income for your family and allow you the extra time like dentistry does. He was right, but that didn't matter. I had clearly heard a different answer from a higher source.

I listened respectfully to all of his persuasive reasoning and then he asked me, "Are you sure of your decision?"

I still knew what I had to do. I said, "I am sure." I thanked him for his time and his considerate response to my decision.

Now, I had to drive back home and tell my father something that would break his heart for a second time. My father had dreamed that his son would take over his dental practice. He had had a very successful practice for years in Long Beach, and was very excited about sharing it with me.

When I told him the news, his eyes filled with tears. He asked me, "What will you do now, John?"

I said, "I don't know what I'm going to do, but I do know that this is the right decision." Once again my wonderful father didn't understand his son's decision, but was in full support and in no way critical. Years later, he told me that I had made the right decision. He said, "Dentistry isn't as fun as it used to be, there is too much paper work."

I often look back and think that it was his example of not trying to criticize me for my decision that strengthened me when I was raising my own children. It's so important to allow your children to fly out of the nest as they feel inspired to choose their own path. I think a parents' responsibility is to do everything they can to help the child succeed, but not in a way to try to criticize or stop their dreams from coming true.

The Spirit had told me to leave dental school, but that same Spirit didn't tell me what I was to do. So I was questioning in my mind, *"What is my career path?"* I thought about all of the careers that were of interest to me. One of them was my interest in the world of business and finance. So I went to a large company that was an investment brokerage. I applied to be a stockbroker. Before I could be hired and trained, I had to take a test. The test was a two hour preference test. The test asked question after question about my preferences covering a broad range of possibilities.

After I completed the test, and it was scored, the counselor sat down with me and said, "John, you're not a stockbroker."

I said, "What am I?"

He calmly replied, "You are a religion teacher."

I was again shocked and amazed at the results of that test. The test results would now propel me in a new direction.

Once you drop out of dental school, you are no longer exempt from the draft. This was during the Vietnam War, so I was concerned about that. I ended up writing the draft board and telling them that I would not be a dentist, but my desires were to become a teacher. I explained that I thought a teacher was as valuable as a dentist. I asked for a continued exemption from the draft, but I never heard back from the draft board. I was never drafted.

I applied to attend BYU Graduate School for a Master's Degree in Theology, and went back to pursue studies in becoming a religion teacher for the church. At that point, BYU had a degree in theology. That degree was later terminated before I could finish the thesis and complete the degree. However, I completed all the coursework and was accepted into the Church Educational System (CES) to become a seminary teacher.

Even though I never finished the theology degree, I still gained so much from the coursework. It required me to read the two

authorized volumes, "The History of the Church", a seven-volume
set, and "The Comprehensive History of the Church", a six-volume
set. I was required to pass a thorough verbal test on church history,
one on one, with my professor. I carried all the volumes into his
office and placed them on his desk. He would pick a volume and
open it to a random page. He would ask me questions from the
material on the page to make sure I had studied and remembered it.
Even though I never received a master's degree, the intense study of
the history of the restored Church of Jesus Christ would become
very valuable to my future.

Chapter 9
Combined Priesthood Lesson
(Michael)

It was decided that I would give a lesson to the combined priesthood, consisting of the High Priests and Elders, on the Sunday following my confirmation. My lesson would be taught in the chapel, with every adult male attending church that day present.

I was standing in front of all the pews, with a music stand for all my notes and a portable blackboard behind me with the title of the lesson written on it, "How Do You Really Gather Israel?" One of the pieces of paper on the music stand had an outline of my talk on it, but I didn't think it contained enough information to fill the 45 minutes that had been set aside for my lesson. My plan was to go over each bullet point and write on the chalkboard as an emphasis for each point.

There were about 40 brothers in the room as I started my lesson. I was very nervous and immediately started to sweat. As I mentioned before, I didn't like speaking in front of people. Nevertheless, I started out by speaking about how we should strive to understand the Jewish people in order to understand the origins of the ordinances that we do today as Mormons. I knew that a few of the brothers might be shocked by the things that I was about to say, and I didn't know how well it would be received by the others.

First, I read and talked about the passage, Mormon 5:14, from the Book of Mormon. I had been awakened at 4 a.m. a few nights previous and was inspired by the Holy Spirit to read the following verse:

"14 And behold, they shall go unto the unbelieving of the Jews; and for this intent shall they go—that they may be persuaded that Jesus is the Christ, the Son of the living God; that the Father may bring about, through his most Beloved, his great and eternal purpose, in restoring the Jews, or all the house of Israel, to the land of their inheritance, which the Lord their God hath given them, unto the fulfilling of his covenant;"

Mormon 5:14

I then quoted Ezekiel 36:16-19. I told them that I had been inspired again at 4 a.m. a different night to read this passage. As I read the passage, the Spirit reminded me again, "This passage describes you." I told the group that I understood that this passage meant the joining together of The Book of Mormon and the Bible (Ephraim and Judah). I also told them that it meant the coming together of the Mormons and Jews in the last days. I felt that the passage had a personal message just for me, but it wasn't clear yet as to how it would apply to me.

I explained that my father was an Orthodox Jew and my mother was a Christian Scientist, who had converted to Judaism when I was born. She did this so that my brother and I could be raised in the Jewish faith, and there would be no religious conflict in our home.

I then related my experience about receiving the Book of Mormon and being told "The book is true." I described how that remarkable event initiated my decision to move to Mesa and investigate the LDS Church in depth. Although I didn't relate it to them at that time, I knew that receiving the Book of Mormon in that way was to be a major turning point in my life.

I continued on, talking about the origins of baptism as I had been taught in Judaism. I taught, "Baptism as a rite of immersion and cleansing was not begun by Christians, but was taken from ancient Hebrew rituals. The immersion pool or font was called a 'mikveh'. Mikveh in Hebrew means a gathering of waters."

I then said, "The building of the mikveh was so important in ancient times, it was to take precedence over the construction of a synagogue. If necessary, holy scrolls were to be sold to finance the building of a mikveh. When building a mikveh, Jewish law states that it must be connected to 'living water', such as an underground spring, to be valid. To be living water, the water must be moving to continually cleanse itself, thereby being able to cleanse anyone immersing themselves in it."

I stopped for a brief pause and looked around the chapel. Everyone was looking directly at me and no one said a word. You could hear a pin drop in the room. I thought, *"If they don't like what they are hearing and I get excommunicated, it might as well be in the beginning of my joining the Church!"*

I forged ahead, "Total immersion in this 'living water' was so important that it occurred before the High Priests conducted the Temple service on the Day of Atonement. It also occurred before the High Priests participated in the Temple service, before each person entered the Temple complex, and before a scribe wrote the name of God. According to Jewish law, immersion is required for both men and women when converting to Orthodox Judaism. In the LDS church, we call it baptism."

"The individual would immerse himself and this was witnessed by three Holy Men (High Priests, Rabbis). Jewish law states that not one hair on the top of the head may be above the water for the immersion to be valid. The subject immersed himself or herself by squatting at the knees until completely covered and then coming up straightway out of the water." I quoted:

> "16 And Jesus, when he was baptized, went up straightway out of the water: and, lo, the heavens were opened unto him, and he saw the Spirit of God descending like a dove, and lighting upon him."   Matthew 3:16

I continued, "Jesus and John were in the river Jordan fulfilling the ancient Hebrew commandment of immersing oneself in a mikveh filled with 'living water'. This was normally done to be cleansed of their sins, but in this case, Jesus had no sin."

"John recognized that, hesitated, and Jesus said unto him,

"Suffer it to be so now: for thus it becometh us to fulfill all righteousness." Jesus did it to follow his Father's plan, provide an example, and make it available to all. To fulfill the ancient law, Jesus himself was the "living water" and is the only source capable of cleansing us of our sins. Baptism is the ordinance of obedience to God's law.

Certificate of Michael's Conversion from
Reform Judaism to Orthodox Judaism 1974
Document of Halacha (Jewish Law)

I passed around my certificate, which is a document of Jewish law, that recorded the event of my immersion in a mikveh as I converted from Reform Judaism to Orthodox Judaism when I was 18-years old.

The document states:

Certificate Of Conversion

This certifies that on the 20th day of the month of Iyar in the year 5734, corresponding to the 12th day of the month of May in the year 1974, there came before the undersigned, constituted as a Beth Din,

Michael LeRoy Morton   5021 W. 60th Terr.   and declared his desire to become a member of the Jewish people. He accepted upon himself the commandments of the Torah, and cast his lot with the Jewish people in all times, in all places, and under all conditions. Upon questioning him we found him sincere in his declarations and possessing a fair knowledge of our holy Torah. He was circumcised in anticipation of and for the purpose of conversion. He immersed himself in a mikveh in the manner prescribed for converts by Halacha, and has taken to himself the name Michael, son of Abraham, by which he shall henceforth be known among the Jewish people.

Done this day in the city of Kansas City in the state of Missouri Signed by two Orthodox Rabbis and an Orthodox Cantor.

I concluded my lesson with the words, "In the name of Jesus Christ. Amen" That was the first time that I had ended a talk or lesson in His name. I sat down and realized that I was so nervous about speaking in front of such a large group that I forgot to write on the chalkboard at all!

I had told them that my lesson had been "How Do You Really Gather Israel?" It occurred to me that I had tried to teach them the importance of understanding the Jews and the origins of some of their ordinances. I thought, *"If you are really trying to educate and gather Israel, shouldn't you know their history and try to understand them first?"*

Teaching this lesson was a huge event for me, because it was the first time that I had given a religious talk as an adult. The only other time that I had given one was at my Bar Mitzvah at the age of 13, when I helped conduct a religious service as a rite of passage in the Jewish religion. Becoming a Bar Mitzvah and conducting a service in Judaism included reading from the Holy Torah in Hebrew, then translating the passage into English and acting as an assistant to the Rabbi during the entire service.

Even though I didn't know it at that time, my first teaching experience in the LDS Church would turn out to be a rite of passage also. My lesson had turned into a theme that I would carry forward throughout many future talks. The theme was about how close these two tribes of Israel really were to each other in their ordinances and commitment to Heavenly Father.

After the lesson, several brothers came up and congratulated me on a great lesson. One of the brothers said, "You should really be doing a fireside." I thought, *"What is a fireside? Do you stand next to somebody's fireplace and give a lesson?"* I said, "Ok," since I remembered what someone had said about volunteering, instead of getting assigned something anyway!

I made an appointment with my bishop for the following week to discuss what this fireside thing was all about. When we met, we decided that I would be the featured speaker at a fireside in a few weeks on October 20th in our chapel. I was excited as I left his office until the thought hit me, *"I need to attend a fireside so I can see what one is supposed to be like."* I suddenly realized that I had just agreed to do a fireside even though I was clueless as to what a fireside even was.

Aaronic Priesthood

I was taught that there were two priesthoods within the Church, the Aaronic Priesthood and the Melchizedek Priesthood. As a new convert, I was to go through the Aaronic Priesthood to understand how it worked within the church before progressing into the Melchizedek Priesthood. I visited Bishop Holman, and it was decided that I would receive my Aaronic Priesthood Ordination on

May 12. We discussed the role that the Aaronic Priesthood plays in the church.

Worthy male members may receive the Aaronic Priesthood beginning at age 12. These young men, typically ages 12–18, receive many opportunities to participate in sacred priesthood ordinances and give service. As they worthily fulfill their duties, they act in the name of the Lord to help others receive the blessings of the gospel.

The offices of the Aaronic Priesthood are deacon, priest, teacher and bishop. With the authorization of the presiding priesthood leader (usually the bishop), deacons pass the sacrament. They help the bishop watch over Church members by giving service and assisting with temporal matters, such as gathering fast offerings. They also prepare the sacramental bread and water, and serve as home teachers.

The Aaronic Priesthood is often called the preparatory priesthood. As a priesthood holder serves in the Aaronic Priesthood, he prepares to receive the Melchizedek Priesthood, to receive the blessings of the temple, to serve a full-time mission, to be a loving husband and father, and to continue in lifelong service to the Lord.

I thought, *"What a great system of service they are teaching these young men."*

It was explained to me that the definition of priest craft is using the priesthood and being paid for it. All of my service in using the Aaronic Priesthood would be for one purpose only: to bless and serve the recipient without any monetary gain.

May 12th arrived, and I went to Bishop Holman's office for my Aaronic Priesthood ordination. This time there were not as many men standing in the circle around the chair that I was sitting in. The bishop conferred upon me the Aaronic Priesthood, ordained me a priest, and gave me a blessing. So I began my journey into the realm of the LDS Priesthood structure.

Heavenly Parents

A concept that I hadn't thought about was presented to me one afternoon by a friend, Don, in his office. Another friend, Mark, was there also. I was presented with the idea of heavenly parents. We discussed having a Heavenly Father and a Heavenly Mother. This was a mind-blowing concept to me. I don't think that I had ever thought of the possibility of having a Heavenly Mother.

They asked me, "Have you ever known anyone that was born without a mother?" That made perfect sense.

I asked, "Why doesn't anyone talk about this?" I was told that Heavenly Father did not want those who didn't appreciate this truth to know that there was a Heavenly Mother. He was protecting her from having her name taken in vain, as His and Jesus' names have been.

A few days later Don called me and said, "You need to come see a young man open his mission call."

I asked, "What is a mission call?" He explained that a mission call is when a young man or woman gets their letter from the church stating what geographical area that they will be called to for their mission.

So I met Don and Mark at Don's cousins' house for the event. There were at least 50 people in the house waiting for Don's cousin to open up his letter from the First Presidency of the LDS Church. There were cell phones around the room to capture the moment so that other relatives, not present, could celebrate this sacred call to service.

Then the envelope was opened, and the letter was read. The letter was from the President of the Church. I don't remember where the young man was going, but I do remember what one line said, "As you serve with all your heart, mind, and strength, the Lord will lead you to those who are prepared to be baptized." This sentence was shocking to me. I thought that the missionaries were like door-to-door salesmen that worked off the law of averages. If they knocked on so many doors, they would baptize a certain percentage of the people they met. This calling from a Prophet of God indicated otherwise. His missionaries would instead be led by the Spirit of God to those who were looking for the truth.

I had just witnessed the LDS Church's missionary system in action. There were over 90,000 young missionaries all over the world, at that time. Each one had left behind attending college, job opportunities, families, boyfriends, and girlfriends for two years to serve the Lord at their own expense. To me, this was incredible. There is no other church on earth that comes close to achieving this level of service among its young people.

Chapter 10
Brain Robbers
(John)

My first seminary teaching assignment for the Church was in a small town in Utah. It was a little all-Mormon town. I was single, in my mid-20s, and excited to teach seminary for the first time. The church seminary building was adjacent to the public high school. For one hour each day, the LDS students were released from public school and came to seminary class for their religious education.

Having never attended seminary class myself, I envisioned the classroom filling up with eager-to-learn LDS kids. I thought that I would roll out the gospel, and they would soak it up like sponges. Little did I know how it would really be? My first warning of how things really were came in the form of two students telling me a joke on my first day. I stood out in front of the seminary building to greet some of the students, two of the young men came up to me. I introduced myself to them as their new seminary teacher.

They said, "Brother Wudel, we have a question for you."

I replied, "What is it?"

They questioned, "Do you know why it takes two minutes to walk from the seminary building to our school building, and only one minute to walk from the school to the seminary?"

I answered, "No, why?"

They had big grins on their faces as they answered, "It's because seminary sucks!"

I felt like I had just been punched in the stomach. I tried to understand the humor in what they were saying. I thought, *"Why would they say such a tasteless remark."* It wouldn't be long until I found out what they really thought about seminary.

There were two teachers in the seminary, the principal and myself. The principal, an older gentleman taught all the young students, and he gave me, the rookie, the juniors and hard-core seniors. Just prior to my coming, the Relief Society sisters had given a gift to the seminary. They had donated a beautiful, large potted plant to help decorate the lobby of the seminary building. Within one day, a few of the students had set it on fire and killed it.

My seminary career started when the first class filed in, and eight cowboys filled the back row. One of them, named Cody, had eight toothpicks sticking out of his mouth. It wasn't difficult to identify their leader, David, the biggest senior. He was 6' 3" and 200 pounds of muscle. He leaned back in his desk and put his muddy boots up on the desk in front of him. He was the first one to speak.

He said, "We dare you to teach us anything." The rest of the cowboys just laughed. I was stunned and started mentally questioning my career choice.

I made my first mistake when I stepped out of the classroom to get some chalk, not knowing that they had removed all of the classroom chalk on purpose. In the few minutes that I was gone, they moved the entire bank of bookshelves in front of the door, so I couldn't get back in. I had to climb over the shelves in order to reenter the classroom. I quickly determined that I would never, ever leave the room during class time again.

The second day, I came to my classroom, and the heavy wooden door was shut. Little did I know that the students had removed the pins in the hinges. When I went to open the door, it fell on the floor with a mighty crash. At first, I was mystified by their behavior. There was a total lack of respect for authority, no respect for the seminary building, or for the seminary teacher. It seemed that they didn't even have any respect for the gospel of Jesus Christ.

I wondered, *"What would cause this to happen in this Mormon town?"*

One day, while shopping the local grocery store, I noticed the factory representative for coffee was filling the shelves with product. I asked him, "How big of a territory do you cover?"

He answered, "Three states."

I said, "This must be one of your worst accounts."

He replied, "Just the opposite, this is one of my best accounts. They drink more coffee per capita here, than just about anywhere else that I cover."

I wondered, *"How could that be possible?"* I later found out the answer, when I saw some of the adults stand up in church during testimony meeting. They would testify how much they loved the Lord and the Church. These adults would then go home after church and brew up a big pot of coffee. In the LDS Church, one of the commandments is to abstain from drinking coffee. The children from these families were able to see, firsthand, the hypocrisy of it all. The result was that they thought the church and seminary class was a joke. They acted accordingly.

Their clueless parents were mystified at their children's bad behavior. These parents were basically wonderful folks; they had just relaxed on one of the important principles of the gospel. The Word of Wisdom counsels us to abstain from alcohol, tobacco, coffee, tea, and any other substance that may be harmful to our bodies. The parents hadn't realized that there were consequences to their own actions of breaking these commandments. They simply blamed this bad behavior on their children without realizing that their own behavior was part of the problem. I found out that this was not a new problem for this community.

Many years before, Brigham Young had sent J. Golden Kimball to this very community. He was a member of the LDS Quorum of the Seventy and was to speak at the stake conference. J. Golden Kimball had a great sense of humor. Before he arrived, he had sent down word that he would be speaking on "The Mysteries of God." When he arrived on that Sunday morning, the building was packed. It was standing room only. He got up and began his talk on "Tithes and Offerings."

A few minutes into his talk, a brother yelled out from the audience, "Brother Kimball, you said that you would be talking on the "Mysteries of God" but instead you are talking about tithing."

J. Golden answered, "I am talking about the "Mysteries of God." It's a mystery to God where your tithing is." The burst of laughter was followed by a stunned reality.

These people were not obeying the Word of Wisdom, or the Law of Tithing and Offerings. Like the Nephites in the Book of Mormon, some of these modern members had strayed off of the straight and narrow path. They were also ignoring the Lord's warning in the "Parable of the 10 Virgins." One-half of all of the church will not be prepared spiritually at the Savior's second coming when the earth will be cleansed by fire. The old joke that paying tithing is like buying fire insurance, might be more true than not.

That was 47 years ago in that small town. My seminary story does have a happy ending; however, it got worse before it got better. During class, the cowboys were so rude that they were constantly talking to each other and laughing while I was trying to teach them. They would make fun of both me and the gospel. I would prepare a gospel lesson that I had worked on for hours the night before. As I tried to teach what I had prepared, these boys would constantly interrupt with what they thought were funny comments, followed by their rude laughter.

As I looked into the eyes of the good students in the class, there were some that had blank looks on their faces. I was especially troubled when I looked at the girls and saw the sad looks on their faces. I thought, *"The good students are here to learn about their Savior and are being robbed of that opportunity."*

After class, I boldly told the unruly boys that they were "Brain Robbers." They were robbing the other students of the important gospel knowledge that they would need in order to make good decisions as they moved forward with their lives.

I told the disruptive students, "It is my responsibility to not allow you to get away with destroying this seminary class."

I warned them that I was going to act, if they didn't stop their disruptive and rude behavior. It didn't stop, so finally, I gave them my last warning.

I told them, "If you don't stop your bad behavior, I will remove you from seminary class."

They replied, "You can't do that; our parents won't let you."

The next day I posted a list of nineteen names of boys that had lost the privilege of attending seminary. Some of those boys were shocked and asked, "Where will we go?"

I responded, "I don't care where you go, but don't come back here. You are not welcome here until you repent and change your bad attitudes and behavior."

The principal of the high school was upset that I had let loose, during school hours, nineteen juvenile delinquent cowboys. The LDS community leadership was also concerned, as were the local police. I wasn't concerned, because for the first time since I had gotten there, there was peace in my seminary class, and I could actually teach.

A week went by, and one day during class, a white flag on a pole was lifted up to the window of my classroom. Eighteen of the nineteen delinquent cowboys wanted a truce. At our truce meeting, with a smile, I explained, "The way this will work from now on is really quite simple. When the teacher is talking, you are quiet and listening. When you want to say something, you will raise your hand. If I call on you, then you can speak. No more passing nasty notes or any notes at all during class." I gave them a couple of more rules and said, "Will you follow these rules?"

The cowboys all said that they would. I turned to Cody, who still had eight toothpicks in his mouth, and said, "Okay Cody, will you take over the audio visual department? Whenever we show a movie, filmstrip, or play a tape, you will be in charge of it. Can you handle that?"

His face lit up as he answered, "Yep!"

So after that exchange, my eighteen unruly cowboys were allowed back in class. I believe that I had made my point, and they knew that if they didn't follow the rules I'd expel them again, without hesitation. Their attitudes changed from that point on. As the year progressed, the days were filled with gospel truths being discussed and mixed with small miracles. The miracles were tiny, but very real and oh, so powerful.

One Small Miracle, One Huge Difference

An example of one of these little miracles occurred the day I was trying to teach about the events just prior to the Second Coming of Christ. Now that I had them quieted down and they were actually listening to me, I wanted to frighten the bejabbers out of them. So I had them turn to Doctrine and Covenants 29:17-18.

As I started to read this scary scripture, a large fly flew through the open window and proceeded to circle my head. As I read, I was trying to swoosh the fly away, with no success. The scripture describes in detail how the Lord will send flies upon the wicked. The flies shall take hold of the wicked and eat their flesh. At the perfect moment during my reading, this large fly had landed on my forehead and wouldn't go away. The students started to laugh. The more I tried to swoosh the fly away, the more it kept landing on my head. It just wouldn't go away.

The students kept laughing harder and were almost rolling out of their chairs. At this point I started laughing with them and said, "Okay, okay I give up. The fly wins. Let's talk about something else."

It was obvious to all of us that were present that day, that we had just witnessed a small, but wonderful miracle. That miracle came in the form of a large persistent fly. The students left that day, convinced that God had a great sense of humor. He had sent that fly into his seminary to give everyone a good laugh. I don't think that God wanted me to try to scare his children into being good. I agreed with this conclusion and never again tried that method of teaching. I still won't teach the gospel by using fear as a motivator to be good. That day a little determined fly had taught me a very important lesson.

That experience along with several more, touched the minds and hearts of those kids. It turned them around from anti-seminary to pro-seminary. By the end of the year, the respect was restored for the seminary teachers and its building. At the last high school assembly, I was invited as a special guest of the high school. As I entered the filled auditorium, the school band played my favorite song, "To Dream the Impossible Dream." It was against the district policy, but the high school had awarded a seminary teacher the "Teacher of the Year Award." It had been voted upon by the whole student body. I was stunned and with a tear in my eyes walked up on the stage and accepted the award.

What had really taken place here was the example of the power of the gospel of Jesus Christ. The gospel had overcome the negative examples of the disobedient parents and redirected the lives of their children. Some of those young cowboys went on to become law enforcement officers, Highway Patrol, and city police.

The largest one, David, the one that said, "We dare you to teach us anything", went on to become the county sheriff. David was named Utah's Sheriff of the Year twice in six years. When they presented him his award, they said, "David truly exemplifies what a sheriff serving his citizens should be." After twenty-one years of service, he was named "Utah's Lawman of the Year." This award meant that out of all of the law enforcement officers in the entire state, he was rated number one. He received many other awards during his tenure for his outstanding drug enforcement, public service, and distinguished service to the children and youth of the county.

I am still amazed at how that young man had changed. I'm so grateful that I had David and all of the other young cowboys and sweet girls as students. I like to think that kicking some of them out of seminary and then taking them back was the best thing I could have ever done for them. The experience that I had teaching that first year taught me one of life's important lessons. The lax parents were saying one thing, but doing just the opposite. I learned that year to care what people say, but now I watch more closely what they do. I believe that God also watches what we do and what we say. This is why it is important that we do more than just accept Jesus verbally. It really isn't enough. It is also about what we do to serve. Jesus taught us, "If thou lovest me thou shalt serve me and keep all my commandments."

"I remember President Uchtdorf saying;

Perhaps this is why Jesus asked the people to listen to and follow the words of the Pharisees and scribes, but not to follow their example. These religious teachers did not walk the talk. They loved to talk about religion, but sadly they missed its essence."

President Dieter F. Uchtdorf Ensign September 2016

Chapter 11
Who Is This Guy?
(Michael and John)

We thought back to the first time that we had met each other.

Michael was looking to produce a recipe for a new frozen dessert. He had been in either real estate or food service for a good portion of his life and being entrepreneurial in nature, was seeking out someone that could help put this formula together. Michael had connections with a couple of frozen dessert shops, and they were looking for a better frozen treat that had a unique taste and consistency.

At this point in John's career, he owned and operated an international food development company, which exported frozen treats to over 92 countries. He had used his chemistry experience to become a food formulator.

One of the brothers in Michael's ward knew John and suggested that they be introduced. One day, Michael went over to John's office and met with John and his two sons.

Michael said, "I remember going to John's office and meeting him one day. John and his two sons, David and Johny, ran his international frozen treat business. I was taken into a room where John and his sons were finishing up one of their usual business meetings."

"John was sitting across the table from me with a white lab coat on, looking like he was the professor of a chemistry lab. We visited for a while and he asked me about my background. I told John that I had been raised Jewish and was now going through the conversion process in the LDS Church. He seemed to have a surprised look on his face when I told him this. I thought, *"Why is he so surprised."*

John remembered, "When I first met Michael and found out that he was a Jewish convert, I was amazed and shocked at the same time. I said to him, 'You mean to tell me that you went from being raised Jewish to believing in Christ, and you are now converting to Mormonism?'"

Michael replied, "That's not entirely right. It wasn't until God revealed to me that the Book of Mormon is true that I began to investigate and have an appreciation for who Christ really was, the messiah."

When John heard that, he thought, *"This is a very unusual individual. I need to get to know him and find out how this came about."*

"I thanked Michael for coming and told him that we would be in touch. We decided to meet for lunch in the near future. In my mind, I thought, *'I can't wait to talk to him and find out more about how this happened.'*"

"Michael invited me to his fireside that was being held at his ward in a few weeks. That really made me think, *'Who is this guy? He just joined the Church and he's already giving two fireside talks?'*"

Mission Presidents Fireside (Michael)

I was asked to give my testimony at a Mission President's Fireside in September. I was told to prepare a talk based upon how I decided to convert to the LDS faith. So the first fireside that I would see would be the one that I would give my testimony in, only a month before my fireside which had been scheduled for October 20th.

The night of the Mission President's Fireside arrived. I showed up early at the stake center for a quick meeting with a member of the Stake Presidency before the fireside started. I had prepared about a 20 minute talk on the decisions that led me to join the church.

I was taken to an office to meet with him, and there were a few other people in the room that I did not recognize. There were two of us that would give our testimonies that night. The other speaker was a young woman in her late 20s. We were told to try and keep our talks to within a twelve minute time limit. I thought, *"I'm going to have to make some quick revisions to cut down my talk."*

We were taken back into the chapel and seated on the stand. I sat in my chair looking out upon the congregation as they started to fill the pews. I quickly started crossing out portions of my outline that I had written so that I could shorten my talk to the 12 minute time limit.

I started to get nervous. As I said before, I start to sweat when I get really nervous. I looked out on the people coming in to the chapel and didn't recognize anybody. That seemed to make me more nervous than I already was. It was about five minutes before the fireside was to start when I saw a few of my ward members come in to the chapel. Then, as I had my head down revising my talk, a member of my ward, Joey, sat down next to me. He had been assigned the opening prayer. He said, "How are you doing?"

I answered, "Nervous!"

He said, "You'll be fine."

I thought, *"How does he know? Fine...I don't think so."*

Programs were handed out, and I saw that Evelyn was singing after my talk that night. She was the eight-year-old girl from my ward who sang at my baptism. I thought, *"If an eight-year-old girl can get up in front of this crowd, then I certainly should be able to as well."*

The young sister gave her talk first. It was a heart-wrenching story of all the tragedies that she had gone through, including the loss of her child. Somehow, she was introduced to a couple of missionaries, and her life changed after a few lessons. She was a convert of a few years, while I was a convert of a few months.

I thought, *"How can I follow this? My talk has two or three jokes in it; how can I joke around after such a heartfelt testimony?"* Now, I was really nervous. I got up and went to the podium. I had never spoken in front of such a large group nor had I spoken in this chapel, or any chapel, except for the combined Priesthood meeting.

As I stood at the podium, the microphone seemed to be right in my view, almost like a cobra that was right in front of my face, poised to strike. I didn't know if the microphone could be moved or not, so I didn't touch it. I stepped slightly to the left, so that only half of my body was behind the podium. I must have looked ridiculous, but I was petrified as I launched into my talk.

I started out with the story of how I went to the Visitors' Center, saw the Joseph Smith movie, and how it made me feel. I then related how I received the book of Mormon in the construction trailer. I also told them that I was a Jew who had converted to the LDS Church.

People seemed to be riveted by what I was saying. I have to admit that I can't remember more than the first half of my talk. After that it was all a blur, even though members from my ward said that I spoke very well.

Since it was the Mission President's Fireside, there were a lot of missionaries attending that evening. During my talk, there was laughter, and people seemed to be enjoying it. I ended my talk with a heartfelt testimony and said, "In the name of Jesus Christ, Amen." I went back to my seat on the stand and sat down. The young sister that had spoken before me turned to me and said, "That was really great." I thanked her and told her how wonderful I thought her talk was, as well.

Next on the program was Evelyn's musical number. Evelyn went up to the podium to sing her song and immediately grabbed the microphone and bent it down out of her way. I shook my head in disbelief. I didn't know that I could move the microphone. I realized what a rookie move I had made to stand there giving my talk halfway outside the podium, instead of moving the microphone.

The fireside ended, and I got up and shook hands with those presiding. I turned around and the missionaries had formed a line, waiting to talk to me. There were questions like, "How do we talk to Jews?", "Did you really feel something when you were handed the Book of Mormon?" and "Can you teach us Hebrew?" In fact, there were so many questions and so many people up on the stand waiting in line to talk to me, that I didn't leave the stand for almost 45 minutes. I couldn't believe it. I thought I had messed up the whole talk, and yet they wanted to know more.

The line ended, and I stepped down off the stand, headed towards the exit. There were a few more people that had waited around to talk to me. I stopped and talked to them for a few minutes. I couldn't imagine why they were so interested. I then realized, *"I have to prepare something even better than this for my fireside and it's only a little over a month away!"*

First Fireside (Michael)

That month passed quickly. I have always thought that music is very important to enrich the soul. So I decided to have a couple of special musical numbers at my fireside. Since Evelyn sang at my baptism and the Mission President's Fireside, I thought that having her sing for my fireside would be good luck.

I was incredibly nervous and had only been to one fireside, but I thought that I could pull it off since I was getting so much help from the Spirit.

The fireside was only announced in my ward. I also invited friends that lived in other parts of the city, including John. I didn't expect very many people to show up. All in all, around 65 people attended. I was amazed that anyone showed up at all.

October 20, 2013, was a Sunday evening. The fireside was to start at 7 p.m. and I got to the chapel at about 6 p.m. to make sure that we were ready to start on time. Evelyn and her mother, Hillary, showed up early and went to one of the classrooms to practice their special musical numbers.

I was really nervous, even though I knew that the majority of the people showing up that night to hear my message were my friends. A member of the bishopric was presiding that evening. He came up to me about 10 minutes before I was to start and said, "Are you ready for this?"

I replied, "I think so."

He said, "Who is giving the opening and closing prayers and the opening and closing hymns?"

I asked, "What opening and closing prayers and hymns? I prepared a talk for about 40 or 45 minutes, and then Evelyn is going to sing two special musical numbers, one before I speak and one after I speak. I didn't realize that there were prayers and hymns that I was supposed to pick."

He had a quizzical look on his face as he said, "We always start with an opening hymn and an opening prayer and conclude with a closing hymn and a closing prayer for a fireside."

One of the members of the ward, Lance, overheard us. He, his wife, Judy, their son, Dallin and daughter, Lizzie, jumped up and volunteered to help. Judy picked out an opening and closing hymn and volunteered to be the chorister to lead the music. Lance said he would give the opening prayer and Dallin his son, volunteered to run the microphone around for questions and answers. Lizzie volunteered to help her mother pick the opening and closing hymns. I chose someone else for the closing prayer.

Seven o'clock came quickly. An opening hymn was sung and an opening prayer was said. Evelyn sang a beautiful musical number, with her mother Hillary accompanying on the piano. Time for my talk came, and I walked up to the podium.

I started my talk, "For those of you that don't know me, my name is Michael Morton. It is a pleasure and a privilege to speak before you this evening. I thought, *"I should start off with something humorous!"*

"To give you a little of my background, I was born on April 8th in Kansas City, Missouri which lies in Jackson County at St. Mary's Catholic Hospital, to a Christian Scientist mother and an Orthodox Jewish father. I was delivered by a Jewish pediatrician and two Catholic nuns who were nurses. In the waiting room were my Christian Scientist grandmother, Protestant and Jewish aunts and uncles and an assortment of Jewish and Christian friends and neighbors."

"I can safely say that: ALL THE MAJOR RELIGIOUS FOOD GROUPS WERE PRESENT AT MY BIRTH!" This brought a laugh from the audience.

"My mother converted to Judaism when I was born, and I was brought up Jewish. As a family, we read the Bible, we never read the New Testament, and we never spoke of Jesus. I loved growing up Jewish. From the food, to the songs, to the culture that surrounded me as I grew up, I loved it all. I am so grateful that I grew up in the Jewish faith and still consider myself Jewish to this day."

Michael Morton Bar Mitzvah
Rabbi Opher, Michael, Mom, Dad, Mr. Rich

"Discovering that Jesus was the Messiah that we, as Jews, were waiting for and converting to the LDS church was the icing on the cake for me."

"I was baptized this last April, and now I'm doing a fireside. The Mormons sure put you on a fast track when they get a hold of you, don't they?" People were laughing, and I thought I got off to a pretty good start.

I continued, "Honestly, I've been asking the bishop to do this fireside, because I keep getting promptings to teach the similarities that I have discovered between Judaism and the LDS faith. These promptings seem to come at three or four in the morning, sometimes several days in a row."

"Typically, I wake up out of a deep sleep, and I am impressed to turn to a specific scripture that would answer a question that I had been pondering."

I had prepared a PowerPoint presentation that followed along with the talk. It was much more than I had prepared for the combined priesthood lesson or the Mission President's Fireside. The first slide of the PowerPoint was an abridged copy of the title page from the Book of Mormon. This page was also part of the last leaf of the golden plates written by Moroni.

"Wherefore, it is an abridgment of the record of the people of Nephi, and also of the Lamanites --- Written to the Lamanites, who are a remnant of the house of Israel; and also to Jew and Gentile --- Written by way of commandment, and also by the spirit of prophecy and of revelation... Written and sealed up, and hid up unto the Lord, that they might not be destroyed."

"Which is to show unto the remnant of the House of Israel what great things the Lord has done for their fathers; and that they may know the covenants of the Lord, that they are not cast off forever--- And also to the convincing of the Jew and Gentile that JESUS is the CHRIST, the ETERNAL GOD, manifesting himself unto all nations ----"

Book of Mormon Title Page

My first question to the group was a rhetorical question. "Why are the Jews mentioned so prominently on the first page of the Book of Mormon?"

This was a question that had perplexed me from the first time that I read it. I thought that the answer might come from the following scripture.

I then had someone in the audience read Ezekiel 37:15-19.

After the scripture was read, I explained, "This scripture is clearly about two written records. The record produced by Ephraim, or the stick of Joseph, is the Book of Mormon. The record produced by Judah is the Bible. These two records have literally come together as one in our hand to fulfill Ezekiel's prophesy. In addition to the two sticks representing the Book of Mormon and the Bible, it was the foretelling of the coming together of Ephraim and Judah. I believe that it is also talking about me."

I thought, *"I wasn't sure about that last statement. Why did I still feel that Ephraim and Judah were alive within me? Was it because my mother was born Christian and my father was born Jewish?"*

The answer to those questions came as a startling discovery that was revealed through my Patriarchal Blessing.

I then told them about the mezuzah. "The mezuzah is placed on the door post of every Jewish home. It is placed there to have God bless and protect those who reside inside that home. What makes it important is the concept that the door post is the dividing line between the chaos of the outside world and the sanctity and safe haven of our homes."

I told them that this sounded like a Mormon concept as much as it was a Jewish concept. I then continued with a quote by Maimonides, a great Jewish sage, who lived during the 12th century.

"Whenever one enters or leaves a home with the mezuzah on the door post, he will be confronted with the declaration of God's unity. And will be aroused from his foolish absorption in temporal vanities. He will realize that nothing endures through all eternity save knowledge of the ruler of the universe."

I asked, "Is this not what we also feel as Mormons? Don't we also try to make our homes a special place, a place of safety, family unity, and learning about God?"

My questions brought some great answers from the people attending. I continued with an explanation of the Jewish prayer that is the Shema.

"Contained in the mezuzah is the Shema, a tightly-rolled piece of parchment made from the skin of a ritually clean animal on which is hand written in 22 lines, words from Deuteronomy, the last of the five books of Moses. The passages are from Chapter 6, verses 4 through 9 and in Chapter 11, verses 13 through 21. The parchment is rolled from the end to the beginning, so that the first word, Shema, is showing on top. The parchment is checked twice every seven years to ensure that it is rolled properly.

"The first line of the Shema reads:"

"Shema Yisrael Adonai Elohenu Adonai Echad
Hear, O Israel, The Lord Our God, The Lord Is One."

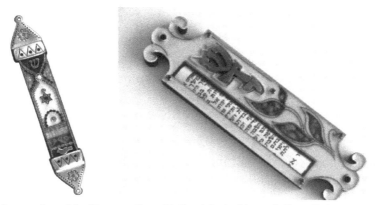

Mezuzah with Shema Scroll (inside left) and Scroll (exposed right)

I continued, "The Shema is one of only two prayers that are specifically commanded in the Torah (5 Books of Moses). The other prayer is Birkat Ha-Mazon, which is grace after meals. The Shema is the oldest fixed daily prayer in Judaism, recited morning and night since ancient times and consists of three biblical passages. Two passages say to speak of these things 'when you lie down and when you rise up.' It is the first prayer that Jewish children learn.

"It is safe to say that many of Jesus' teachings had their roots in Hebrew rituals. To understand this better, let's read Mark 12:28 through 30." I then had someone in the audience read the following:

28 And one of the scribes came, and having heard them reasoning together, and perceiving that he had answered them well, asked him, Which is the first commandment of all?
29 And Jesus answered him, The first of all the commandments is, Here, O Israel; the Lord our God is one Lord:
30. And thou shalt love the Lord thy God with all thy heart and with all thy soul, and with all thy mind, and with all thy strength: this is the first commandment.

Mark 12:28-30

"The third verse of the Shema is almost identical to Mark 12:30:"

"And you shall love the Lord your God with all your heart
and with all your soul and with all your might."

Shema 3rd Verse

"So I believe that Jesus was bringing that ancient Hebrew commandments forward to all the masses. I continued, "The next similarity comes from one of the most important Jewish holidays. Jewish holidays, as part of the Jewish calendar, are based on the lunar cycle. The Gregorian calendar that we use today is based upon the solar cycle. The difference is that the Jewish days start at sundown and going to the next sundown, instead of starting the day with the sunrise."

"For the service on Rosh Hashanah, I remember our Rabbi cradling the Torah (the first five books of Moses) in his arms and in a commanding voice saying:" (I recited the Shema again.)

"Shema Yisroel Adonai Elohenu, Adonai Echad
Here, O Israel, The Lord Our God The Lord Is One"

"This is a very emotional time in the service. Rosh Hashanah is commonly known as the Jewish New Year. The Jewish New Year is a time to begin introspection, looking back at the mistakes of the past year, and planning the changes to make in the New Year. Rosh Hashanah is usually held in September."

"The shofar (ram's horn) is also blown on this holiday. It sounds somewhat like a trumpet. One of the most important observances of this holiday is hearing the sounding of the shofar in the synagogue. A total of 100 notes are sounded each day."

"No work is permitted on Rosh Hashanah. Much of the day is spent in the synagogue. A popular observance during this holiday is eating apples dipped in honey, a symbol of our wish for a sweet new year. Another popular practice of the holiday is Tashlikh, which means 'casting off.' We walk to flowing water (living water), such as a creek or river, on the afternoon of the first day and empty our pockets into the river. By doing so we are symbolically casting off our sins. Small pieces of bread are commonly put in your pocket to cast off. This practice is not discussed in the Bible, but it's a long-standing Jewish custom."

"Before the first century, Rosh Hashanah was called 'The Feast of the Trumpets'. When the shofar was sounded it would signify the last or final harvest. It was blown outside the great temple. The shofar was usually gold plated and two silver trumpets were blown on either side of the shofar. Jewish scholars believed that The Feast of the Trumpets signified:

1. The beginning of Israel's final harvest.
2. The day God has set to remember his ancient promises to regather Israel.
3. A time for new revelation that would lead to a new covenant with Israel.

4. A time to prepare for the millennium."

I changed the slide. "What does this date signify? September 22, 1827. It was the date that Moroni gave the golden plates to Joseph Smith. It is also the first day of Rosh Hashanah in 1827."

"It is common Jewish thought that on Rosh Hashanah, God would eventually move from his seat of judgment concerning Israel and sit instead upon the seat of mercy, remembering his covenants with their fathers, and begin to restore them as his covenant people."

"I believe that the final harvest has been initiated with the sounding of the shofar. On September 22, 1827, God's trumpets (shofars) sounded throughout the world in every synagogue. It was the day the Prophet Joseph Smith would receive the golden plates, which would help fulfill God's promise to remember and gather Israel in these latter days. On that day, God began the final harvest of all the souls here on earth."

The Shofar - God's Trumpet

"Thank you all for coming this evening. I know this church is true. I say these things in the name of Jesus Christ. Amen."

Evelyn beautifully sang the final musical number, and my first fireside came to an end. I breathed a huge sigh of relief.

Chapter 12
Fresh View
(Michael and John in Booth One)

John had attended my first fireside, and I wanted to find out what he thought of it. I gave him a call at his office and asked if we could meet sometime to discuss any thoughts that he might have after listening to me the previous night.

We decided to meet for lunch at John's favorite restaurant, in his favorite booth for an enjoyable lunch together. I asked John why he loved to come to this particular restaurant more than anywhere else.

John said, "This is the best hamburger place on earth."

When the food was delivered, John and Michael looked at the lettuce-wrapped burgers and agreed that these were really salads disguised as hamburgers. They included extra tomatoes, fresh onions, grilled onions, and chopped banana chilies combined with a fresh patty of meat covered with cheese, seasoned with special sauce and all wrapped in lettuce! As if that wasn't enough, they added French fries made from fresh potatoes fried to four-minute perfection.

Michael and John's Booth One

John always preferred to sit in the first booth of this hamburger place, which he called Booth One. As we sat down to eat, John said, "I want to tell you how much I enjoyed your talk. It is unusual to have someone give a Jewish perspective to what's currently happening in relation to the doctrine of the Mormon Church. The thing that hit me the most was when you drew a comparison to the final harvest, The Feast of the Trumpets, which is a traditional Jewish holiday celebration, to Joseph Smith receiving the Golden Plates on the same day."

As we discussed that thought, Michael explained some additional thoughts on the same subject.

"I really don't know how I pulled that fireside off. There were so many marvelous thoughts coming into my head as I was talking, that it was hard to sort them out. I had printed off my talk word-for-word so that I wouldn't make any mistakes. As I was giving what I had prepared, the Spirit was giving me a flood of confirmation that what I was teaching was the truth. The Spirit wasn't trying to confuse me during my talk, he was confirming what I had already prepared."

"The confusing part to me was; Why am I the one delivering these messages? I'm not a Jewish scholar and I'm not good at quoting scripture. I'm just an average person that has made an amazing discovery and now I'm being prompted to talk about it."

John replied, "Michael, remember God picked an obscure farm boy, Joseph Smith, to restore His Church here on earth. Who would have ever imagined that was possible? Whoever God chooses, God qualifies. He picked you for a specific purpose. You might look at yourself as average, but God does not. We know that the time of the Gentiles will end and the Gospel will be taken to the Jews and the time of the Jews will begin. The Lord said that 'The first will be last and the last will be first.' I think that you are a part of the time of the Jews that has been prophesized. Tell me more about these amazing similarities between the LDS Church and Judaism. Few are as poignant as the story that you were referring to, of Joseph Smith receiving the Golden Plates on Rosh Hashanah."

Michael explained, "I see many similarities between Judaism and the LDS Church. The following story of Passover in 1836 is another one. These two historical events caused me to think seriously about the true purpose of Joseph Smith as a Prophet."

"For the holiday of Passover, a place setting at the table and a cup of wine is set aside for the prophet Elijah. He is to herald the coming of the Messiah for Jews and will come on Passover to fulfill this prophesy. In Jewish tradition, the front door is then opened to invite Elijah into our homes on the second night of Passover."

"As a child growing up with this tradition, it was a very important time in the Passover Seder dinner. We always looked forward to that time in the Seder when one of the children was chosen to open the door for Elijah, as prayers were said to invite him in. Growing up Jewish, we were taught that he would herald the coming of the Messiah and the redeeming of the Jewish people. As an adult, it was shocking to me to learn that Elijah had already come. I thought, *'How had he come back without any Jews knowing that it had happened?'"*

"The truth as I have come to understand it was the long-awaited return of Elijah had occurred in the LDS Kirtland Temple on April 3, 1836. First, Jesus appeared, followed by Moses, then Elias, and finally Elijah. It was also the second day of Passover and Easter Sunday. On Passover, Jews are praying about Moses redeeming and delivering them from bondage, and Elijah returns to signal the Messiah is coming. Instead of this happening in front of Jews, they all appeared to Joseph Smith and Oliver Cowdery."

John said, "This reminds me of what I have taught many times in seminary classes. Listen to this:"

"11 After this vision closed, the heavens were again opened unto us; and Moses appeared before us, and committed unto us the keys of the gathering of Israel from the four parts of" "the earth, and the leading of the ten tribes from the land of the north.

12 After this, Elias appeared, and committed the dispensation of the gospel of Abraham, saying that in us and our seed all generations after us should be blessed.

13 After this vision had closed, another great and glorious vision burst upon us; for Elijah the prophet, who was taken to heaven without tasting death, stood before us, and said:

14 Behold, the time has fully come, which was spoken of by the mouth of Malachi—testifying that he [Elijah] should be sent, before the great and dreadful day of the Lord come—

15 To turn the hearts of the fathers to the children, and the children to the fathers, lest the whole earth be smitten with a curse.

16 Therefore, the keys of this dispensation are committed into your hands; and by this ye may know that the great and dreadful day of the Lord is near, even at the doors."

Doctrine and Covenants 110:11-16

John continued, "The Spirit of Elijah is the desire to search out our ancestors through genealogical research and connect ourselves with them. This is done by going to the Temple and performing the saving ordinances for our departed family members starting with baptism for the dead and ending with sealing families together for eternity. The Lord revealed in Doctrine & Covenants:"

"15 These are principles in relation to the dead and the living that cannot be lightly passed over. ...For their salvation is necessary and essential to our salvation...they without us cannot be made perfect---neither can we without our dead be made perfect."

Doctrine & Covenants 128:15

Michael thought, "*What would be more joyful than being with your family for all eternity? Death and separation from your loved ones was no longer to be feared.*" A sense of calm came over me at these thoughts.

"Michael", John said, "what's exciting about all of this is that you're bringing something to the table that is a totally fresh view of things. When you tell me about how you grew up with these traditions, I can help you see how these traditions have been fulfilled, or how they're going to be fulfilled. Both sides of this are so important to understand the whole."

Chapter 13
Two Gather In My Name
(Michael and John in Booth One)

John and Michael met to enjoy an amazing lunch in Booth One. As time went on, meeting for lunch in Booth One would turn into a habit. These meetings would become a source of great spiritual nourishment for both of them.

Michael began, "I have been continually prompted by the Spirit to write a book of my conversion experiences since the fireside. I've tried to write a manuscript several times, but I tear each one up. None of them sound right. I wonder if I will ever be able to write this book."

John replied, "Quit messing around with this book idea and focus on your employment!

Michael answered, "Ok, I'll try to get my real estate career back on track."

John and Michael met a few days later in Booth One for lunch.

"John said, "I went home the other night, thought about it, and decided that you were right! Do you have a manuscript yet?"

Michael looked at John in disbelief and thought, *"Is this guy crazy? He just told me a few days ago to NOT write the book and now he is telling me to write the book. Which is it?'* Are you kidding me, John? I can't even get my thoughts onto paper when I sit down to write."

John replied, "Your story is too important not to have it written and published. So get to it!"

Michael said, "I'll try and see if it works. There is a scripture that keeps coming to mind and I don't understand what it means."

19 Again I say unto you, that if two of you shall agree on earth as touching anything that they shall ask, it shall be done for them of my Father which is in heaven.
20 For where two or three are gathered together in my name, there am I in the midst of them.

Matthew 18:19-20

John responded, "I know what it means. The reason it keeps coming up is that you are trying to write this book alone. I have a suggestion that is going to be a lot of work and probably some sacrifice for both of us."

"I suggest that we meet at 6:30 a.m. at my office, two or three times a week for two hours at a time. We will start with one meeting and if we both feel that the Spirit is with us, we will continue. If this book helps one person to find the truth, then it is worth writing."

Michael asked, "Ok, but do you have the time to put into this? You have just expanded your business and moved into a new office. This doesn't seem like the right timing for you."

John replied, "In my experience, when God asks you to do something, there never seems to be a convenient time to do it. When you know something is right, you just need to jump in. So let's do it!"

John and Michael started writing Michael's book. After a month of meeting three times a week, Michael noticed that John had some very unusual stories about his own conversion at age 19.

Three Questions

As time went on, Michael finally said to John, "We should include your stories as well. We are including some of our Booth One conversations anyway."

John said, "No, no, Michael this is your story and should be your book."

Michael replied, "It would be a much better book if we were to include some of your experiences to provide a balance to my stories."

John thought for a moment and said, "I don't know, I'll have to pray about it. When I get stuck in a project and can't seem to find an answer, I add fasting to my prayers. What fasting does is sharpen your focus and increase the intensity of your prayers. Maybe you ought to fast and pray about it."

Michael said, "John, I have some other things to pray about too. I actually have three big questions and how to write the book isn't one of them. Could you add a few more questions to your prayers also?"

John asked, "What are they?"

Michael replied, "The three questions that I have are:

1. How do I get my career on track?
2. How do I find my eternal companion?
3. How do I help build God's kingdom here on earth?"

John laughed, as he grabbed another fry, "Really Michael, you want me to pray about who you should marry? Please, I'll just pray about how to write the book."

Michael said, "Ok, I'll pray about my three questions myself."

John called Michael a few days later. "Michael, have you prayed and gotten your answers to your 3 questions yet?

Michael answered, "I sure did. I received answers, but not the answers I thought I would get."

John replied, "Michael, I can't wait to hear your answers, and also I have an idea to run by you. Let's meet in Booth One for lunch. I hope you turn down my idea and say no, because it will save me a lot of work."

Michael said, "Ok, see you then."

John and Michael met in Booth One for lunch. John was excited to hear Michael's answers.

Michael explained his experience, "I fasted and prayed about the three questions and here are the answers."

"Number 1: How do I get my career on track?
     The answer was, **'Write The Book.'**"
"Number 2: How do I find my eternal companion?
     The answer was, **'Write The Book.'**"
"Number 3: How do I help build the kingdom here on
     earth?
     The answer was: **'Write The Book.'**"

John smiled and asked, "Michael, do you think you should 'write the book?'"

Michael laughed, "Ya think?"

John recalled, "This reminds me of the story of the guy that was trapped in a flood. A man was trapped on his rooftop by a massive flood. So he prayed to God to be saved. A short time later a boat came by and asked him if he needed any help. He thought to himself, *'I prayed to God that He will save me, so I don't need this help.'* A little while later two other boats came by and offered their help. He turned them down one by one. Night came, the water rose and the man drowned. When he met the Lord in the spirit world, the man asked Him, 'Why didn't you save me?' The Lord said, 'I tried, I sent you three boats!'"

"Three boats and three answers to write the book, Michael added. Now that I have my answers, tell me about your idea."

John answered, "Michael, what I am about to suggest to you is not necessarily an inspired idea at all. Anyway, I hope you say no to it. If you say yes to it, it will require a whole lot more work on my part. Trust me, I'm busy enough as it is. My idea is, what if we make this a book about two converts? One converted from Judaism and one converted from Protestant Christianity. One converted early in his life at 19 years old and the other converted later in life at 57 years old. They eventually meet and both of them end up strengthening each other. This book then becomes a co-authored book between you and me. **Please say no to this idea!**"

Michael's response was without hesitation, "That's a great idea! I had been hoping that was the direction that this book would go. I think that your conversion story adds more depth to the overall book. Was this idea really the result of prayer?"

John answered, "It was, Michael, but I didn't want to present it that way. I didn't want to take away your ability to decide. I wanted it to be easier for you to say no! This is going to be a lot of work."

As funny as this exchange between them was, they both felt the same thing. This was the direction that the Lord wanted them to go with this book. This became a game changer for both Michael and John. They felt an urgency to move forward and before long they started meeting five times a week, for two hours each morning, before the work day started. This went on for another six months.

The first time that they met for the new co-authored format, Michael asked, "John, give me an overview of what you would like to put in the book."

John said, "Michael, I too am a convert to the Church. When I joined at 19, I felt that I was way behind in gospel knowledge. I never had the opportunity to attend primary, Sunday school, seminary, or any other church meeting. I changed my career path, left dental school at UCLA, started my Master's degree at BYU, and became a seminary and institute teacher for 10 years. A seminary and institute teacher is employed by the LDS Church Education System (CES) as a full-time teacher.

"During those ten years, I married a wonderful woman, Nanci Twitty, and started a family. I immersed myself in the revealed truths of the gospel. After leaving CES, I went on to start a successful business, but along the way I had learned an important principle. I believe that the responsibility of seasoned senior members of the Church is to help mentor those new converts so that they are able to see more clearly and understand the path that Heavenly Father wants them to follow. If I can help you write this book, it would be my privilege."

Michael replied, "Thank you John." I thought, *"How could I be so lucky as to have this kind of enrichment added to this book?"*

As they were talking, Michael remembered what Matthew said would happen when two or three were gathered in Christ's name. It seemed that the scripture was defining what the two of them were about to do.

Chapter 14
Who Wrote The Book
(Michael and John in Booth One)

Michael and John sat in Booth One together for some more "fine dining."

Michael asked, "John I've always wondered how did you get your witness that the Book of Mormon is true?"

John answered, "Michael, I've never known anyone that got a direct answer from God declaring that 'the book is true' like you did. You didn't even ask God if it was true and you were given a vision that convinced you instantly that you were holding the truth in your hands. That is not the typical way a testimony of the Book of Mormon comes to a person seeking the truth of the book. My path to that truth was very different, let me explain."

John continued, "When the missionaries gave me a copy of the Book of Mormon, they asked me to read it, pray, and ask God if it's true. That is the way most people come to know that it is true. Moroni outlined the steps in Moroni:"

> 4 And when ye shall receive these things, I would exhort you that ye would ask God, the Eternal Father, in the name of Christ, if these things are not true; and if ye shall ask with a sincere heart, with real intent, having faith in Christ, he will manifest the truth of it unto you, by the power of the Holy Ghost.
> 5 And by the power of the Holy Ghost ye may know the truth of all things. Moroni 10:4-5

"If anyone will study the Book of Mormon and then ask God with a sincere heart and real intent having faith in Christ the Holy Ghost will manifest that the book is true."

"However in my case I was afraid that it was true. I was worried that if the Book of Mormon was true, I would have to change my entire goals in life. So instead of reading it, I began to look for evidence that it wasn't true. The first thing that became apparent was that it was not written by Joseph Smith. Joseph was a farm boy and had only a 3rd grade education. When he received the golden plates and started to translate the book, Joseph's wife Emma said he wasn't capable of writing a complete sentence. How could he create a 531 page literary masterpiece in just over 65 days? To make it even more impossible, he did it without any rewriting. When he started and stopped during the translation of the Book of Mormon, he never asked his scribe where he had left off. That is impossible!"

Michael said, "John, you are exactly right. We haven't been able to write this book without several rewrites, and this book isn't exactly a literary masterpiece!"

John laughed and then continued, "So I had to ask myself, *'If Joseph Smith didn't write the Book of Mormon, then who did?'* My investigation turned to the anti-Mormons. I wondered what the "antis" had to say as to who wrote the Book of Mormon. I knew that anti-Mormons had their own agenda to discredit the book and thereby try to destroy the Church."

"As I investigated the anti-Mormon explanation as to who really wrote the Book of Mormon, I soon realized that these folks were as clueless as I was. Their explanations as to who wrote the book were impossible to believe, even more than thinking that Joseph Smith wasn't capable of writing it. I won't waste the space here to describe their ridiculous claims. In the end, I was still left asking the question, 'Who really wrote the Book of Mormon?'"

"Eventually, I came to the conclusion that there is only one possible answer to my question. That would be the one Joseph Smith gave, that the book is written by the ancient inhabitants of America who lived from 600 BC to 400 AD. It was written in a lost language and needed a prophet of God, a Seer, to translate it correctly. Joseph Smith was chosen to accomplish this task. It was important for Joseph to be illiterate at this point in his life so that no one could convincingly suggest that he wrote it himself. I found that once a person accepts the only possible explanation as to who really wrote the book, the magic starts to happen."

"Over the years I have had the wonderful opportunity to study and teach the Book of Mormon in various high school Seminaries, college Institutes of Religion, and in several Gospel Doctrine classes in Sunday school. I have come to know that what Joseph Smith said is true: 'The Book of Mormon is the most correct of any book on earth and the keystone of our religion and a man would get nearer to God by abiding by its precepts than by any other book.'"

"During those years of teaching, I have felt the power of this amazing book to open minds and change lives for the better. I now try to read something from the Book of Mormon every day, even if it is just one verse."

"Michael, I, too, know that the book is true, it just came to me in a different way than it came to you. For me, that knowledge is the best example of 'You shall know the truth and the truth shall make you free.'"

"Since the Book of Mormon is true, it follows that Joseph was and is a true Prophet of God. As a prophet, Joseph restored the original Church of Jesus Christ (set up in these latter-days) and the only true church on the face of the earth. The Church provides ordinances of exaltation and the full truth regarding the real purpose of this life. Both you and I are now free to move forward without fear of the future. That is real freedom. I thank God every day for the Book of Mormon."

Chapter 15
Is There Humor In Heaven?
(Michael and John in Booth One)

John called Michael and said "Let's meet for lunch tomorrow. Remember, we have that awesome place where we can have the best hamburgers in the universe." John and Michael agreed to meet the next day for lunch in Booth One.

At lunch the next day, John said, "Michael, one of the fun things about you is your sense of humor. You have the same sense of humor that I do, and I enjoy it very much. Where did that come from?"

Michael gave an amazing answer, "When you grow up Jewish, you have to figure out how you're going to deal with the persecution that comes with the territory. You have to find a way to deflect the barbs that are thrown at you every day for being Jewish. You decide whether you are going to become a fighter, or whether you are going to become a comedian. I decided to become a comedian, because using humor to neutralize anger is one of the best ways to survive. Growing up, I remember my uncles and family members always enjoying a good laugh when they got together. They were always telling a joke to bring humor into the conversation. They would tell me that a Jewish boy has a Rabbi on one shoulder and a Jewish comedian on the other."

John laughed and said, "Really? I was told that I had a devil on one shoulder and an angel on the other. No wonder we were both messed up as little kids!"

Michael smiled and replied, "I always try and put a lighthearted joke at the beginning of my firesides to get everyone laughing and loosen up the crowd. The time goes by a lot faster when you can teach with laughter and joy. John, do you think there is much humor in heaven?"

John answered, "Humor is one of the joys of life and we are assured that all that is good in this life will be magnified in the next life."

"If you've ever spent time around the General Authorities and other leaders of the Church you'll find them to be men and women of good will and good humor. They all seem to have a great sense of humor and often use it as a effective teaching tool.

"Over the years I have had some of my most important prayers answered in such a wonderful way that I couldn't help but chuckle with both amazement and amusement. We know that loud laughter and light mindedness are not a part of Heaven, but I believe that good humor will be. Let me share an example of what I mean."

"I was teaching seminary at a high school in Utah, right after I first got married. There was one student, Cindy that I was very worried about. Cindy didn't seem to have many friends. She had a very low self-image and didn't seem to be happy about her life. She had a deep sadness about her."

"It was the beginning of the school year, and I was the new seminary teacher. Because I went out of my way to be so nice to her, Cindy would often come to have lunch in my office with other students almost every day. I imagined that she ate lunch with me because she couldn't bear the humiliation of sitting all alone in the cafeteria."

"I was very concerned for Cindy, so I decided to pray and ask for promptings as to how I could help her."

"One morning, Cindy walked into my office. She had something behind her back, and she said, 'Brother Wudel, you said in class yesterday that your favorite dessert is a chocolate cream pie, so I stayed up late last night making you your favorite pie!' Then Cindy brought the pie around in front of her, to hand it to me. I looked down at the pie, put my hand under Cindy's hand, and then without even thinking, I brought it up and pushed it squarely in her face."

"The office was full of other students, who all gave a collective gasp. They watched in horror as Cindy stood there with chocolate pudding and whipped cream dripping down her face onto the newly replaced carpet! As Cindy blinked her eyes open through the pie filling, she asked in astonishment, 'Brother Wudel, why did you do that?'"

"To my total shock, I heard myself actually say, 'Cindy, some pies fit some faces and this pie fits yours.' The students who were present couldn't believe what they had just seen and heard. I couldn't believe it either."

Chocolate Cream Pie

"I went home that night, still stunned at what I had done. When I walked in the door, I told Nanci, 'I think I'm going to be fired from teaching seminary.'"

"She asked, 'Why on earth would you be fired?'"

"I replied, 'Because I did something so inappropriate that I'm sure I will be terminated. One of my favorite students brought me a gift of a chocolate cream pie. I pushed it in her face, and it fell all over the new carpet of the seminary.'"

"With a shocked look on her face, Nanci asked; 'Why would you DO that?'"

"I said, 'I don't know why I did it. I really think that I was compelled to do it. I really don't know why!'"

"When I returned to school the next day, I found out that the story of this incident had spread like a brushfire throughout the school. By 6th hour, everyone at the high school knew who Cindy was. Kids would stop her in the hallway and say, 'Did a teacher hit you in the face with a pie?'"

"Cindy became an instant celebrity. For the rest of the week, the most popular kids couldn't wait to eat lunch with Cindy. They wanted to help her plan how she could 'get even with Brother Wudel.' They had such a good time planning the retaliation that they came to know what a fun person Cindy really was."

John continued, "This new acceptance of Cindy by all of her student peers gave her a new sense of confidence. With her new found self-esteem came her ability to have the courage to do things that she never thought she would do. During her senior year, she ended up participating in all of the activities, as well as being one of the leads in the school play. She bloomed as a person, right in front of our eyes, in the most amazing way. It really was a miracle."

"Two days after graduation, I was in my office packing up the last of my things, because I had been transferred to another high school. Cindy came into my office with a whole group of excited new friends behind her. She said, 'Brother Wudel, I have something for you.' Then from behind her back, she brought out a homemade chocolate cream pie with extra whipped cream. She cocked it ready to throw, then brought it down and handed it to me with tears in her eyes. She said just two words, 'Thank you.'"

"Michael, many years have gone by since that incident occurred. As I've thought about this, I've come to the conclusion that there is humor in heaven. I can almost imagine a ministering angel with his hand under my hand causing that pie to go into Cindy's face. Can you imagine how that angel felt when he got that assignment?"

"It amazes me how well our Father in Heaven knows us and knows our needs. If we are humble and prayerful, He will find ways to help us grow to our full potential. It took a pie in Cindy's face to reach that goal for her. I have come to believe that sometimes personal growth can be accelerated by heavenly humor."

Chapter 16
Presidential Tour
(Michael)

The Gilbert Temple, where I received the Book of Mormon in the construction trailer, was in its final stage of completion. My friend, Stu, a member of my Ward, was the lead electrician in charge of the installation of all the lighting in the temple. He stood up one Sunday in combined Priesthood session and asked for volunteers to go to the Gilbert Temple site and build shelves in the access tunnel under the parking lot.

This temple was in the final stages of completion. So that nothing would interrupt the sacredness of the temple, the heating and air conditioning units were in a building in the parking lot. An access tunnel was built under the parking lot connecting the HVAC duct work from the units to the temple.

I volunteered to show up on the next Saturday morning at 6 a.m. The tunnel was 300 feet long and had electrical and plumbing running down one side of the tunnel. We were to build shelves down the other side for storage. As a real estate broker, I had an open house scheduled that day at 10 a.m., so I was leaving around 9:30. I came up out of the tunnel and walked over to Stu's truck to thank him for letting me help build the shelving units.

As we stood in the parking lot talking, a member of our Stake Presidency pulled into the temple parking lot.

I said, "Hi President, how are you doing?"

The President shook hands with both of us and said to Stu, "Are you ready for my tour of the temple?"

Without thinking, I said, "That sounds great. Can I go too?" All of the sudden my open house didn't seem that important.

They both looked at me and Stu said, "Sure."

I hadn't been ordained an elder, so I wasn't allowed in a LDS Temple yet. Since this temple was under construction and had not been dedicated, I was allowed to tag along. We proceeded to go through the entire temple from the top floor down to the basement. A lot of wood and marble was used, and the craftsmanship was incredible.

I was told that members of The Church of Jesus Christ of Latter-day Saints perform sacred ordinances which take place only within their temples. These ordinances are not secret, but they are sacred. These ordinances may be performed either on behalf of the participant, or by "proxy" on behalf of the dead. Some of these ordinances, like baptism, are normally performed outside of temples, but when performed on behalf of the dead, they must be performed inside the temple. Some of the ordinances include baptisms for the dead, confirmation, ordination to the priesthood, and sealings.

The first thing that I noticed was that it was not like a typical construction site. There was no loud music, no one was smoking, and the construction workers talked in whispers or low voices. When I asked about this, I was told that the workers were reverent because this was a sacred site. As we went from room to room, Stu would point out the different rooms and what they were used for. When we came to a room that I wasn't supposed to know about yet, the other men would say, "We can't tell you what goes on in that room until you hold the priesthood."

We entered a large room with ceilings that were at least 30 feet high. Stu said, "This is the Celestial Room." I had heard about the Celestial Room before. I was told that in finished temples, the Celestial Room represents the highest degree of heaven. As we walked in, I immediately noticed that the room was very bright.

I said, "Why is it so bright in here?"

They turned to me and questioned, "What do you mean bright?" At that point, I was squinting my eyes. I looked around, but couldn't see any light source other than the light coming through the stained glass windows. Stu explained to us that there would be a giant chandelier mounted in the middle of the room when it was completed.

I asked again, "How did you get this room so bright? Is the lighting hidden?" No one answered, so I kept my mouth shut.

As we were leaving the room, I turned and looked back, still wondering how they could get this room so full of light without any visible light fixtures. I stood there for a moment as the rest of the group continued on. A gentle calm feeling swept over me. The Spirit spoke to me and said, "You are in the House of the Lord." I lingered for another moment and then hurried to catch up with the tour.

Baptize The Dead?

I found out that I could get a temporary temple recommend and go to the Mesa Arizona Temple to do baptisms for the dead. Members are required to have a temporary temple recommend from their bishop before entering a temple. This temporary temple recommend can be obtained after a few months' membership and allows the member to do baptisms for the dead.

A permanent temple recommend requires that an individual be a member for one year. Some of the requirements are to pay tithing, live the Word of Wisdom, follow the commandments, and remain morally clean.

The recommend is obtained from and signed by a member of the bishopric after passing a one-on-one worthiness interview, in which one's commitment to the gospel is reviewed. The recommend is also signed by a member of the stake presidency, after a second one-on-one worthiness interview, and finally by the member themselves. By signing his or her own recommend, the member acknowledges their responsibility to ensure that they remain worthy to hold the recommend. Once issued, a recommend remains valid for a period of two years.

So I met with my bishop to find out the procedure to get a temporary temple recommend. He explained that we as Latter Day Saints believe that baptism is essential for salvation. It is a covenant with God to obey his commandments. Jesus taught that we all must be baptized. Some people die without being baptized or knowing about the Church of Jesus Christ of Latter-day Saints. They must also have an opportunity for salvation. Those who have died are taught the gospel in the world of the spirits.

Baptism is an earthly ordinance, so we can perform that ordinance for them. By being baptized for them, just as Jesus died for us, as a proxy for us, we can be baptized for others. This is authorized by Jesus in His Church to be performed in the temples. The person who died can either receive this proxy baptism or reject it. They still have their agency (ability to choose). The New Testament records that the members during Jesus' time on earth were also doing baptisms for the dead.

> 29 Else what shall they do which are baptized for the dead, if the dead rise not at all? why are they then baptized for the dead?
>
> 1 Corinthians 15:29

After receiving my temporary temple recommend, I arranged to go to the Mesa Arizona Temple for the first time to do baptisms for the dead. I arrived at the baptistery and changed into a white jumpsuit, which was just like the one that I had been baptized in. I entered the room with the baptismal font in it and proceeded to get into the warm water in the font."

Sitting on the bench on one side of the room, was a sister dressed in white waiting with her family names. I was then asked to be baptized by proxy for a few extra names, because that sister was waiting to take her family member's records through all the different ordinances in the temple that day. I agreed and the baptisms proceeded. After being baptized for several temple names and the sister's personal family names, I got out of the font. The temple workers then put towels on a chair and confirmed me for the sister's family names right there in the baptismal room.

I then got up and headed to the entrance of the men's changing room. As I did so, the sister that had brought her names to the temple came over to shake my hand. She looked directly into my eyes and said, "Thank you, Brother, for your service." Her voice trembled, and there were tears in her eyes as she shook my hand. I could feel the intense emotion of that moment and the sister's deep gratitude for my help in performing those sacred ordinances for her departed family members. I didn't know her name, but I could feel the Spirit as I went through the ordinances for her posterity.

As I changed my clothes, I realized that I had just participated in a holy ordinance given to us by God. I thought about what this must have meant to that sister and her family. The temple suddenly had a different meaning for me. I had been a part of performing a sacred ordinance, just as my ancestors had thousands of years before. I felt the presence of the Spirit inside me and all around me as I left the temple that day.

Bonds Through Service

I was assigned to work with Jim, a High Priest, for home teaching. Jim was a great example of someone who genuinely cares about people. He had an easy style of getting to know each person individually. He would end each visit with, "How can we help you? Do you have everything you need?" This very direct concept of caring for each other was unfamiliar to me. I always have cared about others, but not as specific as the Mormons do. It was like we, as home teachers, were watching over that family.

Home teaching is done in pairs, and each pair of brothers is usually assigned two or three families to home teach every month. Jim explained to me that home teaching is the responsibility of all Melchizedek Priesthood holders and of those who are teachers and priests in the Aaronic Priesthood. It is part of their responsibility to watch over the members of the Church. Home teachers visit their assigned families at least once each month to teach and strengthen them. Home teachers establish a relationship of trust with those families, so that the families can call upon them in times of need.

Brothers do home teaching, and the Sisters do visiting teaching. This is a great system within the church and keeps the members connected. It really forms a bond between families and encourages members to take care of each other.

To help take care of families in need, there is the bishop's storehouse. A bishop's storehouse refers to a commodity resource center that is used by bishops of the Church to provide goods to needy individuals. The storehouses stock basic foods and essential household items.

Most of the goods in the storehouse are purchased with fast offering funds or produced on LDS Church-owned agricultural property. The storehouses are staffed by volunteers or church missionaries. Bishop's storehouses are located throughout the world. Persons in need, whether members of the church or not, can access the storehouse by approaching a bishop or local Relief Society president. The bishop decides whether or not the person will be given assistance and works with the Relief Society President in determining what the person will be given. The usual practice is to ask the recipient to work or render some form of service in exchange for the goods that are given to them. Goods are generally not for sale to the public.

In the bishop's storehouse, there is also a food cannery. Part of our service within the church is volunteering to work in the cannery. I volunteered one afternoon to help. That day, they were canning raspberry jam. We made raspberry jam in big vats and then it was canned on an assembly line to be used in the bishop's storehouse. Most of the people working that day were volunteers. I got to meet people from other wards in the area. All in all, it felt really good to volunteer my time to help others. Since the Church is a lay ministry, the majority of the workers are not paid, but willingly volunteer their time. Out of fifteen storehouses in the states surrounding Arizona, there are only a few paid employees.

I didn't know it before I joined the church, but as one of the largest supporters for the Red Cross, the LDS Church is a first responder for many natural disasters around the world. It is apparent to me that Jesus' Church has been reestablished here on this earth. It is based on the same things that he taught while he was here on earth. Love is the motivation of what we should do in unselfish service to our fellow man.

I have heard people of different Christian sects say that they are sacrificing something in helping their fellow man. My personal opinion is that this isn't true. I don't look at it like it is a sacrifice. Neither did Jesus. It is really "service unto the Lord." Jesus didn't view what he was doing in being placed on the cross as a sacrifice. He looked at it as a service to his Father in Heaven and to his fellow man. When we serve, we are helping our fellow man and helping God build his kingdom here on earth.

Chapter 17
Growth Through Service
(Michael and John in Booth One)

Sitting in Booth One with Michael, enjoying the world's most delicious hamburger, John said, "Michael, congratulations on receiving your first calling in the Kingdom of God. Home teaching is one of the greatest callings of service that you will ever have in your life. In addition to home teaching, there will be many other callings as you stay active in the Church. The Lord's way is to call his members to all different levels of service for their personal growth. The Book of Mormon says it this way:

17 I tell you these things that ye may learn wisdom: that ye may learn that when you are in the service of your fellow beings ye are only in the service of your God.   Mosiah 2:17

"Let me show you a list of all the callings that I have had over the years. I have never turned down a calling. Notice that I have been called to the same calling more than once. Remember, if you don't get it right the first time, you might get asked to do it again." John handed Michael the following list:

John's Church Callings, from 1961 to 2016:
1. Priest Quorum Teacher – BYU
2. Sunday School Teacher Course #14
3. Gospel Doctrine Teacher – BYU
4. Full-time Missionary (2 Years)
5. Training Elder
6. Senior Companion
7. District Leader
8. Assistant to the Mission President
9. Zone Leader

10. Stake Missionary
11. Ward Missionary
12. 70's Group Leader
13. Stake Missionary Presidency
14. Full-time Seminary Teacher (6 High Schools, 5.5 Years)
15. Full-Time Institute Teacher (3 Colleges, 4 Years)
16. Institute Director (2 Years)
17. Early-Morning Seminary Coordinator (2 Years)
18. Sunday School Teacher Course 16 – 17
19. Gospel Doctrine Teacher (3 Years)
20. Primary Teacher – CRT B
21. Cub Scout Den Leader
22. Elders Quorum Teacher – BYU
23. Gospel Essentials Teacher
24. Stake Sunday School Presidency
25. Temple Ordinance Worker (6 Years)
26. Temple Assistant Veil Coordinator
27. Temple Veil Coordinator
28. Stake High Council
29. Bishopric 2nd Counselor (2 Years)
30. Bishop (6 Years)
31. Stake, Know Your Religion Teacher (1 Year)
32. High Priest Group Leadership (3 Years)
33. Gospel Doctrine Teacher
34. Word Activities Committee (2 Years)
35. High Priest Group Leader 2nd Counselor
36. Home Teacher (55+ Years)
37. Sunday School Assistant Teacher Course 15
38. Gospel Doctrine Teacher (2 Years)
39. Volunteer Institute Teacher MCC (2 Years)
40. Easter Pageant Narrator (2 Years)
41. Easter Pageant Apostle (1 Year)
42. Volunteer: Cannery, Stake Farm, Building Cleaning
43. Mesa Arizona Temple Ordinance Worker (2 Years)

44. Gospel Doctrine Teacher (3 Years)
45. Primary Teacher - 11 Year Olds
46. Gospel Doctrine Teacher

John suggested, "Michael, if you look at this list, it represents an example of the genius of the Lord's Church. This church is run with a lay ministry. The growth that has come to me through service in the Church, over all the years, has been irreplaceable. That growth was made possible through accepting these callings and be willing to help others. The same opportunity will be presented to you. The Lord makes these calls through inspired Priesthood leaders. My advice to you, Michael, is that you never turn down a calling from the Lord."

Michael responded, "That sounds like good advice. I agree, I will never turn down a calling. Looking over your list, why do you sometimes go from big responsibilities to small ones? Why isn't it more of a progression?"

John continued, "In the Mormon Church there is no vertical ascension. For example, when a bishop is released, he can be called to the nursery for his next calling. These callings are from God through your inspired priesthood leaders. God inspires the bishop or stake president to call you to a position where you can not only serve the best but benefit the most."

Michael thought for a moment and then replied, "That isn't like any other organization that I have ever seen. Most of the religious organizations that I have seen would promote you moving up the ladder to more important callings. It seems that the Lord's way is just the opposite. John, you mentioned that you grew a lot from these callings. Was there anything else that you gained from these callings besides personal growth?"

John replied, "When you accept a calling in the Lord's Church, you become a partner with Him in His work. That gives you access to a spiritual power that is very real. That spirituality that comes to you enriches your life and the lives of those around you in a way that is indescribable. There is no high like the high that you feel when the Spirit helps you to perform a task for the Lord."

Michael said, "I know exactly what you are saying. I have felt the very same way every time I give a fireside. The opposite of that feeling is how the rest of the world tries to get high. Alcohol and drugs never leave you with a feeling that you are fulfilled. You always feel empty afterwards and want to do more because you feel so empty. When you feel the power of the Spirit in your life, it is so fulfilling that you are always building on it. It is like you are always reaching new heights that you never dreamed were possible."

John added, "If the people that are looking for a high from drugs understood all of this, they would set their drugs aside and ask for a calling to serve in the Lord's kingdom."

The Day Winnipeg Was Paralyzed

John and Michael met again for lunch in Booth One. Michael asked John, "The meaning of service has been on my mind a lot lately. Can you give me a personal example of significant service that you have seen in the Church?"

John reflected for a moment and replied, "Here is one example that I experienced while serving a mission. It occurred on Friday, March 4, 1966. Winnipeg, Manitoba Canada was shut down by a snow storm like never before."

"Snowmobiles took nurses and doctors to work, and thousands of people were stuck downtown and slept overnight at Eaton's Department Store and the Hudson's Bay Company."

"That particular winter in Canada of 1966 was the third coldest winter of the century. In February 1966, Winnipeg reached minus 49 degrees, the lowest February temperature ever recorded, and the second coldest day ever. Winnipeg did not see the temperature go above zero for 90 days."

Winnipeg, Canada Picture
Courtesy of Snow Storm News Photo by IMGUR

"Snow started to fall after midnight on Thursday and despite the heavy snow, on Friday morning March 4, people still went to work. By my mid-morning, the streets were impassable. The buses were called in by 11:00 a.m. and would not return to the streets till the next Saturday morning. Schools closed for that Friday and the following Monday, as did stores, restaurants and theatres. The big storm piled up 14.6 inches of snow and was driven by winds gusting up to 70 miles an hour. This was the worst winter storm since March 1902. Eight foot high drifts were reported, and plows created 12 foot high walls of snow along Ness Avenue, a main street in Winnipeg. Hundreds of cars were reported stranded."

"Soon those who could not walk home were stuck wherever they were. Thousands of people were stranded at City Hall. 1600 people were reported stranded at Eaton's and Hudson's Bay. Eaton's took care of 700 of its staff and 400 customers. The women slept on the ninth floor and the men on the seventh."

"Snowmobiles were given to the police and volunteers operated additional snowmobiles to take people to hospitals and to deliver drugs to patients. Two policemen delivered a baby in the North End of Winnipeg. They got there with their own front-end loader leading the path. The two police men took instruction from a doctor over the phone and helped the mother with the delivery of her baby boy."

"In this amazing situation, I was serving as the Assistant to the President of the North Central States Mission for the Church of Jesus Christ of Latter-day Saints. It was my responsibility to direct the activities of the LDS missionaries in Winnipeg. I know what you're thinking; of course you don't send the missionaries out in this horrific weather. Even the Canadian Army was told to stand down and stay inside. That's conventional military. I was dealing with an unconventional army, the Lord's Army. I was trained that these missionaries are the Lord's, so I decided to ask Him what to do with them. I then got down on my knees and prayed."

"My prayers were answered, and I made two decisions that later proved to be very significant under these circumstances. The first decision was to send the missionaries out into the cold. I told them to go forth and to tract and they would be blessed. Tracting is going door to door inviting people to hear a Gospel message. This was in spite of such strong winds and freezing temperatures with a wind chill that was minus 90 degrees."

"Tracting usually doesn't work very well. Most people don't want to be bothered so they say they are not interested and shut the door. My thought was if the missionaries would go door to door in this storm, they would get in every door that they knocked on, because the folks would feel so sorry for them. It worked. I'm not sure how many Elders followed that advice, but my companion and I did. Every house let us in and usually tried to warm us up with hot chocolate. I will mention just one of those homes that my companion and I were invited into."

"As we were walking door to door it was very important to keep your eye on your companion's face. Frostbite would start as a small white spot especially on the nose and ears that must remain covered if possible. When the frostbite thawed out it was like a burn and was very painful. The tears from your eyes would freeze immediately as they ran down your cheeks. We presented such a pitiful sight standing on everyone's door step that we were always quickly invited inside to warm up."

"We knocked on one lady's door who was shocked that we would be out in such a storm. We told her that we had a message for her from Jesus Christ. She immediately invited us in. After we warmed up and gave her the message that the Lord had restored His Church again to the earth, she thanked us for coming. We had been instructed by our mission president that we should never leave a home that had invited us in without leaving a priesthood blessing on that home. I asked the dear lady if we could please say a prayer and leave a priesthood blessing on her and her home before we left. She said we could."

"Before I prayed I asked her if there was anything that she was particularly concerned about that we could include in the prayer. She said that she was worried about her husband who was a traveling salesman driving home in the storm. She was very concerned as she had not heard from him. We all knelt down in her front room, and I prayed that by the power and authority of the Holy Melchizedek Priesthood that her husband would be safe on his return trip and that her home would be safe in the storm. After the prayer, she stood up with tears in her eyes, thanked us and bid us farewell. Off into the cold we went, having no idea what was about to transpire because of that prayer."

"Days later, we learned that a phone call came to the mission home in Minneapolis from the same lady in Winnipeg. We were told that the conversation went something like this:
'Is this the Church that sends out young men with messages from God?'"

"The secretary of the mission home replied, 'If you mean our missionaries, yes it is. How can I help you?'"

"The lady said, 'Two of your young men came by my home during the storm last week. Before they left, they knelt down and blessed my husband and me with some kind of Mel...chez...ic? priesthood. My husband was away at the time on a business trip and was caught in the storm. He was involved in a terrible head-on collision during the storm and should have been killed. By some miracle, he returned home fine and does not have a scratch on him. I know that it is only because of the blessing that those two boys left in our behalf that my husband was saved. I can't thank those two boys enough.'"

"The secretary said that it sounded like she was in tears on the phone. The lady then asked how she could learn more about the Mormon Church. The sister that took the call reported that story to us. We never saw that lady again, but I know that someday, in the next life, we'll meet again with tears and a big hug, because two young missionaries went forth in spite of the storm."

"The second decision involved the entire city of Winnipeg. I called the city offices to volunteer the services of the missionaries. I was told that if we could get down to the Hudson Bay Company they could really use our help in taking all the phone calls that were coming from people stranded and needing their medications. About four sets of Elders, including my companion and I, were able to get downtown. We were immediately put to use on the department store phone system, taking incoming calls from desperate people that were running out of their medications and supplies."

"We quickly organized a plan. We would answer their calls; record their addresses, phone numbers and what medications they needed. A runner would come by every few minutes and gather this information and process it. The needed medications were delivered by young people driving snowmobiles. We loved helping out and even got some good will for the Church out of it."

Missionaries in the Hudson's Bay Company
(John Wudel, front right)

"One local newspaper exaggerated a bit with a headline of:

'MORMON MISSIONARIES SAVE WINNIPEG'"

"Two quotes come to mind. A fellow missionary serving in Boston once said,

'Serve every day of your mission in such a way that when you get out of bed every morning, Satan says, Oh no... HE'S AWAKE!'

Elder Richard G. Scott said, 'No missionary can determine the lasting effects of his or her labors.'"

Chapter 18
Elder Ordination
(Michael)

The next step in my conversion journey was my Elder ordination. I had a meeting with my bishop and then one of the members of my Stake Presidency. At each meeting, we discussed my adherence to the commandments. Any person who receives the Melchizedek Priesthood is ordained to the office of elder. This is done for male members who are at least 18 years old. In order to be ordained, I had to be determined worthy by my bishop and stake president. I passed and started to make arrangements for the ordination ceremony. I also needed the consent of the other priesthood holders in my ward and stake.

Some of the duties of an elder are to teach, baptize, and watch over the Church. Elders have the authority to administer to and bless the sick; to confirm those who are baptized into the Church by the laying on of hands for the Baptism of Fire and the Holy Ghost; to give others the Aaronic or Melchizedek Priesthood as directed by priesthood leaders. An elder may also ordain others to the priesthood offices of deacon, teacher, priest or elder.

Typically, you would choose a Melchizedek Priesthood holder, either a high priest or an elder, to give the blessing for the Elder Ordination. Other Melchizedek Priesthood holders are requested to stand in a circle. Just like the Aaronic Priesthood Ordination, the member receiving the ordination would sit in a chair and each Melchizedek Priesthood holder would put his right hand on the member's head for the blessing. This is called "laying on of the hands." Each man would put his right hand on the members head and his left hand on the brother's shoulder next to him. Usually you have about six or seven men, plus the person giving the blessing standing in a circle around the chair that the person receiving the blessing would be sitting in.

I talked to my friend, Sam Woodruff, to see if he would ordain me an elder. Sam had been asked to be the bishop of a local singles ward, a ward solely for unmarried men and women, between 18 and 32 years of age.

Sam agreed to perform the ordination and we decided on an appropriate date. The bishop went over with me what would happen during this ordination and what it meant to accept the Melchizedek Priesthood.

I believe that during my first year as a new member, Heavenly Father placed certain brothers and sisters in my path to help counsel and guide me through my conversion experience. Sam was one of those important brothers. I found out later that Sam was the great, great grandson of Wilford Woodruff. Wilford Woodruff was the third President of the Church and a Prophet of God.

Sam was to conduct the ordination. We also needed a representative from the Stake Presidency to preside over the ceremony. A high councilman was assigned to preside over my ordination.

The ordination had been set up for Sunday evening, January 26, 2014, after the church services had ended in the building. Usually ordinations were held in the bishop's office. As we were waiting for the high councilman to show up to preside, people started filing in the door of the chapel building to attend the ceremony. There ended up being 30 or 40 brothers and sisters attending. I realized, as everyone was standing in the foyer of the chapel, that there would be too many people to fit into the bishop's office. Our high councilman arrived and as we shook hands, he said, "How many of these people are here for your Elder Ordination?"

I replied, "All of them." I think he was a bit surprised.

Since there were so many people, he thought it would be best to hold the ceremony in the chapel. Sam stood up and gave a great introduction as to how important it was to become an elder in the Church of Jesus Christ of Latter-day Saints. I was a little nervous because so many people had shown up for the ceremony. Usually an elder ordination is attended by members of that person's family and a few friends that come to observe and participate.

After the introduction, Sam asked for all of the members that were participating to come forward. Almost every man in the room got up to come forward to stand in the circle. There were at least 15, counting Sam. Sam said, "Let's be careful of Michael's head, since there are so many in the circle tonight."

As the blessing was being given, I could again feel the power of the Spirit coursing through my body from my head to my toes. The blessing ended and I became an Elder in the Church of Jesus Christ of Latter-day Saints. As I got up from the chair, I shook each man's hand and thanked those who had participated. I felt like I was walking on pillows, sort of like after my baptism. I have been told about similar experiences by several other Jewish converts.

I couldn't fall asleep that night, thinking about this new responsibility that I had taken upon myself. I felt a great sense of peace and calm, even though I couldn't fall asleep. I wondered when I would be asked to give my first blessing and be asked for the first time to baptize someone.

Temple Preparation

The next step in my conversion, now that I was an elder, would be to receive a temple recommend. With a temple recommend, I would be allowed to go to any of the LDS temples and perform ordinances. At that time, there were about 147 operating temples in the world.

One of the requirements was to go to a temple preparation class. Our ward did not have a class planned for at least another month. So I called Sam and asked him if there was any other way that I could start studying sooner to complete this step. He said, "If you don't have a temple prep class in your ward presently, you are welcome to come to my young singles adult ward (YSA) and attend classes here." I thought that was a great idea and arranged to start attending classes at his YSA ward and started the following Sunday.

A YSA ward is attended only by members that are 18 to 32 years of age. Since all of the members are single, all of the activities are geared towards single young adults. The leaders of the ward, including the bishop and his two counselors, are married adults. I decided to attend their sacrament meeting and see what it was like, before attending their temple prep class. There was an incredible energy in the room and I could feel that the spirit was very strong. After sacrament meeting, I proceeded to the classroom where the temple prep class was being held.

A sister, Debra, was teaching the class. She was in my age group, but everyone else in the class, besides me, was in their early 20s. Temple prep class would consist of seven sessions in which I would be taught about preparing myself to go to the temple. Attending the temple and participating in ordinances is one of the cornerstones of the LDS faith. Sam's wife, Cherri, sat in on several of the classes with me. I appreciated her and Debra's kindness in helping me to understand the lessons. I think they may have also felt sorry for me, because I was the only "old" guy in the room.

Everyone else in the room had either converted as a child or grown up in the faith and seemed to know a lot more than I did about going to the temple. The following are the seven classes that I attended:

Lesson 1: The Temple Teaches About the Great Plan Of Salvation
Lesson 2: We Must Be Worthy to Enter the Temple
Lesson 3: Temple Work Brings Great Blessings into Our Lives
Lesson 4: Receiving Temple Ordinances and Covenants
Lesson 5: Learning From the Lord through Symbols
Lesson 6: Preparing To Enter the Holy Temple
Lesson 7: Continuing To Enjoy the Blessings of Temple Attendance

As we went through each lesson, I realized and felt the great reverence that LDS members have for their holy temples.

Again the similarities between Judaism and the LDS faith came to mind. In ancient times, the temple was the center of my ancestors worship, from Moses' tabernacle in the wilderness; to the magnificent temple that Solomon built; to Herod's great temple in the time of Jesus.

I was now prepared to attend a temple that would be the center of my modern day worship. I was amazed that the holy temple, the House of the Lord, had once again been restored to the earth.

Blessing of Comfort

My first calling in the church was Elders Quorum Secretary. The elders quorum meets each Sunday to study the gospel and be instructed in their duties. In our quorum presidency meeting before church, we decided to have one elder go to the front of the room before each Sunday lesson started and tell the rest of the group about themselves and their families.

It was during these elder introductions that I came up with a profound question for each elder. At the end of the questions for each elder, I would ask, "Have you ever had a spiritual experience that was so compelling that it changed your life?" This query became the elder's favorite question when someone was giving a brief introduction of themselves and their families. These heartfelt and tender stories of personal experiences brought a new spiritual depth into our weekly Sunday meetings.

When the bishop called me into his office and told me that my first calling would be the Elders Quorum Secretary, I said, "I don't know if I'm qualified for this. Wouldn't I be better suited as a hall monitor or something similar?"

He chuckled and replied, "No, I think you could help the elders quorum as the secretary. Meet with Timo, and he will show you what your duties are."

Timo was the ward clerk and sang in the ward choir with me. So we arranged to meet one evening in the clerk's office in the ward building. There, we could go over how I would keep track of the home teaching and attendance for the Sunday meetings of the elders quorum. I would turn in the numbers each month, and then those numbers would be reviewed by the bishop and the stake presidency.

We met that evening at 7 p.m. in the clerk's office. Any other activities in the building were winding down, and the last person in the building would let us know when they were leaving. We locked all the doors and went back in the clerk's office to go over my duties.

We left the door to the clerk's office open. About 45 minutes later, we were startled when someone knocked on the door jam. We turned from the desk to see who it was and were surprised to see a young man in his early 30s. He was obviously very upset. He said, "I used to attend church in this ward building and wondered if anyone was still here so that I could get a blessing."

We said in unison, "Come in and have a seat." He immediately started pouring his heart out to us.

He immediately poured out his concerns, "I was thrown out of my house, and I can't see my children. My wife wants a divorce." I could see by the look on Timo's face that he was a little shocked.

The young man proceeded to tell us a heart-wrenching story of how he had come home one day to the locks changed on his home. His wife looked out the window and started yelling at him from behind the glass. He could hear his children crying and calling out to him in the background. In a few minutes, the police arrived, and he was escorted off the property.

He was served with papers the next day that accused him of abusing his wife and children. He told us that he did not have a police record, nor had the police ever been called to his house. He said that he had never abused his wife and children.

As he spoke, tears welled up in his eyes. He said he was from Tucson, but was staying with his brother in Mesa. His court hearing to start the process of deciding his children's custody was going to be the next morning. Since his wife had emptied their bank accounts, he didn't have any money for a lawyer and didn't know what to do. He could only assume that his wife had been planning this scenario for some time.

With tears in his eyes, he said, "Have you ever heard of anything like this? I don't know what to do."

Timo remarked, "I've never heard of anything like that."

I stated, "I have." Timo looked at me in disbelief. I had been in a similar situation, not that long ago, and I knew exactly how he felt.

I questioned, "Did it seem like everything was well-rehearsed, like she had been planning this for a while?"

He replied, "I had no warning. Our bank account was emptied and the locks on the house were changed on the same day. Since then she has cut me off from the children, like she had pre-planned this, step by step."

When I went through my divorce and experienced something similar to this, I responded by volunteering with a couple of different nonprofit support groups. These groups tried to help others avoid losing their children and navigate the divorce system. In one self-help group that I worked with, we saw many people, men and women being taken advantage of in the corrupt divorce court system.

Even though he didn't know it, this young man was only at the beginning of experiencing the heartbreak of a broken family.

Timo asked, "Would you still like a blessing?"

He pleaded, "Yes, please."

Timo looked at me and said, "You give this blessing."

I replied, "I haven't given a blessing yet."

Timo said, "You know more about this than I do." He was referring to the man's problems.

We had the man sit in a chair and placed our hands upon his head. Timo nodded to me, and I began. First, I tried to clear my mind and listen to the Spirit. I suddenly realized that I now held the Melchizedek Priesthood and that I had the authority from Heavenly Father to give a blessing to this brother in need. I began with the words, "By the authority of the Melchizedek Priesthood..........."

I continued with a blessing asking for peace and love within this man's heart, so that he could receive the help of Heavenly Father. I prayed for his children, that they would be safe and reunited with him. I prayed that he would have the clarity of thought to be able to represent himself and that the judge would rule with fairness and compassion. The blessing went on for a few minutes, and then I concluded with "In the name of Jesus Christ. Amen."

He looked relieved as he got up. We wrote down the young man's name and phone number so that we could have one of our members, who was a divorce attorney, give him a call and offer some advice.

After the young man left, I asked Timo if I had done a good enough job with the blessing. He answered, "You did great. Just like you were an old pro." I smiled. He said, "Did you really experience some of the same things that he was describing?"

I replied, "Unfortunately, I have. We live in a time where there is so much turmoil going on in this world and inside ourselves that we have lost our peace of mind. Families are being continually torn apart. There is so much contention between husbands and wives that we have forgotten how to forgive each other and get along."

I didn't realize it at that time, but the words of Jesus Christ have never had more meaning than when he said in John:

27 Peace I leave with you, my peace I give unto you: not as the world giveth, give I unto you. Let not your heart be troubled, neither let it be afraid.   John 14:27

Through giving my first priesthood blessing of comfort, I was able to impart His peace to this troubled brother.

I had felt the Spirit in the room and so had Timo. I realized how much we all need help from time to time and how important it is that the keys to the priesthood have been restored here on the earth to provide that help. I could feel the gravity of the responsibility that we as priesthood holders have. We must be true to our faith and to help others, so that we can be ready at any time to perform a blessing for those who need it.

Early the next morning, a member of our ward, a divorce lawyer, gave the young man a call to offer advice. Timo let me know that the young man had said that he was amazed that the judge had shown fairness and compassion just as the blessing had promised. The young man was given an extension so that he could have time to prepare his case.

When I heard this, my heart rejoiced at the thought that Heavenly Father knew what this young man needed, had heard, and had honored our inspired blessing.

Chapter 19
John's First Priesthood Blessing
(Michael and John in Booth One)

John and Michael met again in Booth One for lunch. Michael related to John the story of his first priesthood blessing.

"My first blessing was such a powerful experience for me. Can you remember your first priesthood blessing?"

John replied, "Yes, I'll never forget it." He then related the following story:

"I joined the Church and received the Aaronic Priesthood in 1961. I later received the Melchizedek Priesthood and was ordained an Elder. I had the authority to give a priesthood blessing, but I was not asked to do so until 1965. It's hard to believe that four years had gone by before I ever participated in giving a priesthood blessing."

"I was serving a mission in Rochester, Minnesota. I was a district leader over four sets of missionaries. On the day of one of our zone conferences (a zone includes about four to six districts), held in the Rochester chapel, I was sitting in the audience of about sixty missionaries listening to the speaker, when I was tapped on the shoulder. Our mission president had requested me to follow him into an adjoining classroom. Upon entering the classroom, he introduced me to a woman who was sitting in a chair waiting for us. This woman was about 40 years old and had a gauze bandage wrapped around her head covering her eyes."

"The mission president explained that this was a sister who had been driven up from a city in Wisconsin to receive a blessing from him. She was losing her eyesight from a very painful malady. I assumed that she had to wear the bandages to keep out the light to reduce the pain. She had come a fair distance to receive this blessing, and my mission president had chosen me to assist him."

"I think that the mission president knew that I was a convert and had little experience in using the priesthood. Because I was a college graduate, he also had his eye on me to eventually become his assistant. He wanted to give me as much spiritual training as he could. I was grateful for that, but I could never have imagined what was about to happen."

John continued, "I was asked to anoint the sister with holy oil that had been consecrated and blessed for the healing of the sick. Then the mission president placed his hands on the anointed head of the sister, and I placed my hands on top of his. As soon as my hands were in place, a power came upon me from the Spirit. It entered the top of my head and moved down thru my body and out my arms and hands."

"When the mission president began the blessing I couldn't believe what I was hearing. It went something like this:"

"'Dear Sister, you are going blind for a reason. You are the wife of the branch president [a branch is a small unit of the Church]. You are in a position where you can help build the Kingdom of God.'"

"'You, however, are doing just the opposite. Your gossiping about the members of the branch is undermining your husband's good efforts. If you don't stop the evil speaking against your branch members you will go completely blind. If you choose to repent and stop this backbiting, your sight will be returned to you.' He then promised her this in the name of Jesus Christ and closed the blessing."

"I stood there in shock. I'd heard several priesthood blessing over the years but never anything like this. This sister stood up, and I saw the tears coming from under the bandages and rolling down her cheeks as she said nothing, but thanked us both. At the time I thought, *This sister could leave the Church over this.*'"

"The mission president said nothing to me but asked me to return to the meeting in progress. I wondered what would happen to this sister over the next few weeks. I found out what happened a month later at the next zone conference. Again I was called out of the meeting and was ushered into the same class room as before."

"There stood in the middle of the room the sister we had blessed. Her face radiated with joy, and her eyes appeared normal. She expressed the deepest appreciation for the blessing she had received. Without saying anything, it was apparent that she had taken the warning in the blessing to heart and changed her ways. She was freed from more than just the blindness. She was given the truth and became free from her own negative attitude and behavior."

John concluded, "Over the years I have had the privilege of giving dozens of priesthood blessings, but never have I experienced anything close to that first blessing that I was privileged to take part in. That blessing left an indelible impression that comes to mind every time I'm giving a blessing. It reminds me of how much our Father in Heaven loves us all in spite of our faults and will do anything necessary to help us succeed. Priesthood blessings are a source of power and revelation that are only available because of the restoration of the Lord's Church. This is one of the restored truths that will help make us free, as it did for this good sister."

Michael responded, "Wow, each of our first blessings were amazing!"

Conflicted

Michael said, "John, I have enjoyed speaking at a few family home evenings for members of my ward."

A family home evening is a time to strengthen your family's bonds. By learning the gospel together and listening to each other's feelings, thoughts and ideas, a family can build closer ties. Family home evenings (FHE) are usually held each Monday night. It is the responsibility of the parents or hosts to plan enjoyable activities. No church meetings are allowed on Monday nights to disturb this family time.

Michael continued, "Now, I have an invitation to a luncheon in a different stake to teach all the missionaries serving in that stake about some of the similarities between Judaism and the LDS church and how to start a conversation with a Jewish person. I don't feel comfortable teaching the missionaries how to proselytize Jewish people. I feel that in some way, I would be disrespecting my heritage by doing so. I still consider myself a Jew, and Jews are taught not to proselyte. I love the Jewish faith, and I loved growing up Jewish, with all the holidays, learning the ordinances and principles of which the Jewish people live by." I thought, *"I now have the ancient foundation of Judaism that is being added upon. Joining the LDS Church is like the icing on the cake for me."*

John said, "I think you are right."

Michael replied, "The personal revelations that I have received during the past year have impressed upon me that I am being exposed to something very special. I am being given the truth, the truth about the gospel of Jesus Christ. I have to find out a few answers, before I can go to the missionary luncheon. That's why I called you, John."

"Why are you so conflicted?", John asked. "God gave you a revelation where he showed you the Jewish prayer book and the Book of Mormon together in the same vision. He then told you the Book of Mormon is true. You have been given additional truth than what you grew up with and received revelation to confirm this truth."

"Isn't it your obligation to now share this with others? You know Michael, your story reminds me a little of Paul, who was a Jew and is an example of this conflict that you are experiencing. Paul was schooled in the ancient traditions of Judaism to the highest degree. He was against Christ, until he met the Savior on the road to Damascus. Then he became the greatest missionary that Christ ever had, because he had learned the truth."

"Our missionaries go out to deliver a message of truth. They're not there to take away what people already have, but just add to it. If they knock on the door and the people that answer are looking for additional truth, further light and knowledge, they will be interested to listen to the message. If they believe that they have all the truth that they need, they won't be interested in what the missionaries have to say. The missionaries aren't there to convert anybody; they are there to deliver a message. It's the spirit of God that converts people."

Michael asked, "What is the message to a Jew as opposed to a Christian?"

John replied, "To a Christian," John answered, "it is that the original Church of Jesus Christ has been restored. The Church was taken off the earth for a period of time during the dark ages. A modern prophet has been called in these latter days, and the church has been restored."

"To a Jew, the missionaries will tell them that the promised Messiah has restored His kingdom to the earth in preparation for His coming. Both of those messages to Christians and Jews are nothing but positive. If they want to know more, then the missionaries are there to teach them. They are there to teach the gospel of Jesus Christ as it is been restored by these latter day prophets."

John continued, "If you can help the missionaries understand the traditions of Judaism, you empower them to be more effective in delivering their message. That's not being a traitor to your Jewish brothers and sisters. That's just helping the missionaries share the joy that you have received through the gospel of Jesus Christ and giving it to God's covenant people."

Michael replied, "Thanks, John. That is a better way to look at this. I'll let you know what happens."

A few days later, Michael reported back to John that the missionary lesson went off without a hitch. The missionaries received a lot of new information in their understanding of the beliefs of the Jewish people.

Chapter 20
Living Endowment
(Michael)

I picked the Gilbert Arizona Temple as the temple that I would receive my personal living endowment on April 17, 2014. My stake is in the Mesa Arizona Temple District, but I chose to have my endowments done in the Gilbert Arizona Temple, because that is where I had received the Book of Mormon, and the spirit told me that the "book is true."

Before you attend the temple to receive your own endowment, you want to prepare yourself spiritually to make your covenants with God in the temple. The preparations include: taking the temple prep class, being interviewed by your priesthood leaders to receive a temple recommend, making an appointment with the temple, inviting someone to be your escort during the ordinance, and purchasing your temple garments. Family members and friends who are temple worthy are also invited.

I was grateful to be allowed to go to the temple. It is such a sacred place and truly the House of the Lord. I felt another one of those moments where I recognize the similarities between the Jewish and LDS faiths. My Jewish ancestors were commanded to build temples and perform sacred ordinances.

> 8 And let them make me a sanctuary; that I may dwell among them.   Exodus 25:8

> 12 And thou shalt bring Aaron and his sons unto the door of the tabernacle of the congregation, and wash them with water. 13 And thou shalt put upon Aaron the holy garments, and anoint him, and sanctify him; that he may minister unto me in the priest's office.   Exodus 40:12-13

Inscribed on each LDS Temple are the words "Holiness to the Lord." This statement about holiness is about both the temple and its purposes. The temple is the House of the Lord.

I picked Sam Woodruff as my guide through the sacred ordinance. The Sunday before we were going to go through the temple, an announcement was made at sacrament meeting about receiving my personal endowments. I invited everyone in my ward and many other LDS friends that I had in the area.

Sam and I showed up at the temple early so that he could prepare me for the ordinance. A member of the temple presidency welcomed us to the temple and spoke with us briefly to prepare us for what was to come. We went to the ordinance room, sat in the front row, and waited for the ceremony to start. Since we were in the front row, I didn't notice the other people being seated behind us. As it turned out, 30 or 40 friends showed up to share this important event with me.

When we progressed into the Celestial Room, one friend after another came up to shake my hand and congratulate me. The Celestial Room was the same room that I had been in when the temple was under construction and I couldn't believe how brightly lit it was. This time it was finished, and there was a giant chandelier hanging in the middle of the room. I marveled at how beautiful the craftsmanship was in every detail of that room.

After I was through shaking hands, Sam told me to sit down on one of the couches for a minute. He said, "Now that you have seen all of your friends who came to support you, just sit here for a minute and take it all in." I sat there with Sam and his wife, Cherri, and said a silent prayer of thanks to Heavenly Father for allowing me to enter his holy temple and receive my personal endowment.

I was overwhelmed to see how many people had showed up for this important event and expressed such love and friendship for me. I was grateful to Heavenly Father for guiding me to receive this priceless blessing. As I went through the ceremony, I was amazed to see so many similarities relating to the Jewish religion. I came out of that sacred experience feeling empowered with the gift of knowledge of the truth.

> 31 Then said Jesus to those Jews which believed in him, If ye continue in my word, then are ye my disciples indeed;
> 32 And ye shall know the truth, and the truth shall make you free.   John 8:31-32

I now felt free from any doubt about following Christ and in reaching my full potential in this life as a faithful son of God.

Second Fireside

I talked to my bishop and got approved for a second fireside on May 18, 2014, at our ward building. I had learned from the first fireside that I didn't want to ask questions during the talk. Instead I would have a 30-minute question and answer session after the last special musical number. I sent out emails and tried to advertise this one a little bit more than the first one. I asked Evelyn's parents, Amos and Hillary, if Evelyn could sing again, and they said yes. This time they brought Evelyn's brother and sisters, Porter, Kira, Ruth and Blakely. Evelyn sang beautifully as always.

The fireside was to start at 7 p.m. and there were very few people there at 6:50 p.m. At about two minutes till, people started coming in. There ended up being about 100 people attending. I recognized a few people from my ward, but most of the people were new. I was very nervous, but the words started to flow after I got started. I won't go into the full fireside other than to say that I reworked the first fireside and included additional similarities. I concluded with the following:

"In concluding my talk tonight, I would like to relate a story of a great Rabbi. Rabbi Yitzhak Kaduri was one of the most beloved Rabbi's in the world and lived in Jerusalem. In the Jewish worldwide community, he would be of the stature of the First Presidency."

"The following are excerpts from a story that first appeared in the April 2007 issue of Israel Today Magazine;

"A few months before he died, one of the nation's most prominent Rabbis, Yitzhak Kaduri, supposedly wrote the name of the Messiah on a small note which he requested would remain sealed until now. When the note was unsealed, it revealed what many have known for centuries: Yehoshua, or Yeshua (Jesus), is the Messiah."

"With the biblical name of Jesus, the Rabbi and kabbalist described the Messiah using six words and hinting that the initial letters form the name of the Messiah. The secret note said:

'Concerning the letter abbreviation of the Messiah's name, He will lift the people and prove that his word and law are valid. This I have signed in the month of mercy, Yitzhak Kaduri.'"

"Before Kaduri died at the age of 108, he surprised his followers when he told them that he met the Messiah. Kaduri gave a talk in his synagogue on Yom Kippur, the Day of Atonement, teaching how to recognize the Messiah. He also mentioned that the Messiah would appear to Israel after Ariel Sharon's death. (The former prime minister was still in a coma at the time after suffering a massive stroke more than a year previous.) Other Rabbis predicted the same, including Rabbi Haim Cohen, kabbalist Nir Ben Artzi and the wife of Rabbi Haim Kneiveskzy. Kaduri's grandson, Rabbi Yosef Kaduri, said his grandfather spoke many times during his last days about the coming of the Messiah and redemption through the Messiah. His spiritual portrayals of the Messiah—reminiscent of New Testament accounts—were published on the website Kaduri.net:"

"It is hard for many good people in the society to understand the person of the Messiah. The leadership and order of a Messiah of flesh and blood is hard to accept for many in the nation. As leader, the Messiah will not hold any office, but will be among the people and use the media to communicate. His reign will be pure and without personal or political desire. During his dominion, only righteousness and truth will reign."

"Will all believe in the Messiah right away? No, in the beginning some of us will believe in him and some not. It will be easier for non-religious people to follow the Messiah than for Orthodox people."

"The revelation of the Messiah will be fulfilled in two stages: First, he will actively confirm his position as Messiah without knowing himself that he is the Messiah. Then he will reveal himself to some Jews, not necessarily to wise Torah scholars. It can be even simple people. Only then he will reveal himself to the whole nation. The people will wonder and say: 'What, that's the Messiah?' Many have known his name but have not believed that he is the Messiah."

April 2007 Israel Today Magazine

I continued, "I think that it is pretty amazing that a revered Orthodox Rabbi claimed to have spoken with Jesus and confirmed that he was the Messiah. It shows us all how close we all are to each other in religion and thought."

"Thank you for joining us this evening. I say these things in the name of Jesus Christ. Amen."

Then came the special musical number followed by 30 minutes of questions and answers.

As I was collecting my speech and computer, people started lining up to speak to me once I left the stage. The line extended all the way back to the last cushioned pew. I was amazed as I started shaking hands and talking to people in the line. I thought, *"Why were they lining up to talk to me afterwards?"* One by one people moved forward to shake my hand and tell me where they were from. Many had driven 20 or 30 minutes to hear me speak. Two couples moved forward to shake my hand. One couple said, "We are members of the Church. That was a very interesting talk. We brought our Jewish neighbors."

I thought, *"Here we go. They are going to say something like,*

'Why would you leave the Jewish faith?'" I shook hands with them both, carefully watching their faces for an advance sign of their disappointment with my talk. Instead, they said, "We live in a cul-de-sac surrounded by Mormon families. We have always wondered about their religion. Your talk was such a great insight into some similarities between the two religions. We loved it!"

I'm sure that I looked like I was in shock as I blurted out, "Thank you. I'm so glad you enjoyed it." I was relieved that I had reached out to some of my Jewish brothers and sisters who had not been critical of my message. I continued to shake hands and talk to people for a good 45 minutes after the actual fireside and question and answer period ended.

I've read that the Mormon Church is strong on continuing education. You're encouraged to continually be looking for additional light and truth no matter where you can find it. That means that you're encouraged not just to read the scriptures every day, but study them, to attend Sunday school once a week, to have family home evening on Monday nights to teach your children, to discuss gospel principles with your family members, and to continue to learn how to apply the gospel principles in your life.

Mormons should be interested in all religions, because all religions have some part of the truth in them. You should gather the truth from wherever you can find it. A Mormon's main source of direction in this life is a living prophet. The 12 apostles, just as in Jesus' time, receive revelation and teach the truth, but the living prophet is the only one authorized to speak for the entire church.

I went home and thought, *"I'm so exhausted, I think I will go right to bed."* The problem was that I couldn't sleep. Within a few minutes, I started receiving instruction from the Spirit about my fireside.

I don't remember if I was talking out loud or not to answer what I was being told. If anyone else had been in my room, it would have been a weird scene that looked like I was talking to myself. This particular exchange went on for quite some time.

It was like I was being told how to improve it for the next one. I thought, *"Another one. Are you kidding me? I did two of these and that's enough."* I would find out later that Heavenly Father had a different idea in mind.

Chapter 21
The Voice
(Michael and John in Booth One)

As Michael and John sat in Booth One waiting for their burgers and fries to be served, Michael asked about "the voice."

"John, before I heard the voice in my head telling me to move to Mesa, I always thought that it was my intuition. The voice wouldn't stop directing me until I actually started to move. It came back again when I held the Book of Mormon and it declared 'The book is true.' It wasn't an audible voice that I could hear with my ears, so I think even a deaf person could hear it. I know now that it is the Spirit of God talking to me. Have you ever experienced anything like that when you hadn't even asked for it?"

John replied, "Yes I have, and it's always amazing to me how the Spirit of God can speak to anyone like that. The Spirit will only speak in soft tones, never loud, unless you are refusing to listen to it. It will only speak the truth and will never tell you a lie. Sometimes it will tell you things that seem impossible. Let me tell you one example."

"In 1983, Nanci and I and our four kids were living in Orem, Utah. I was serving my 6th year as bishop of the 27th Ward. Nanci's health was not good due to the Utah winters. She was told by her doctor to move south and get out of the cold. I reapplied to the Church Education System to teach seminary once again. I was offered the opportunity to teach seminary at Arcadia High School in Phoenix, Arizona. This move would get us out of the cold, so I accepted it. This would be my last assignment in a blessed 10-year career of teaching for the Church."

"The Church provided two air plane tickets for Nanci and I to fly to Phoenix to look for housing. We left over a weekend without telling anyone we were moving and arrived in Arizona on a Saturday. During the flight the Spirit spoke to me and said, 'You are going to trade your house with someone that wants to move to Utah.'

I turned to Nanci who was quietly reading a book and said, "You're not going to believe this, but we are going to trade our house with someone that wants to move to Utah." She looked at me with a questioning expression and said, 'Really, what are the chances of that, a million to one?' Like you Michael, we often first doubt what we are told. Experience teaches us that when the Spirit speaks we should follow it, as nothing is impossible for God."

"The next day was Sunday and we decided to attend the ward closest to the high school. Armed with the truth I had been given on the plane, I found the bishop and asked him who in the ward had their house up for sale. He told me that there were three members of the ward with homes for sale. When I asked him who they were, he named off the first one and said, 'Forget about this one, because as a seminary teacher you would not be able to afford it. This sister just went through a painful divorce, and she wants to sell the family estate and move to Utah.' I asked the bishop where I could find the owner of that home, and he told me she was teaching the Gospel Doctrine class next hour. Nanci and I attended her class and watched this remarkable sister teach a powerful lesson. After class I introduced us, told her that I was the new seminary teacher and was looking for a house in the Arcadia area."

"She told us that following the finalizing of her divorce she and her daughter had decided to go on a cruise to help her sort things out to decide what to do next. She was praying intently for guidance and while on the cruise one clear night, she was outside enjoying the beauty of the ocean when the Spirit spoke to her. She was told that when she returned home to immediately put her house up for sale by owner. She was also told to not list her home with a realtor. She followed that prompting only a few days before we came to Arizona. When she heard that I hadn't listed my home for sale she said, 'Let's you and I just trade houses.' Can you imagine our shock at how fast the prophesy given to us on the plane was fulfilled?"

"To shorten this amazing story, we worked out the details, and she moved into our home on Sunny Lane in Orem. We then moved into her upscale home in the Arcadia area of Phoenix. We made this exchange of homes and never had to use a Realtor, which amounted to saving thousands of dollars. The bishop was right. I couldn't afford her house on a seminary teacher's salary, but the Spirit knew better and made it happen."

Michael said, "Wow, John, I've sold real estate for 16 years, and I've never heard of anything like that. That deal was made in heaven."

"Exactly Michael. If there's one thing we both have learned out of all of these experiences, it's this: When the spirit speaks to you, believe what he tells you to do and just DO IT!"

Michael asked, "Did you have any other experiences with the Spirit?"

John smiled and said, "Many others over the years, but some are just too sacred to talk about. The Gift of the Holy Ghost is real and one of God's greatest gifts to his children. It will sometimes tell you things but warn you not to talk about it."

Michael asked, "John, do you think that some of the visions and things that have happened to me are too sacred to write about in my book?"

"Michael, that is something only you can decide as you are prompted by the Spirit. Be prayerful, I am sure that the answer will come to you. It seems to me that your experiences can help provide others with an example that it is never too late to change, if you have the faith to follow the Spirit."

"Tell me about it," Michael responded. "Being 56 years old when I was baptized and changing the entire direction of my spiritual life has been huge. I first started writing this book when I was prompted to do so after my first fireside. As I was writing about the different visions and promptings that I have had, the Spirit would fill me with the most wonderful feeling of joy. I had the same question about whether to include the visions and promptings in this book and prayed many days and nights for an answer."

"The Spirit revealed to me that I was to include these visions and promptings to enable me to touch the lives of those who otherwise may not have understood certain truths that lead to eternal salvation. This book had to include most of the experiences that I have written about. However, the Spirit has constrained me to not include all of the things that I have experienced."

John agreed, "I think it is important that you include these sacred experiences in the book for the benefit of others. This will help you to be the example that you are supposed to be. Your stories have already strengthened my faith as I'm sure they will many others."

Chapter 22
Patriarchal Blessing
(Michael)

The patriarch of my stake called me and set an appointment in August for my patriarchal blessing. I was looking forward to my blessing, because I had been told by many members that a blessing given through the patriarch comes directly from God.

During our phone conversation, I asked: "Brother, what is the proper way to address you?" I didn't know whether to call him patriarch or brother.

The patriarch chuckled and replied: "Michael, you are a little bit "older" than the usual person that I give blessings to. Please address me by my first name, Ron."

I thanked him as we ended our phone call.

Every worthy, baptized member of the LDS Church is entitled to a patriarchal blessing. Each person receives one blessing in their lifetime. This blessing provides inspired direction and personal counsel from the Lord.

In biblical times, Jacob was the grandson of Abraham and his name was changed to Israel. Jacob, or Israel, had twelve sons. Their descendants became the Twelve Tribes of Israel. Today, the bloodlines of those twelve tribes are scattered around the earth. A patriarchal blessing includes a declaration of a person's lineage from one of the Twelve Tribes of Israel, as a descendant of Abraham.

Many people that have the blood of Israel in them are not even aware of it. When they join the Church, they have the opportunity to get a patriarchal blessing which will declare to them their dominant bloodline. Many Latter-day Saints are from the tribe of Ephraim, which is the leadership tribe today. Ephraim is given the primary responsibility to lead the latter-day work of gathering and building God's kingdom here on earth.

As a member studies his or her patriarchal blessing and follows the message it contains, it will provide guidance, comfort, and protection. It provides the opportunity to realize an individual's full potential while here on earth.

Ron called me around July 1 and told me that he had a cancellation on Sunday, July 6th. He asked me if I would be available for my blessing on that Sunday. I said yes.

"Usually, I would have you come to my home for the blessing, but we have company that weekend, Ron explained"

I replied, "I feel the need to do this in a spiritually clean place, so since your home is not available, would you meet me at my ward building? I'm sure that I can get permission to have the blessing performed in one of the classrooms."

"That would be fine," Ron answered, "I will see you Sunday night July 6th at 6 p.m.."

I immediately called John to tell him the good news. "John, my patriarchal blessing has been moved up to July 6th."

John asked, "Can I come?"

"I'm not sure," I said, "Is it okay if you come, or is it just between me and the patriarch?"

John replied, "You can have family and close friends attend, if you choose."

I was excited, "It's fine with me. I would appreciate it if you would come."

Since no one in my family was a member of the LDS Church, I really didn't know what to expect. I never had the privilege of witnessing or hearing a patriarchal blessing. Church members considered their blessings to be sacred and would rarely share them with anyone.

Sunday, July 6th at sacrament meeting, I told Bishop Holman that the appointment for my blessing had been moved up. I asked his permission to use one of the classrooms in the ward building. He told me instead to use his office, and he would have the ward clerk open it for me. I thanked him and thought, *"That was really generous of him to let me use his office."*

Sunday evening came, and I went to the ward building at 6 p.m. The patriarch and John met me there. The ward clerk was there to let us into the bishop's office for the blessing.

There were three of us in the bishop's office: Ron, the patriarch, John, and myself. Ron was the patriarch for our stake and stood at least 6 foot 4 inches tall. He said he was in his 70s and that being called as a patriarch was a calling for the rest of your life.

John and I sat down as Ron prepared his recorders. Ron started, "Years ago we used cassette recorders. Since cassette tapes would break once in a while, we would set up three separate cassette recorders so that we could record the blessing. If one of the recorders or tapes broke, we would still have two more to record it."

He then took three digital recorders and three microphones out of his bag and set them on the desk. He said, "I don't think that one of these will break down, but I have gotten in the habit of having three recorders! I will give you your blessing, and then I will transcribe your blessing onto paper later and send it to you in about a week or so."

I asked, "Do you want to know anything about me before we start?"

Ron answered, "I'd rather not. Everything will be revealed in the blessing. Michael, would you please come over and sit in this chair." He had pulled a chair to the center of the room.

I sat down in the chair, bowed my head, and Ron placed his hands on my head and began the blessing. "Brother Michael LeRoy Morton, ... I lay my hands upon your head and bestow upon you your patriarchal blessing."

Since my blessing is sacred, I will not repeat it here. I can tell you that as I was given my blessing, I again felt incredible power surging through me. The intensity was much greater than I felt at both my baptism and my elder ordination. In fact, the intensity was so profound that my hands were shaking as if an electric current was coursing through my body. The blessing lasted a little over 20 minutes. As long as I live, I will never forget the feeling that accompanied that blessing. The patriarchal blessing is the only blessing within the church that is recorded. A copy is sent to Salt Lake City and stored in the Church's granite vaults as a permanent record. If you lose your written copy, it can be restored to you.

As Ron finished, he sealed the blessing upon me in the name of Jesus Christ. Ron took his hands off my head, and I got up out of the chair. Tears were streaming down my face as I contemplated the incredible blessing that I had just received.

I turned to see Ron wiping tears from his eyes. Ron said, "That was a very powerful blessing." I looked at John, who with tears in his eyes, remarked, "That was a beautiful blessing."

I stated, "You couldn't have been talking about me. I have not been a righteous man. Do you just say nice things to people in these blessings?"

Ron chuckled and said, "No, we don't just say nice things. The blessing that you just heard was from your Heavenly Father."

Then he asked if we had a few minutes, so that he could explain a few things. I said, "Yes, please." Little did any of the three of us know, that those few minutes would turn into over two hours of conversation.

Ron explained, "I wanted to explain the declaration of your tribe to you. When I named your tribe during the blessing, I hesitated for a moment. The reason that I hesitated was because it was hard to decipher which tribe was the strongest."

I replied, "You said that I was from the tribe of Judah and that makes complete sense to me. Is that a good thing or a bad thing that you hesitated?"

He chuckled and said, "As a patriarch, when we give a blessing, we can only name the dominant tribe. Sometimes, there is a little bit of a second tribe within people. In your case, there were two tribes of almost equal strength. The tribe of Judah won out by this much."

He held his hand up with his forefinger and his thumb, just barely apart.

Then he continued, "I have never experienced this in any blessing that I have given, nor have I heard of this from any other patriarch. The two tribes that are of almost equal strength are Judah and Ephraim. Do you know what the tribe of Ephraim is?"

I answered, "Ephraim is the tribe of leadership."

Ron replied, "That is right. You have within you two choice bloodlines. You have the ancient wisdom of the tribe of Judah and the leadership of the tribe of Ephraim. You are very special and have a special purpose while you are here in mortality. You have a great journey ahead of you."

I just sat there shaking my head in disbelief. I was not special at all. I had made so many mistakes in my life, to have a wonderful blessing like this, was mind blowing.

As he said his remarks to me, I suddenly remembered how many times I had been prompted to read the following:

15 The word of the LORD came again unto me, saying,
16 Moreover, thou son of man, take thee one stick, and write upon it, for Judah, and for the children of Israel his companions: then take another stick, and write upon it, for Joseph, the stick of Ephraim, and for all the house of Israel his companions:
17 And join them one to another into one stick; and they shall become one in thine hand.
18 And when the children of thy people shall speak unto thee, saying, Wilt thou not shew us what thou meanest by these?
19 Say unto them, Thus saith the Lord GOD; Behold, I will take the stick of Joseph, which is in the hand of Ephraim, and the tribes of Israel his fellows, and will put them with him, even with the stick of Judah, and make them one stick, and they shall be one in mine hand.   Ezekiel 37:15-19

After I would read the scripture, the Spirit would say to me, "This is describing you." Ron's explanation about the two bloodlines of almost equal strength coming together in me, clarified the meaning of what I had been told by the Spirit.

Ron continued, "I feel inclined to tell you a story of a young missionary. The story takes place years ago before cell phones and the Internet. This young missionary did not believe completely that his patriarchal blessing came from Heavenly Father. So when he went to his mission training center, they asked if anyone still needed to have their patriarchal blessing. This young man raised his hand. Even though he had his patriarchal blessing before he left home, he wanted to have another one and see if they were really identical thereby proving that they were from God. They believed this young man and took him at his word. So this young missionary had his second blessing. When he received the transcript of the blessing he compared it with the first one and they were the same exact blessing except for a few words. Those few words had the same meaning as the words in the first blessing." I thought, *"The Jews have a word for what this young man had done and that word is 'chutzpah' (audacity)."*

Ron explained, "I felt compelled to tell you this so that you would know that your patriarchal blessing comes from your Father in Heaven and not from me telling you a lot of nice things."

I stated, "I don't deserve this, you can't be talking about me."

Ron stated, "You will bring great blessings to many people. This blessing IS about you."

Ron then related many things about my life that he could not have known. He told me of many more opportunities that Heavenly Father would offer me and wanted me to accomplish in the time that I had left here on earth. I thought, *"How am I supposed to accomplish all these things?"*

Ron continued, "You should write the book that you're working on. It should be written in a style that is easy to read and in a format that can be read on a tablet or other mobile devices. Your book should have plenty of pictures in it, and will be read by people of all ages."

I sat there with my mouth open, not believing what I was hearing. I thought, *"How could he know that I wanted to write a book about my experiences?"*

Ron admonished, "You should continue with your talks, as there are many that need to hear your message."

I took that remark to mean my firesides, although I knew that he had never attended any of them.

Many more possibilities were revealed that my Father in Heaven wanted me to understand. As it all unfolded, even though I was 58 years old, I realized that I had a lot more work to do. My life suddenly had purpose and possibilities.

I looked at the clock and we had been in the bishop's office from 6 p.m. until 9 p.m.. We had been in the bishop's office for three hours!

We all stood up and Ron walked over to stand directly in front of me. He suddenly grabbed both of my arms, looked down into my eyes with a piercing stare and said, "I see no darkness in you, only light."

Our conversation had come to an end as Ron let go of my arms, walked back to the desk and proceeded to pack up his three recorders and microphones to leave.

We all walked out to the parking lot, and John and I said goodbye to Ron. As he drove off, I turned to John and said, "This has been unbelievable. He couldn't have been talking about me. He was describing a person who would achieve great things. There is no way that I can achieve even half of what he told us tonight."

John turned to me and replied, "You had better stop saying you aren't the right person and figure out how you can start believing that you are the person that Heavenly Father described."

John softened and said, "Michael, I want to thank you for inviting me to be here tonight. That is one of the most unique Patriarchal Blessings that I have ever witnessed."

John and I parted company and I went home. I couldn't sleep, instead I just kept pacing back and forth in my room. I thought, *"How can I achieve the things that were described to me tonight?"* That question has haunted me ever since.

Chapter 23
Beautiful System
(Michael)

The time came for our stake priesthood meeting. Our stake consisted of eight wards, and all of the men of priesthood age met at our stake building. The purpose of a stake priesthood meeting is to teach the priesthood their responsibilities and strengthen their faith.

The stake presidency gave us four bullet points to guide us:

- Pray
- Ponder
- Plan
- Perform

I thought about this for a moment and realized how valuable these four bullet points were. They gave us a plan to follow for almost every question that we had in our daily lives.

There were several messages from the Old and New Testaments that evening from our stake presidency. The message from the Old Testament was, "be strong and of good courage."

5 There shall not any man be able to stand before thee all the days of thy life: as I was with Moses, *so* I will be with thee: I will not fail thee, nor forsake thee.
6 Be strong and of a good courage: for unto this people shalt thou divide for an inheritance the land, which I swear unto their fathers to give them.
7 Only be thou strong and very courageous, that thou mayest observe to do according to all the law, which Moses my servant commanded thee: turn not from it *to* the right hand or *to* the left, that thou mayest prosper whithersoever thou goest.

8 This book of the law shall not depart out of thy mouth; but thou shalt meditate therein day and night, that thou mayest observe to do according to all that is written therein: for then thou shalt make thy way prosperous, and then thou shalt have good success.

9 Have not I commanded thee? Be strong and of good courage; be not afraid, neither be thou dismayed: for the Lord thy God is with thee whithersoever thou goest.   Joshua 1:5-9

It made me think that I needed to trust in Heavenly Father, to not be afraid, but to be strong and of great courage. From the New Testament, Ephesians 6 was quoted to teach us about putting on our armor to keep us safe from the adversary. The adversary, being Satan, is always waiting for us to let our guard down.

10 Finally, my brethren, be strong in the Lord, and in the power of his might.

11 Put on the whole armour of God, that ye may be able to stand against the wiles of the devil.

12 For we wrestle not against flesh and blood, but against principalities, against powers, against the rulers of the darkness of this world, against spiritual wickedness in high places.

13 Wherefore take unto you the whole armour of God that ye may be able to withstand in the evil day, and having done all, to stand.

14 Stand therefore, having your loins girt about with truth, and having on the breastplate of righteousness;

15 And your feet shod with the preparation of the gospel of peace;

16 Above all, taking the shield of faith, wherewith ye shall be able to quench all the fiery darts of the wicked.

17 And take the helmet of salvation, and the sword of the Spirit, which is the word of God:

18 Praying always with all prayer and supplication in the Spirit, and watching thereunto with all perseverance and supplication for all saints;   Ephesians 6:10-18

As I was sitting there thinking about the fiery darts contained in the messages of that evening, I reflected on all of those who had hit me over my lifetime. What came to mind was growing up with Anti-Semitism, the darts of a painful divorce, and everything in between.

The Spirit then asked me a question: "Are we also cleansed of the damage of those who have sinned against us when we are baptized?" This question was confusing and profound at the same time. I know that we are cleansed of our personal sins when we are baptized, but what about the damage done to us by the sins of others? Do their sins against us continually torture us?

The modern terminology might be post traumatic syndrome. Has anyone ever done anything to you that was so terrible that you can't seem to let it go?

We are told in Ephesians 6:10-18, that we can defend ourselves against these fiery darts. If some of them hit us, are these sins from others stuck in a never ending loop in our minds? Can we be healed of this?

The profound part of this for me was that God, through the Spirit, was asking me questions and expecting me to come up with the answers. If I could answer these, it would help heal me from the persecutions of the past and help me move forward with a clear mind. I could then let go of the burdens of the past and become the person that God wanted me to be.

The only way that the damage done to us by the sins of others can be completely healed and removed is through the Gospel of Jesus Christ or in the Savior's words, "The balm of Gilead."

President Monson, in his talk from General Conference, October 1987, titled "A Doorway Called Love" said,

"President Ezra Taft Benson has often stated, 'We live in a wicked world.' The Apostle Paul warned, 'Men shall be lovers of their own selves, covetous, boasters, proud, blasphemers, disobedient to parents, unthankful, unholy. … lovers of pleasures more than lovers of God.'(2 Timothy. 3:2–4). Must we suffer the same fate as those who lived in the cities of the plain? Can we not learn the lesson taught in the time of Noah? 'Is there no balm in Gilead?' (Jeremiah 8:22) Or is there a doorway that leads us from the morass of worldliness onward and upward to the high ground of righteousness? There echoes ever so gently to the honest mind that personal invitation of the Lord: 'Behold, I stand at the door, and knock: if any man hear my voice, and open the door, I will come in to him' (Rev. 3:20). Does that doorway have a name? It surely does. I have chosen to call it 'the doorway of love.'"

"Love is the catalyst that causes change. Love is the balm that brings healing to the soul. But love doesn't grow like weeds or fall like rain. Love has its price. 'God so loved the world, that he gave his only begotten Son, that whosoever believeth in him should not perish, but have everlasting life' (John 3:16). That Son, even the Lord Jesus Christ, gave His life that we might have eternal life, so great was His love for His Father and for us."

I thought, *"The Spirit asked me a question and the question was, 'Are we also cleansed of the damage of those who have sinned against us when we are baptized?'"* The Spirit had given me the answer to that question, and the answer is LOVE. As we learn to love God, to love ourselves, to love our neighbors, the damage is healed.

The stake priesthood meeting ended, and again I was reminded of the beautiful system that the LDS Church has for its members. It is a system that teaches and empowers us to follow the Lord and provides us the opportunity to develop the pure love of Jesus Christ.

Chapter 24
Prayer for Judah
(Michael)

David, a brother from my ward, called me and said that someone he worked with invited him to go to a Rosh Hashanah service at a local Orthodox Jewish Synagogue. He invited me to go with him. David was curious about the Jewish New Year and how Jews celebrate it.

I thought, *"This is the first time in my life, that I have ever been invited to a Jewish service by a Mormon!"* So I knew that this was going to be a once in a lifetime event.

I said yes and David picked me up to go to the synagogue. When we entered the foyer, there was a table with a basket on it, full of yarmulkes. A yarmulke (Yiddish) or kippah (Hebrew) are words for a skullcap. Jewish law requires men to cover their heads as a sign of respect and reverence for God when praying, studying Torah, saying a blessing, or entering a synagogue. This practice has its roots in biblical times, when the High Priests in the temple were instructed to cover their heads. When a Jewish man or boy wears a yarmulke, it signifies a symbol of their awareness of, and submission to, or respect for, a higher entity.

As the service began, I was pleased to hear and speak Hebrew again. I knew all of the Jewish prayers since I was a child and recited them all with ease. This Rosh Hashanah service would go on for two or three hours.

The sanctuary of the synagogue was set up so that the women and girls sat on the left, while the men and boys sat on the right. There was a 5-foot-high partition that ran down the middle of the sanctuary separating the women from the men.

The prayer books are written so that you read from right to left, and from the back of the book to the front. When you open the prayer book, the page on the left is in English, and the page on the right is in Hebrew. The service is mostly in Hebrew, and the chanting of the scriptures goes so fast that a man in the front of the synagogue would call out page numbers as they went along. David was thrilled to see the reading of a 2,000-year-old scroll (Torah). I was impressed that he showed so much reverence for such a different religious practice while we were in the synagogue.

About 30 minutes after the service started, I realized that I was pointing out things in the prayer book to David that related to LDS principles. I knew what the Hebrew prayers meant, but I was relating to them from an LDS point of view. This was a little shocking to me.

I suddenly realized that my whole paradigm had changed!

After about an hour, I realized that I didn't feel the Spirit of the Lord as I had felt it when I was a child. As a child, I could feel a connection with Heavenly Father every time I was in a synagogue.

Rabbi Reading from the Holy Torah
Photo Courtesy of Wikipedia

Another hour went by. Then, as the Rabbi read from the Torah, the ancient scroll containing the Five Books of Moses, I realized that they were reading the same Torah portion that they had always read at this time of year during this holiday. I then had a feeling that I never had before. I felt that the Jews were just marking time, as they had for thousands of years. They were repeating the same cycle over and over again and waiting for Heavenly Father to redeem them as promised in the scriptures.

I was trying to comprehend this new paradigm shift, when the time came in the service for the children to gather in front of the Rabbi for the blowing of the Shofar (ram's horn). The blowing of the Shofar would signal the final harvest of the year and the beginning of the New Year. As the Rabbi sounded the shofar, I finally felt the Spirit of the Lord.

The Spirit then spoke to me saying:

"As God's trumpet is sounded, Ephraim will help raise up God's Covenant People and they shall be redeemed."

Tears came to my eyes as the Spirit told me this. The Shofar has been called God's trumpet throughout history. I knew what God's trumpet was since I was a little boy and had heard the Shofar blown many times. Now it was about to be sounded right in front of us. This brought to mind a scripture that I had recently read:

30 And then shall appear the Son of man in heaven: and then shall all the tribes of the earth mourn, and they shall see the Son of man coming in the clouds of heaven with power and great glory.

31 And he shall send his angels with the great sound of the trumpet and they shall gather together his elect from the four winds, from one end of heaven to the other.

Matthew 24:30-31

The Shofar, God's Trumpet

When the Rabbi sounded the Shofar, the Spirit spoke to me again, saying: "Pray for your Jewish brothers and sisters."

From my patriarchal blessing, I knew that I had the bloodline of both the tribes of Judah and Ephraim in me in almost equal strength, and I suddenly felt an overwhelming obligation to do what I was just commanded to do. So I bowed my head in the middle of the synagogue on this holiest of Jewish holidays and prayed to Heavenly Father.

"Heavenly Father, I am so grateful for the enlightenment that you have shown me and for the journey that I am on. I know that you had David ask me to come here today, so that I could understand the faith of my childhood through different eyes. I also know that you are a kind and benevolent God. Please redeem my people, your Covenant People, for keeping the Jewish faith alive, through so many trials of persecution, over thousands of years. Please bless them and forgive those who do not believe that your Son, Jesus, was and is the Messiah of the world. Heavenly Father, please enlighten my Jewish brothers and sisters with the same gift of enlightenment that you have given me. Let them feel your light and love as they come to know who the Messiah truly is."

I then ended my prayer with "I humbly pray for these things in the name of Jesus Christ. Amen."

I quickly wiped away the tears on my face and looked around to make sure that I hadn't said that prayer out loud, especially the last part, "In the name of Jesus Christ." I didn't want David to be a witness to me being removed from a synagogue on such a Holy Day. I looked to either side of me and luckily no one but Heavenly Father had heard me, as I had said my prayer in silence.

I have heard people say many times over the years, "The Jews missed it, They missed the fact that Jesus was the Messiah." In my mind, that simply isn't accurate. The Jewish people of that time were known as Hebrews and lived under Roman rule. Some of the Roman emperors considered themselves to be gods and demanded to be worshiped. The Hebrew leaders, the Pharisees, Sadducees, and the scribes did not recognize Jesus as the Messiah out of fear of what would happen to them by the Romans if they did.

When Jesus or Yeshua (his real Hebrew name) spoke and performed miracles, the Hebrew people flocked to him. I believe they knew that Jesus was very special, and many knew that he was the Messiah. A very important question that often comes up during my firesides is, "Old Testament prophets like Isaiah wrote clearly about the coming of the Messiah. They wrote about how and where he would be born, what he would be like, and how he would be treated. So why didn't the Hebrews recognize him when he came?"

My answer to that is, at that time in history, the Hebrews did not have access to the scriptures as we do today. They only had access to the scriptures through their leaders and their leaders' interpretation. The Hebrew leaders were under tremendous pressure from the Roman Empire. It seemed to me that to be able to preserve the Kingdom of Judah, the iniquities of the Jewish leaders caused them to reject and remove the thought of Jesus being the King of the Jews to avoid the repercussions of Rome.

Every decision had to be thought through by Chiapas, the High Priest, so as not to appear that the leaders, or anyone that they endorsed were greater than the Roman dictators. Acknowledging that Jesus was the Son of God and the "King of the Jews", would have angered the Romans and could have led to the Jewish people's extinction.

The modern day descendants of those early Hebrews, who believed in Jesus, will one day come to know that Jesus is their Messiah, as well. Some will recognize it now, because they will feel it in their hearts. The others will recognize it when Jesus returns and fulfills his promise to gather Israel in the latter days.

9 That was the true Light, which lighteth every man that cometh into the world.
10 He was in the world, and the world was made by him, and the world knew him not.
11 He came unto his own, and his own received him not.
12 But as many as received him, to them gave he power to become the sons of God, even to them that believe on his name.
John 1:9-12

When I got home that evening, I was inspired to do a search on the internet for "Mormons and Jews." I'm not sure what I expected to find, but the search revealed a link to the following article from the LDS Ensign magazine. The article was from the Ensign dated December 1976 and was titled "A Message to Judah from Joseph."

President Ezra Taft Benson said the following, in his address to Mormons, Non-Mormons and Jews at the Jubilee Auditorium in Calgary Alberta, Canada, on May 2, 1976:

"Yes, there is a great affinity for the Jews by the Mormons. The Jews have endured great persecution and suffering. This we understand, for our people have also undergone severe persecution and extermination."
"Indeed, the man we revere as a modern prophet, Joseph Smith, was martyred for his testimony in 1844. In 1846, our people had

to exodus from the United States because of the threat of annihilation. We settled in a desert region similar to the topography around the Dead Sea and the Sea of Galilee. There we have developed our 'land of promise.'"

"Yes, we can empathize with the suffering of the Jews, for we have co-suffered with them. But our affinity toward modern Judah is not prompted merely out of mutual suffering; it is prompted out of a knowledge of our peculiar relationships together—relationships which claim a common heritage."

"Jeremiah has prophesied that in the latter times "the house of Judah shall walk with the house of Israel, and they shall come together."   (Jeremiah 3:18.)

"My prayer is that because of evenings spent together like this one, this prophecy will come to be fulfilled. We need to know more about the Jews, and the Jews ought to know more about the Mormons."

"When we understand one another, then perhaps you will understand why Ben-Gurion said, 'There are no people in the world who understand the Jews like the Mormons.;"

I was so grateful that David had invited me to go with him that day. The feelings that I received in the synagogue were so profound, that it reinforced the truths that had been revealed to me during my conversion process. I realized that the strength of my Jewish roots had empowered me to receive and appreciate these additional truths.

I wondered if I would ever be able to enlighten others as I had been enlightened. I had hope that I would.

Chapter 25
Third Fireside
(Michael)

I was asked by the Phoenix East Stake to give a fireside for their stake. This would be my third fireside. They had read about my conversion in an article in a local LDS newspaper. I asked Hillary and Amos if it would be possible for Evelyn to sing again. I also asked two sisters in my ward, Joy and Linda, to play a special musical number for the closing of the fireside. Joy had played viola for the Salt Lake Symphony for ten years, and Linda played the organ for sacrament meeting and the piano to accompany the choir.

The night of the fireside, August 24, 2014, I arrived at the Phoenix East Stake building early. One of the brothers in my ward, Kade, also came and supplied the audio/video support. I was nervous as usual, but I was confident that I could pull it off.

Evelyn sang beautifully for the opening special musical number and it was time for me to start. As I crafted this speech and power point, I used elements of the two previous firesides and let the Spirit guide me for the rest.

I put a large Star of David on the screen and began with the joke about all the major religious food groups. That drew a big laugh just like in the other firesides.

"My mother converted to Judaism when I was born, and I was brought up in the Jewish faith. My father was pretty strict about us never speaking about Jesus or reading the New Testament. I always had questions about religion that were not being answered, until I discovered the LDS faith last year."

"I was baptized on my birthday in April 2013. So, imagine this, here I am a new convert, I have barely finished reading the book of Mormon and one week after my baptism, I'm giving a combined priesthood lesson on the similarities between Judaism and the LDS faith."

"For those of you that don't know, a combined priesthood lesson is a talk given in front of all the men in the congregation. I wasn't sure if they liked the talk that Sunday until several brothers came up to me afterwards and suggested that I give a fireside. So before I knew it, I was volunteering to give a fireside on the similarities between the two religions."

"The problem was, I had never been to a fireside, nor did I know what a fireside was. I just said okay and volunteered on the spot. This fireside tonight will be my third in the last year and a half."

"Just so you know, I am not a Jewish scholar or an LDS scholar. I cannot quote Bible verses, although I admire those who can. The similarities that I will present tonight are based upon my own personal experiences and revelations. Some of these experiences and promptings seem to come at 3 or 4 a.m., sometimes several nights in a row. I wake up with a start, like a trumpet is sounded in the room and before I know it, I am turning to a specific scripture and the similarities just seemed to appear."

"Let's take a look at a couple of the similarities."

I then told them what a mezuzah is and the tiny scroll with the Shema written on it. I then told them about the shofar (God's trumpet), the feast of the trumpets and how Moroni had visited Joseph Smith on September 22, 1827. On that night Joseph received the golden plates as Jews around the world were celebrating the first night of Rosh Hashanah or the beginning of the final harvest.

The organizers of this fireside had asked me to shorten my talk by about 15 minutes, and I discovered that was too short. People came up afterward disappointed because they wanted to hear more similarities between the two religions. I decided that I still had a lot of work to do to expand my presentation for my next fireside in October.

Crossing The Threshold

The evening of October 19, 2014, my fourth fireside came. It was held in my ward building, and Bishop Holman presided.

Everyone performing the musical numbers that evening had performed with me several times. Evelyn and Hillary did the first number and Sister Joy and Sister Linda did the final musical number. As I listened, I thought about how beautiful the music sounded and how much it added to each of my talks.

As I was about halfway into my talk, I had a brief vision. The vision showed me walking through a doorway and crossing a threshold. The Spirit spoke to me and said, "Well done."

After my talk and a question and answer session, people still lined up for 40 minutes to talk to me. People had come from across the valley to hear my fireside. After I got home, I kept thinking about the vision that I had during my talk. It was a little distracting that it came during my talk, but I thought that it was profound. I felt like I had accomplished something that the Lord was pleased with. I thought, *"Did crossing the threshold mean that this was the last fireside that I would be doing?"*

I believed that I had progressed from the first fireside and was a better speaker. This had been confirmed by different members. Hillary and Amos, who had brought Evelyn to sing at each one of my firesides, said that I looked more comfortable at this one, as if I had been giving talks for years. I could see that my friends were right; I did feel more comfortable giving a fireside. Even though I dreaded public speaking, I thought, *"How is this possible?"*

I believe that Heavenly Father has helped me to progress through giving these talks. It was like the old saying, "life is not about the end game, it is about the journey." Heavenly Father is there for us whenever we need him during our journey here on earth.

This help in life comes through the Holy Spirit and is given to us by God. It will guide us as we face difficult decisions, comfort us when we are sad, influence our minds and feelings, and help us recognize when something is true. God loves each one of us and wants to help us through all the difficulties in life. That is why when we accomplish something that is right, we feel good about it.

Now I felt that I had continually improved in giving these firesides, and Heavenly Father was telling me that I had done a good job. I believe that I was being told, "As one door closes, another would be opened." So far in my journey into the LDS Church, it had been a series of doors opening, allowing me to grow, progress, and improve each time I crossed a new threshold. As I would soon find out, I was mistaken in thinking that crossing the threshold meant that I would never give another fireside.

Let Your Light Shine

As John and Michael met in Booth One for lunch, Michael asked, "John can you believe that two articles have been written about me."

John said, "I think I have heard about one of them. Refresh my memory."

Michael said, "There were two articles that were written about me after I moved to Mesa. One was in a local newspaper. The editor, Cecily, interviewed me one day over lunch. We ended up spending a couple hours together as I told her the story of how I came to move to Mesa and be baptized into the Church of Jesus Christ of Latter-day Saints. She was a member of the Church also and asked me many questions. To tell you the truth, I was a little bit apprehensive to think that my story would be published in a local newspaper. I wished to live a quiet life, a life with meaning, and I didn't think that notoriety went along with my wish. As you have seen throughout my journey, my plan was not exactly Heavenly Father's plan."

"That night, I was awoken by the Spirit to read a passage:

14 Ye are the light of the world. A city that is set on a hill cannot be hid.
15 Neither do men light a candle, and put it under a bushel, but on a candlestick; and it giveth light unto all that are in the house.

16 Let your light so shine before men, that they may see your good works, and glorify your Father which is in heaven."

Matthew 5:14-16

"Then after my fourth fireside, I received a call from your wife, Nanci. She said that she had received a call from a reporter asking if she knew anyone who had a spiritual experience in or around an LDS Temple. Nanci said she had referred the reporter to me, since I had an experience inside the construction trailer during the Gilbert Arizona Temple construction. The reporter called me a couple of days later. Her website published articles about church members from around the world."

"The interview went on for a couple of hours. The reporter told me that she had to submit the interview to her editor, and she would notify me if and when it would be published. When she sent me the finished article, it was beautifully written and did get published during the same time as the Phoenix Temple dedication. John, do you think that these two articles help in fulfilling that scripture?"

John replied, "Absolutely Michael, those articles let your light shine, and I'm sure that you will have many more opportunities in the future. I think that the firesides are doing so much good in bringing to light the similarities between the two religions. It is so rare for people to have a Jewish point of view about the Gospel."

Chapter 26
That Is Impossible
(Michael and John in Booth One)

John and I sat in Booth One, discussing another important subject as we enjoyed our hamburgers.

"John, what do you think about the Muslims?"

John answered, "I think that 90% of them are good people. The radical Muslims have hijacked their religion and are giving them a bad name."

"Recently, Nanci and I went on a cruise with her sister, Becky, and husband, Tom. Part of the trip included Ephesus, Turkey. While there, we had a private tour with a driver and a licensed tour guide. The tour guide was a young lady that was very knowledgeable. I was especially impressed with her grasp of Christian history. In detail, she explained Paul's missionary efforts in Ephesus. She appreciated what a dedicated missionary he was, to risk his life for his belief. She explained why he was almost killed in Ephesus and finally run out of town. I really came to like and respect this young woman in the short time that she spent with us."

"The remarkable part was that this girl was not Christian, she was Muslim. She was very respectful of the beliefs that were opposite from her own. I thought to myself, '*She knows much more about my Christian beliefs, than I do about her Muslim beliefs.*' I decided to ask her a question that would require stepping away from the group for a private one-on-one conversation."

"Once alone, I asked her, 'What does your religion teach concerning Jesus Christ?'"

"She smiled and answered, 'The Koran mentions Mary, Jesus' mother, ten times. No other woman is even mentioned in the Koran.'"

"I was surprised by that fact. She followed up with, 'We don't believe that Jesus was literally the son of God.'"

"I asked, 'Why not?'"

"She said, 'We don't believe that God has a tangible body and therefore can't father Jesus through Mary.'"

"I said, 'Okay, the scripture indicates that the Spirit of God moved upon Mary and she became pregnant. I think it happened in a way we don't understand and we shouldn't make any conclusions without full knowledge.'"

"She made no response to that comment, so I continued. 'What I really want to know is, what Islam teaches about who Jesus was.'"

"She smiled again and answered, 'We believe that he was a great prophet, but not the Son of God.'"

"I smiled back and said, 'That is impossible.'"

"With a mild look of surprise, she asked, 'Impossible, why is that?'"

"I answered, 'It is impossible, because Jesus is either what He said He was, the only begotten son of God in the flesh, or He is a liar. He is either the Messiah, the Savior of the world, or He is a total fraud. He cannot be a great prophet and be a liar or a fraud at the same time.'"

"The conversation went on pause for several moments as she was processing what I had just said. Her facial expression changed to a 'deer in the headlight look', and then to a look revealing that a light had just gone on in her head."

"She said, 'Wow, I have never thought of it that way before.'"

"Our conversation ended there, and we rejoined the group. I had the distinct feeling that a crack had just been created in her religious thought, and this bright Muslim soul had recognized it."

"Truth is a very powerful weapon, when used with respect and love. I wondered what she would do now, with the truth that she had just been given. Time will tell, but I hope that she would take that little seed of truth and let it grow. As our tour ended, I remembered my personal motto, 'Always move forward with love.' I hoped that she would move forward as well."

Michael asked, "John, do you think more Muslims will ever understand this truth?"

"They will, when Jesus returns and teaches it to them", answered John. "The Muslims believe that they are descendants from Abraham. What did Abraham really want? The scriptures answer that question for us in the Pearl of Great Price."

1 In the land of the Chaldeans, at the residence of my fathers, I, Abraham, saw that it was needful for me to obtain another place of residence;

2 And, finding there was greater happiness and peace and rest for me, I sought for the blessings of the fathers, and the right whereunto I should be ordained to administer the same; having been myself a follower of righteousness, desiring also to be one who possessed great knowledge, and to be a greater follower of righteousness, and to possess a greater knowledge, and to be a father of many nations, a prince of peace, and desiring to receive instructions, and to keep the commandments of God, I became a rightful heir, a High Priest, holding the right belonging to the fathers.

3 It was conferred upon me from the fathers; it came down from the fathers, from the beginning of time, yea, even from the beginning, or before the foundation of the earth, down to the present time, even the right of the firstborn, or the first man, who is Adam, or first father, through the fathers unto me.

Abraham 1:1-3

John continued, "Abraham set a great example for all of his descendants, Jews, Christians and Muslims. He desired to know the truth and to follow all the commandments from God. If all of us would share Abraham's desires, maybe we would all be more united in our thinking and in our appreciation of each other."

The Same God

John asked, "Michael, in your firesides you have pointed out significant similarities between Judaism and Mormonism. Why do you think there are so many? Before you answer, let me give you yet another example."

"My daughter Tricia's father-in-law, Lloyd, is an ordinance worker in the Boston Temple. Recently another Orthodox Jewish convert came for the first time. Like you, he is an older adult and had been a practicing Jew his entire life. Upon entering the temple he said to Lloyd, 'Can you please take me to see the baptismal font?' As Lloyd was escorting this new member to the font he remarked, 'The font better be resting on the backs of 12 oxen, with 3 facing north, 3 facing south, 3 facing west and 3 east.' Upon arriving at the font he looked down to view the 12 oxen and smiling his approval said to Lloyd, 'Now let's see what else you've got right in this Temple.'"

"As the tour continued, this newly converted Jew explained that with Moses' portable tabernacle as well as Solomon's magnificent temple in Jerusalem, there was a laver or a Brazen Sea resting on the backs of twelve oxen. These oxen represented the twelve tribes of Israel and the Sea contained the water used to cleanse oneself before entering the temple. Today, baptism is the ordinance of cleansing in preparation of entering the Kingdom of God as a new member of the Church."

"Michael, each oxen represents one of the Twelve Tribes of Israel: Reuben, Simeon, Judah, Issachar, Zebulun, Benjamin, Dan, Naphtali, Gad, Asher, Ephraim and Manasseh."

Michael replied, "The first time that I saw the baptismal font in the temple, I knew exactly what the oxen represented. I first taught this at the combined priesthood lesson that I gave after my baptism."

LDS Temple Baptistery Ogden Utah
Courtesy of The Trumpet Stone

"When I first went to the temple to do baptisms for the dead, I also realized that there were three witnesses for each baptism. At 18, I immersed myself in a mikveh as part of the ceremony of converting from a Reform Jew to an Orthodox Jew. My mother had been allowed to convert 'up the scale' from a Reform Jew to an Orthodox Jew. At that time the thought was that you are the same religion as your mother. So, I was allowed to convert 'up the scale' also."

"At the ceremony, you immerse yourself. No one is in the font with you. Jewish law states that 'not a hair on the top of the head may be above the water' to be fully immersed. Also by Jewish law, the water must be 'living water.' Only being immersed in living water can the subject be cleansed because living water is, by nature, continually cleansing itself, thereby cleansing the subject. There must be 3 holy men as witnesses. At mine there were two Rabbis and a Cantor witnessing the event."

Then John repeated his question, "Michael, why do you think there are so many similarities between Mormonism and Judaism?"

Michael responded, "First of all, Jesus was a Jew. His real name is Yeshua which is Joshua in English. Joshua is a Hebrew name meaning Jehovah is salvation. Jesus with his Jewish twelve apostles organized the church. When the apostles were killed, the church was destroyed."

"Joseph Smith restored that original church which was organized by Jesus which had been lost for 2,000 years, John added."

Without hesitation Michael answered, "I can't believe I'm going to say this, but the two religions must be getting their inspiration from the same God."

"THAT'S IT," John exclaimed. "One of the biggest shocks to me as I was investigating Mormonism was when the missionaries explained that Jehovah, the God of the Old Testament, was none other than Jesus Christ, the God of the New Testament."

"Think of it, the God of Abraham, Isaac and Jacob was really the pre-mortal Messiah. It was Jesus that gave Moses the 10 commandments on Mt. Sinai and the entire Law of Moses. Then when He came to earth, He didn't come to destroy the Law of Moses but to fulfill those laws with the Gospel of Jesus Christ. An example of this transformation is found in the Old Testament "an eye for an eye and a tooth for a tooth" being replaced with "Love thy enemy, and bless those who despitefully use you and turn the other cheek." Where the Law of Moses was a "school master" law of cold justice, the Gospel of Jesus Christ added love, mercy and the ability to repent and be forgiven. To think that both of these sets of laws came from the same God makes it all even better."

Michael said, "That is an interesting thought, John. Although the only way that I can believe that concept as a Jew is to look back at the meaning of His name. Yeshua means Jehovah is salvation."

3 And I appeared unto Abraham, unto Isaac, and unto Jacob by the name of God Almighty, but by my name JEHOVAH was I not known to them.   Exodus 6:3

2 Behold, God is my salvation; I will trust, and not be afraid: for the Lord JEHOVAH is my strength and my song; he also is become my salvation.   Isaiah12:2

Michael concluded, "If you look at all that we've discussed, then it seems possible that Jesus was the God of the Old Testament. This concept is a huge discovery for any Jew to comprehend."

Chapter 27
Brothers From The Same Family
(Michael and John in Booth One)

John called Michael and said, "Michael you have shown me some amazing similarities between Judaism and Mormonism. Thank you for those insights. Let's do more research, put our heads together and come up with some more contrasts and similarities. Let's meet at Booth One in a couple of days and see what we have come up with."

Michael said, "That sounds like a good idea."

John and Michael met at Booth One a few days later and exchanged what they had found.

HOUSE OF ISRAEL:

Judaism claims to be the modern descendants primarily of the ancient Tribe of Judah, one of the twelve tribes of Israel either by blood or adoption.

Mormons consider themselves to the descendants of the House of Israel primarily from the Tribe of Ephraim and Manasseh either by blood or adoption.

The LDS Church includes among its traditional symbols the Star of David, which has been the symbol of Judaism since the 13th century. For the LDS Church, it represents the divine Israelite covenant, Israelite re-gathering, and affinity with Judaism.

NATURE OF GOD:

Judaism believes in one God who is the cause of all existence. Yahweh (YHWH) is the creator of the world and the only power controlling history. God is eternal. He is single, whole and a complete indivisible entity.

Mormons maintain that God the Father (Heavenly Father), Jesus Christ (His Son), and the Holy Ghost are three separate beings yet one in purpose. Humans are literal children of a Father in

Heaven, and through the atonement of Jesus Christ they can return to Him and become like Him.

PROPHECY:

Judaism holds that the words of the prophets are true. Moses was the greatest of the prophets. Prophecy ceased after the death of Malachi and will be restored with the Messianic Age. The Messiah will come and the dead will be resurrected.

Mormons believe that, in addition to the various prophecies from the Old and New Testament, divine prophecy has been restored beginning with Joseph Smith. At the dedication of the Kirtland Temple (first Temple in modern times), Jesus, Moses, Elijah, and Elias appeared to Joseph Smith and Oliver Cowdery. At this time, Joseph and Oliver received the authority to gather Israel, to lead the ten tribes from the north, to administer the Abrahamic dispensation, and to use the keys with the sealing powers.

TEMPLES:

Judaism teaches that Solomon's Temple held the Ark of the Covenant which contained the Ten Commandments in a room of the Temple referred to as the Holy of Holies. The presiding high priest would enter into this room said to contain the presence of God once a year on Yom Kippur. The Temple was used to perform the sacred ordinances of God. The clothing used in ancient Temple worship is similar to the clothing used today in modern LDS Temples.

Mormons maintain that the LDS Church's Salt Lake Temple contains a Holy of Holies wherein the church's president, acting as the Presiding High Priest, enters what is the modern inner sanctuary similar to the one in the Tabernacle and Temple in Jerusalem. The Temples today are also used to perform the sacred ordinances revealed by God for this time in earth's history.

Latter-day Saints believe that the Jews will one day rebuild a temple in Jerusalem, and that the Jews will restore the practice of the

Law of Moses within that temple. Jews also believe that this will happen.

"Michael, this is really amazing," John interjected. "A few years ago, Nanci and I were in Egypt, and we visited the Karnack Temple in Luxor. That ancient temple is one of the largest religious site ever built on earth. It was built thousands of years ago. The Egyptian guide took us into a small stone chamber and told us that this was the Holy of Holies, or the most sacred part of the temple complex."

"We were stunned to see that carved on the sandstone walls of that once sacred room were depictions of some of the signs of the priesthood and ordinances current to the LDS Temples today. As we were taking dozens of pictures of the walls the guide asked, 'Why is it that when I bring Mormons into this room they won't leave without taking so many pictures?' I couldn't answer his question with a lengthy explanation, so instead I smiled and thanked him as I thought how wonderful it is that these beautiful priesthood ordinances are restored in purity today."

PRIESTHOOD:

Judaism maintains that literal descendant of Aaron (Moses' brother) are priests. Other literal male descendants of the Hebrew tribe of Levi form a different order of priesthood. Judaism recognizes no other forms of priesthood.

Mormonism divides the priesthood into two main divisions. The Aaronic, modeled after the priesthood of Aaron the Levite who was the first high priest of the Hebrews, his descendants and Melchizedek priesthood modeled after the authority of the prophet Melchizedek. The Aaronic Priesthood is not a different priesthood; rather, it is the lesser portion of the priesthood dealing with the introductory ordinances and the preparatory commandments like the Law of Moses. The Melchizedek priesthood deals with the higher ordinances such as sealing marriages and families together for eternity.

SCRIPTURES:

Judaism's most holy book is the Torah (First five books of Bible by Moses). Virtually all Jewish congregations own at least one Torah, of which a portion is read every week. Scrolls of the Torah are copied by hand (written on parchment) by specially trained scribes. The Talmud, a collection of doctrines and laws written by ancient Jewish Rabbis, is the basic book of Jewish law.

Mormonism has four books of scripture: The Book of Mormon; The Old and New Testament of the Bible; the Doctrine of Covenants (modern revelation); and The Pearl of Great Price. These comprise the Standard Works of the Church.

John remarked, "I'm so glad the Jews have reverence for the five books of Moses. However, if God loves us still and has the power to reveal more truth to match our modern challenges, it makes sense to me that there would be more scripture given. The Torah was a great beginning of scripture, but I'm so grateful to have the standard works to help me now."

"I know," agreed Michael. There is a lot of important scripture that I wasn't aware of until now. I just learned that there's actually more written about Jesus Christ in the Book of Mormon than in the New Testament."

AFTERLIFE:

Jewish beliefs with regard to an afterlife are highly variable. Physical resurrection of the dead when the Messiah returns is a traditional belief, however, other Jewish sages promote the idea of a purely spiritual resurrection and still others the possibility of reincarnation. Jewish faiths generally agree that reward in the afterlife or world to come, whatever its form, is not exclusive to Jews, and that punishment in the afterlife is not eternal but corrective.

Mormonism teaches of a physical resurrection at the time of the second coming of Christ and continuing through the millennium.

Between the time of an individual's death and the second coming of Christ, the individual inhabits an intermediary afterlife in the Spirit World. The nature of this afterlife depends on the individual. Deceased persons who lived good lives and repented during their life of any major sins are to inhabit Paradise. Spirit Prison is the place in which the spirits of the rebellious and ungodly reside.

After the final judgment, Heaven is divided into three separate kingdoms, Celestial, Terrestrial and Telestial. All three kingdoms of glory are places suitable to the individuals that reside in them based on the desires of their hearts. Baptism is required to enter the Celestial Kingdom.

CONVERSION and PROSELYTIZING:

Jews refrain from active proselytizing and some denominations discourage conversion. In Judaism, conversion is not a requirement or prerequisite to goodness or salvation. Conversion to Orthodox Judaism involves extensive instruction in Jewish law, renouncing of other religious affiliations, immersion in a mikveh, and for males, circumcision. Jews also believe in the law of tithing.

Mormons have a widespread proselytizing program, and with it missionaries are encouraged to invite others to convert and be baptized. Baptism includes not only membership in the church, but also the blessings of the covenants and promises given to the House of Israel by God. In order to be baptized, individuals must agree to repent of their sins; abide by the Word of Wisdom (no coffee, tea, alcohol or harmful drugs); live the law of chastity (no sex outside the bonds of marriage); agree to pay tithes (10% of income); and attend church meetings.

MARRIAGE:

Polygamy in Judaism: The Bible recounts cases of polygamy among the ancient Hebrews. Abraham, Isaac, Jacob (Israel) all had multiple wives to raise a righteous family that would follow Gods commandments. One other source of polygamy was the practice of levirate marriage, wherein a man was required to marry and support his brother's widow. Judaism has not practiced polygamy since a ban was placed on it in the 11th century. When the State of Israel was created in 1948, that ban was enforced and no polygamous marriages are permitted in Israel today.

Polygamy in Mormonism: Early in its history, the LDS Church practiced polygamy referred to as "plural marriage." It was practiced for the same reason that it was anciently, to raise a righteous group of people to establish God's true religion on the earth. Once it had accomplished its purpose, it was stopped in 1890. God commanded it to start and to end.

Today both Judaism and Mormonism allow only marriage between one man and one woman.

John said, "I was teaching Gospel Doctrine last year and I asked the class of over 100 adults how many had come from polygamous roots. At least 75% raised their hands. Even I, a true convert, come from a plural marriage family. Polygamy wasn't easy to live, but it sure served its purpose.

"John, you were like the lost sheep that was brought back to the fold."

"Yes, and my extended family probably think that I'm still lost," concluded John. "Although that's going to change once they learn the truth."

Chapter 28
Two Fathers
(Michael and John in Booth One)

John and Michael met in Booth One for lunch. John had just finished working on recording a song that he had written called, "Two Fathers." Michael was curious about how he came up with the song in the first place and asked him about it.

"John, where did you get the idea for 'Two Fathers?'"

John replied, "Let me explain how it came about. Last October, my friend Gary brought his guitar to our office and played a couple of songs that he had written. I was impressed with what he had done and as I was driving home from work that day, I wondered if I could write a song. As I considered what my song could be about, I started thinking about what my mother first taught me as a little boy."

"As her words came back to me, my eyes filled with tears. When I got home, I got a piece of paper and bent over the kitchen counter to write out my mom's first advice to me. I included what she had taught me so early that completely changed my life. I printed my song in the form of a poem. Included next to my poem was a picture of my mom and dad. I framed it and gave it to all of my children as a Christmas present."

"Then three weeks after Christmas, a remarkable thing happened. Billy Dean, a country music star, came to stay with Nanci and me. He is an award-winning singer and songwriter. Billy was here to perform several concerts in Mesa, and we had requested the privilege of hosting him while he was here."

"One day while he was here, I felt impressed to leave a copy of my poem on his pillow."

"A couple of days later, Billy asked, 'What is this John?'"

"I said, 'This is a poem that I have written, and I wondered if there is a song in it.'"

"Billy said, 'As I'm reading it, it sounds like the lyrics of a song. Let's go to the piano and see what we can do with it.'"

"He sat down at Nanci's grandmother's old piano, and the magic started to happen. He put on his glasses and bent over to study the words I had written. He read the words over and over to start to feel the rhythm. Then he began to play the piano to create the melody. As the melody took shape, he turned back to the lyrics."

"Billy said, 'I think this chorus line needs more information. What if we change this verse just a little?'"

"He looked at what I had written and made several improvements. As I sat there watching this process unfold, I thought to myself, *'This is not just a country music legend doing this, this is an inspired and gifted songwriter at work on my little poem. He is transforming it into a family musical treasure as we sit here together.'"*

Billy Dean and Marvin Goldstein Recording 'Two Fathers'
(Download this recording by going to www.GatheringIsrael.com)
Photo Courtesy of John and Nanci Wudel

"To my total amazement, in one hour, the musical version of 'Two Fathers' was born. This song is not just about my mom teaching me to pray as a young boy. It's about all mothers and the power of their teaching and example to their children. It's also about the importance of engaged and loving fathers in the lives of their children."

"Nanci and I decided to include most of our grandchildren and to have 'Two Fathers' recorded in a first class recording studio. We hired a professional photographer and videoed the session. Even Marvin Goldstein, a wonderful concert pianist, showed up at just the right moment to add his incredible musical talent to the recording."

John continued, "In one of his hit songs, 'The Seed', Billy reminds us that little things, like seeds, can do amazing things. I believe that 'Two Fathers' is one of those little seeds."

"An example of one of those amazing things occurred three days after Billy had gone to the studio and recorded the soundtrack. I had lunch in Booth One, as I usually do."

"Anna, a regular face behind the counter, was at the register to take my order. She said, 'How is your day going, John?'"

"I replied, 'If it was any better, I couldn't stand it, how about yours?'"

"Her answer surprised me. She said, 'Not so good actually.'"

"I asked, 'Why is that?'"

"She said, 'I'm really stressed, because I don't know what to do. I want to continue my education and get a Master's degree in social counseling. If I do that, I must cut back on work. That would mean less money and I'm barely surviving as it is. John, what did you do when you were my age?'"

"When she asked me that, the message of 'Two Fathers' popped into my mind. I answered, 'I followed the advice my mom gave me as a little boy.'"

"She asked, 'What advice was that?'"

"I said, 'My mom told me that I had two fathers, one on earth and one in heaven. She explained that they both loved me and wanted to help me succeed in life. I needed to talk to both of them and tell them what I was doing. I should tell them my fears, concerns and they would listen and help me.'"

"As I spoke these words to Anna, her eyes filled with tears. She said, 'You're making me cry.' When I saw her reaction, I started to tear up and said, 'You're making me cry.' I went to the booth and sat down to wait for my order."

"When Anna brought my food to my booth, her eyes were still full of tears. She said, 'This is a good cry. Thank you for reminding me that I needed to talk to Him.' With that said, she pointed up."

"I saw Anna again a few days later. She looked more at peace when she said, 'I'm talking to Him again, thank you for reminding me.'"

"I thought, *'Billy is right, little seeds really can grow into amazing things. I believe, Two Fathers is one of those little seeds.'*"

Two Fathers
Music by Billy Dean
Lyrics by John Wudel
Produced by J.D. McLelland & Nanci Wudel

When I was just a little boy,
My mother said to me,
"You have two fathers son,
One earthly and one heavenly.
One dad's in the other room;
The other's just as near,
They're listening, so talk to them,
From you they want to hear.
They both love you, oh so much, my son,
Please know that they are here.
So tell them all that you have done,
Your every joy and fear.
One father lives at home with us,
By faith the other's here.
Believe in them with all your heart;
They hold you very dear."
I took my mom's advice that day.
She taught me how to pray.
I passed it down to all my kids
To remind us every day.
They both love you, the Father and the Son,
Please know that they are here.
So tell them all that you have done,
Your every joy and fear.
You changed direction in my life,
That one amazing day.
I owe it all to an angel mom
Who taught me I should pray.
Thank you, mom, for showing me
That fathers I have two,
And one amazing mother,
There's only one like you,
Like you.

Great Example

Still in Booth One, Michael remarked, "That's pretty cool John, you have a recording of Nanci playing the piano and your grandkids singing with a country music superstar. That's a memory that they will never forget."

Michael continued, "Remember when I met Billy Dean with you and Nanci at one of his concerts in the Dutton Theater in Mesa, Arizona? To tell you the truth, I have never cared for country music. After the first time that I saw him on stage, I was so impressed with his musical ability that I bought my first country music CD. The songs that he sang that night had really touched me."

"During Billy's concert, Marvin Goldstein joined him on stage for a couple of songs. Marvin was an old friend of Billy's, and an incredible LDS concert pianist. Billy had given a great performance during the first half of the show. He hadn't brought his whole band with him from Branson, Missouri, where he performed on a regular basis. Instead, he was the sole performer (troubadour style) onstage for his shows during the three or four months that he was here. Marvin was in town on this particular night, so he joined Billy for a couple of songs onstage."

"At intermission, you and Nanci took me back stage to meet the two performers. I shook hands with Billy and Marvin. Marvin said, 'I hear that you're a Jewish convert. I've been a Jewish convert for 30 years.' I said, 'I've only been a Jewish convert for two years, so I guess I'm a slow learner!' Marvin laughed."

"I spent a few minutes talking to them both. I was really impressed with both of their musical abilities, but I was particularly interested in why Billy was so gracious. He was a superstar of country music who had won Grammys and had many number one hits. It was amazing to me that during his intermission, instead of taking a break, he was willing to meet me and spend some time with me."

Michael said, "After the show, I remember talking to you about my curiosity with Billy. He seemed so relaxed, even though he had so many demands on him at once. We continued to watch Billy attend to his many fans that were now lining up to talk to him. Watching Billy that night inspired me to try to understand why he appeared to be so calm and willing to serve others."

Think To Thank

John said, "I was impressed, just like you were with Billy's graciousness to his fans. I was so impressed one night that I asked Billy, 'Was there a time in your life that was a defining moment in your musical career?'"

Billy Dean
Award-Winning Country Music Singer & Songwriter
Photo Courtesy of Billy Dean

Billy thought briefly and said, "Yes there was, John. I was the warm-up act for a well-known band in a concert. The concert hall was filled to capacity with over 15,000 fans for that band. When those concert-goers entered the venue, they were each given a small flashlight. They knew to turn on the flashlight during the concert when they felt impressed by their feelings to do so. As the warm-up act, I started my performance on autopilot. As I was going through the songs that I had sung a 1000 times before, I was thinking to myself, *'These people aren't here to see me or hear me. They don't really care that I'm up here performing. I don't really care either.'* I was thinking these thoughts at the same time that I was performing my songs. I thought, *'Just give me my check, and I'll get out of here.'"*

"I looked up at the people in the balcony, who were visiting with themselves. They were talking, laughing and weren't paying any attention to my performance. I thought, *'They don't really care that I'm here singing. Just give me my paycheck when I finished and I'll leave.'*"

"At that moment, I closed my eyes, and I thought to myself, *'Billy, what's the matter with you. God has given you a talent and a gift, but you don't even care about it. You don't care about what you're doing or the people you're singing to. What an ungrateful person you are.'"*

"When that wake-up call hit me, something happened deep inside, and I thought to myself, *'I should be so grateful for the privilege that I have to sing these beautiful songs to these wonderful people.'* Even with my eyes still closed, my singing changed, and I started to sing from my heart. Something had really changed. I felt a profound difference in me as I opened my eyes. To my total surprise, the audience must have felt something change as well. Starting way up in the balcony, in the darkness of that concert hall, people spontaneously started turning on those little flashlights. Within seconds, 15,000 people had stopped talking and laughing. Now those same flashlights were being shined at me. I immediately realized that something very magical had just happened."

Then I asked Billy "Was that a defining moment that lasted? Did things change from that point forward until now?"

Billy told me, "In that one moment of time, everything changed. I now perform with gratitude and with such a joy in my heart that I have this opportunity given to me."

"Thank you for sharing that Billy. I have to say that if there is one quality to describe your performances it is that you are singing from your heart. That is truly the magic of Billy Dean."

Michael remarked, "John, thank you for telling me that story, it brought tears to my eyes. Words cannot express how I feel right now. This story describes such a profound change from a very talented, kind, and caring man. I think that Billy embodied the true love of Christ."

"There are good people in every walk of life. We are all sons and daughters of the same loving God. Like Billy, I can trace back my incredible change of heart to one specific moment in time, when I received the Book of Mormon and the Spirit said to me, 'the book is true.' That moment changed me for the rest of my life."

Chapter 29
Temple Volunteer
(Michael)

The Mesa Arizona Temple was dedicated on October 23, 1927. It is a beautiful temple that stands in downtown Mesa, just east of the original Mesa town site that was settled by Mormon pioneers. The Visitors' Center sits just north of the temple on meticulously manicured grounds, which feature a cactus garden and large reflection pools.

The Easter season brings thousands of people to the temple grounds every year to watch the "Jesus the Christ" Easter pageant. The Easter pageant is the largest annual, outdoor pageant in the world. John's wife, Nanci, was the director of the pageant for nine years. At Christmas time, the grounds are converted to an incredible display of thousands of Christmas lights.

Before the Mesa Arizona Temple was constructed, Arizona members performed temple ordinances in the St. George Utah Temple. Because of the numerous bridal parties that traveled the wagon road between St. George and Arizona, the well-trod path became known as the "Honeymoon Trail."

After I had received my personal endowment, I got into the habit of going to the Mesa Arizona Temple on Wednesday evenings. John and Nanci served as temple ordinance workers on Wednesday nights. Sometimes I was able to eat with them during their dinner break. I felt a great feeling of peace envelop me each time that I entered the temple.

From the Ensign magazine dated October 2003 is the article, "Mesa Arizona Temple: The Gathering of Israel"

"Sometimes unnoticed amid the overall beauty and power of the Mesa Arizona Temple are dramatic carvings high on its corners. These intricate panels represent the gathering of Israel as spoken in Isaiah 11:12: "And he shall set up an ensign for the nations and shall assemble the outcasts of Israel, and gather together the dispersed of Judah from the four corners of the earth."

Now here I was, with the bloodlines of both the tribe of Judah and the tribe of Ephraim, going to the temple to perform sacred ordinances. How thrilling!

President Monson in his talk, "Blessings Of The Temple" from the LDS General Conference, April 2015 said,

"As I think of temples, my thoughts turn to the many blessings we receive therein. As we enter through the doors of the temple, we leave behind us the distractions and confusion of the world. Inside this sacred sanctuary, we find beauty and order. There is rest for our souls and a respite from the cares of our lives."

"As we attend the temple, there can come to us a dimension of spirituality and a feeling of peace which will transcend any other feeling which could come into the human heart."

"We will grasp the true meaning of the words of the Savior when He said: 'Peace I leave with you, my peace I give unto you. … Let not your heart be troubled, neither let it be afraid.'"

"Such peace can permeate any heart—hearts that are troubled, hearts that are burdened down with grief, hearts that feel confusion, hearts that plead for help."

President Monson's quote was defining my own heart. I had been burdened down with grief and confusion. I was certainly in need of help to discover joy in my life again, the joy that can only be given by drawing close to my Heavenly Father. The answer to discovering that joy would come to me from the Spirit.

Many nights after my endowment, I had been awakened out of a deep sleep to hear the Spirit tell me, "You will work in my holy temple just as your ancient ancestors did." This was yet another commandment from Heavenly Father asking me to serve and teaching me to become a follower of righteousness.

I didn't know if I could fulfill this command, so I called John and told him of these promptings. He said that I should start the process of becoming a temple worker by meeting with my bishop.

So I set up a meeting to talk to my bishop. Bishop Holman told me that there were two types of temple workers, volunteers and ordinance workers. I could either wait to be called as an ordinance worker or go ahead and volunteer to work in the temple. Since I wanted to honor what the Spirit had told me to do, I said, "I'll volunteer." The bishop gave me his approval and started the process. The process would include being approved by the Stake Presidency and then having an interview with the temple presidency.

After a couple of months, I was called to go to the temple and meet with a member of the Mesa Arizona Temple Presidency. During my interview, he told me that temple workers receive many blessings in their personal lives for their service in the temple. Since I was a volunteer, I had four choices of where I could work: the laundry, front desk, the veil, or the baptistery.

The President said, "Where would you like to work?"

I replied, "I would rather have interaction with people, so I would prefer not to work in the laundry. However, any of the other three are fine with me, and I will work wherever you feel inspired to place me."

The President requested, "Before I decide, please tell me your story."

I smiled and said, "I'm not sure we have that much time."

He chuckled, "How about the abbreviated version."

I told him that I was brought up Jewish and the story of receiving the Book of Mormon in the construction trailer outside the

Gilbert Temple where the Spirit testified to me that "the book is true."

When I finished, he said, "I think that the baptistery would be the perfect place for you to work."

We finished our conversation, and the President told me that he would call the baptistery coordinator and see if they could fit me in on Wednesday nights for the third shift.

A few days later, the secretary of the temple called me and said that I would start on Wednesday night, April 8. I was thrilled. I would start working in God's Holy Temple in the baptistery, exactly two years after I was baptized on my birthday. This was not a mere coincidence. Since it happened exactly on my birthday, it was a personal confirmation that Heavenly Father had a specific plan and purpose tailored just for me. I was here on earth at this time in my life to accomplish the plan that was laid out for me that I had agreed to in the Spirit world. That plan was being confirmed with every step that I was taking. The same way that it was confirmed to me when I first held the Book of Mormon in my hands and the Holy Spirit said 'The book is true'. In that moment He had connected my Jewish heritage to the further light and knowledge that I was continuing to obtain in joining the LDS Church.

This journey that I was on would be the greatest journey of my life. I couldn't think of a better 59th birthday present. Here was another door that had opened on my journey, and I was about to discover what amazing blessings would lie beyond that door.

Chapter 30
You Volunteered Me For What?
(Michael)

I was sitting in John's office, one afternoon in late February. We had just had lunch and were chatting about business. John's phone rang, and he answered it. I wasn't really listening to the one-sided conversation until John said, "No, I'm not available, but the guy who will do it is sitting right here in front of me."

I waited until John got off the phone and asked, "Who were you talking to?"

John replied, "I was talking to a high councilman in the Church that I know who is in charge of lining up firesides for the singles in our stake. He asked me if I would fill in as the main speaker at a fireside on March 1st. Their speaker just cancelled. So I told him that you would do it."

I said, "Oh no, John, why did you do that? That's only nine days from now."

John replied, "Just do one of your previous firesides, no one will remember your last one anyway. Plus it should be a whole new crowd."

I shook my head. I said, "Thanks a lot, John." I couldn't believe it. Each fireside that I had done up until then had taken me weeks to put together. How was I going to pull this off and give a quality talk at the same time in what was to become my fifth fireside?

I spent that next week trying to put something together that was a little bit different from the previous four firesides. Nothing that I was preparing sounded right. Then on Saturday, the day before the fireside, I decided to do something completely different. I had requests after each of the previous firesides to put more of my personal experiences into my talks.

I had just given a talk to an empty nester group where I only related my personal experiences. So I started working feverishly to put together a fireside that was mostly made up of those spiritual events that I have had since coming to Mesa on that business trip in November 2012.

The night of the March fireside came. I asked Evelyn to sing again and her family offered me a ride. So, I rode with Hillary, Amos, Evelyn, and Kira, Evelyn's mom, dad and sister to the fireside. We got to the church building where they were holding the fireside an hour early. Joy and Linda also showed up early to practice. Kade arrived to set up the audio/visual portion of the talk and said, "Michael, we can set this one up by ourselves." Everyone was pretty much on autopilot and for the first time, I didn't have to organize anything. I left the chapel and went out into the hallway to look for an empty classroom in which to pray.

I found an empty classroom with the door unlocked and went inside. I knelt down on my knees and said a prayer:

"Heavenly Father, I am grateful for all the abundance that you have brought into my life. Thank you for giving me the courage to stand up before these people tonight and give the talk that I have prepared. Thank you for the inspiration of what to say. Please fill me with the Spirit, so that those who hear my message will know that the Spirit speaks through me. If this talk inspires just one person to seek out the truth and your light and love, then I feel that I will have succeeded. I say these things in the name of Jesus Christ. Amen."

I had tears in my eyes as I finished my prayer. I got to my feet, wiped away my tears, and headed back to the chapel.

I went back into the chapel at around ten minutes until 7 p.m., and Brother Kade said, "Are you ready to get miked up?"

I said, "Let's do it."

I counted 150 people right before I started my talk. More people came in during the first 10 minutes after I started speaking. The musical numbers were beautiful, and everything went off without a hitch. Part of the way through my talk, I realized that I might have put in too many personal experiences and not enough of the similarities between Judaism and the LDS Church. I continued anyway, ended my talk, and went through about 30 minutes of questions and answers.

After everything ended, people lined up to talk to me. This time, the conversation between me and the people that had attended was different than any of my other firesides. The first woman that came up asked me how she was supposed to deal with her sisters not talking to her, now that she had joined the church. The next person was a man that said that he had severe head injuries, almost died, and asked me what he should now do with his life. The next person said that their father and mother wouldn't speak to them after they joined the Church. They were all asking my opinion on what I would suggest for them to do. I have never been asked these types of questions before, and I felt a responsibility to give the proper response. These types of questions concerning loneliness, confusion, and affliction were from several people that came up to meet me following my talk.

I thought of Billy Dean, the country music star. I had seen him in concert a couple of weeks prior to this night and watched how he had graciously treated all of the people that wanted to talk to him or get his autograph after his show. Even though you could tell he was exhausted, he took time with each person and engaged them in meaningful conversation. I thought of my bishop, Bishop Holman, and my friend Bishop Woodruff. How gracious they both were, in their selfless duty to the church and taking time with each member of their congregation to listen to their concerns.

I suddenly realized that the questions that I was being asked were some of the same questions that a bishop or stake president probably deals with on a daily basis. As I thought about this later, I think that the reason that they asked such personal and tender questions of me was because I had shared some of the most private and sacred moments of my conversion story with them. I think that if I would have just given the similarities of the two religions, they wouldn't have felt comfortable in confiding in me their own personal problems.

On the way home, I talked to Amos and Hillary about what had happened when people came up to talk to me at the end of the fireside. Amos said, "I thought that when I heard your talk that you had put too many personal experiences in it. Although, when I saw and heard some of the questions that people asked you afterwards, I realized that the content of your talk was exactly what these people needed to hear."

We talked about it a little bit more. Hillary and Amos had been kind enough to bring Evelyn to sing at each one of my firesides, and I appreciated their counsel afterwards. My main question to them was always the same, "Did I progress from the last fireside?"

Hillary said, "Didn't you see me crying? When I'm touched by the Spirit during your talks, it usually brings tears to my eyes. Thank you for giving another inspiring fireside."

Overall, I found that I needed a blend of both the similarities of the two religions and my personal experiences of my conversion. I knew somehow that Heavenly Father wasn't through with me yet and that I would probably give another fireside in the future.

Chapter 31
Eternal Companion
(Michael and John in Booth One)

Michael and John were in Booth One having another discussion during lunch. Michael said, "John, they keep saying in church, you can only receive the fullness of the gospel when you are married. Are you kidding me? I don't think I'm ready for marriage again."

Michael continued, "In Hebrew, your one and only companion is called "Beshert." A Beshert is the Jewish notion of a soul mate. Beshert means destiny, or your predestined spouse. Some Rabbis teach that according to the Talmud (the basis of Jewish law), forty days before a male child is born, God announces whose daughter he will marry. According to the Kabbalah (Jewish mysticism), God divides a soul in half, into male and female. When they finally meet in holy matrimony, their bond returns. So, what do Mormons think about marriage?"

"Michael, you are only one-half of the whole, and you need to find your other half to be complete. I struggled with the same problem for years. When I returned home from my mission, I was 24 years old. I knew that the next step in my life was to find my other half and be married in the temple. The question that I had was, 'Is there a 'one and only?' Some think in the church that there's only one person for you to marry. Others believe that you could choose one from among several people and be just as happy. I wanted to know for me if there was a 'one and only' or whether there were several to choose from. I turned to the only source that I knew was reliable."

"I fasted and prayed to Heavenly Father and asked the simple question, 'Is there one or several that I could marry and be happy?' The answer came to me very clear that there were several to choose from. If I lived the gospel with any one of them, I would have a happy marriage and a happy life. The impression that I got from the

Spirit was that number one was way ahead of the others. I could see in my mind my number one choice of a person to marry and a large gap between the other choices. With that knowledge came the determination to do whatever it took to find that number one. The result of all of that was several years of dating."

"My married friends were concerned that I was still single and started to set me up with their friends. I went out with many accomplished women who were very talented and righteous. Each time I would take one of these women out, I would feel the same thing. As wonderful as they were, I never felt that I found my number one. After four years went by, my friends began to get discouraged with me. They said, 'You are too picky, John'."

"I remember one day sitting with my mom and asking her, 'Am I too picky, mom?' My mom said, 'No, son you're not too picky, you just haven't found her yet.'"

"I heard a story of someone who began fasting and praying every Sunday to find out who they should marry. I decided that I would do the same thing. Before I started fasting I got down on my knees and said, 'Heavenly Father, I want to find my other half. Please help me find her.' I told God that I was going to begin fasting every Sunday until I found her."

"The first Sunday that I started fasting, I went to my ward building that was just adjacent to the football stadium at BYU. I was sitting under a tree with my roommates. We were watching the young women coming in to church. Nanci, a young woman that had helped me with advertising for a restaurant that my older brother, Jim, and I owned called "JIMBA'S", was walking in with her girlfriends. She looked over at me and smiled. It was such a beautiful smile that it seemed to light up my surroundings and touch me to my core."

"The meeting was a fast and testimony Sunday. Nanci stood up and bore her testimony. I felt impressed to follow her example and bear my testimony. After the meeting ended, I went up to her and asked her if she would like to go on a drive up the canyon. So Nanci and I, with my roommate and his date, drove up to Aspen Grove."

"When we got there, we realized that we were driving by a cabin that was owned by our stake president. We decided to check it out. As we were looking in the back window of the cabin, the stake president and his wife drove up. When they saw four young college students looking into the cabin, they graciously invited us to come in."

"As we all sat in the living room of the cabin, the stake president's wife asked Nanci to go into the kitchen and help prepare some refreshments. Nanci came out with a plate of brownies. She walked up to me and said, 'Would you like a brownie?'"

"For just a moment, I felt like Adam in the Garden of Eden. I thought, *'What do I do? I'm fasting to find my eternal companion, and Nanci's offering me a brownie.'* I hesitated for a moment, looked into her beautiful green eyes, took the brownie, and ate it."

"My fasting had ended, and I would never have to fast again to find out who I should marry. She was standing right in front of me. Now it was as if the Spirit had opened my eyes, and I could see her beauty and appreciate her intelligence and deep spirituality for the very first time. We dated almost every night and in just thirteen days, I proposed to her. I had found my other half and she said, "Yes." We've been married for 46 years; have four wonderful children and sixteen beautiful grandchildren."

"My patriarchal blessing foretold of this meeting. It told me that I would find a companion worthy to take to the temple and be sealed to her for time and all eternity. The opportunity would come for me to become a father in Zion, know the joys of parenthood with my companion, and rear my children in righteousness. By meeting Nanci, the promise of my patriarchal blessing would be fulfilled."

Michael said, "That's a great story. I wonder how I am going to find my eternal companion. I haven't had that much luck yet."

John said, "This is one of life's most important decisions. It shouldn't be made without fasting and prayer."

Michael said, "You're right, I need to start fasting and praying every Sunday until I find her."

John said, "I'm so glad that I believed my mom when she told me that 'I wasn't too picky, I just hadn't found her yet.' That helped me be patient and wait until I discovered my number one."

"Michael, I believe you'll have the same success as I did. Just be patient, your other half is out there somewhere, unless she was killed in the War in Heaven."

Michael, with a surprised look on his face could only say, "What?"

John smiled and said, "Just kidding, that's an old BYU joke. I'm sure you'll find her once this book comes out." Let's eat this amazing burger and fries before they get cold. By the way once the fries get cold they taste like cardboard, so let's partake while they're still hot."

John and Nanci Wudel
Married For Time and Sealed For Eternity October 8, 1970

Chapter 32
The Greatest Thing In The World
(John's Talk)

John recalled, "I received a phone call from a member of my bishopric. He said, 'John, the Church has a new way of choosing the talks for sacrament meeting. It's now up to the ward council to pick the topics. When one of the ward council members suggested this topic, the room went quiet. The topic that you are assigned is: 'How to Strengthen the Relationships between a Husband, a Wife And their Children through the Atonement of Jesus Christ.' You have been given fifteen minutes next Sunday to cover it in. Good luck.'"

"I started my talk with this;

My assigned topic today is "How to Strengthen the Relationships between a Husband, a Wife And their Children Through the Atonement of Jesus Christ.' This is such a profound and important topic that it's impossible to cover it in the time I've been given. In praying about it, I felt impressed to focus on only one aspect; The Power of Love."

"Let me begin with a story. The year Nanci and I got married, I was teaching seminary at a high school in Utah. As the year was ending, I told the students that I had to give them a grade. To be able to grade them I needed to give them a final exam. For the final exam I gave the students a choice between two options;

1. Study all the notes, the handouts, the reading assignments and take an exam, for your final grade.
2. For one week, every time you come to a decision, pray and ask, 'What would Jesus do?' You must then do what He would do and record it in a journal. You turn the journal in at the end of the week, and I'll decide your final grade."

"To all of the students, the second choice seemed like the easiest. They started on the next Monday and were to finish on the following Sunday. About Wednesday, our phone started to ring. Astonished parents were all asking me the same question: 'What have you done to my child?'"

"I said, 'What do you mean what have I done?' The different parents said, 'Tommy actually makes his bed now before he goes to school. Susie stopped fighting with her sisters. Billy cleans up his room before he goes out with his friends. Judy asked me if she could clear the table and do the dishes after dinner. Then she asked me what she could do to help me with tomorrow's dinner.'"

"The temper tantrums had stopped; the bad attitudes ended. They were all asking, 'What have you done to our kids?' I told them that I really didn't do anything. I explained the assignment I had given, and they told me it was the best thing that had ever happened in their home in years. They explained that a peace had entered their homes, a new lack of contention, reduced arguing, a new kindness, a spirit of being sensitive to others' feelings brought a renewed love into the entire family. They were all amazed."

"What they were describing was the effects of the power of love. The example set by Jesus Christ is one of pure love. He is the perfect example of what love really is, and how it operates in action. What those families were observing, for that one magic week, was the power of the Atonement of Jesus Christ."

"The Atonement was and always will be the greatest example of pure love that has ever been given to this earth. A God was sent to earth to be sacrificed. Think about it. A God actually volunteered to come to earth to be killed. Before Jesus came here He was already perfect. He was the God of the Old Testament, Jehovah. He lived in a Celestial realm with those who honored and loved Him for who He was. He left the presence of His perfect Heavenly Home and Parents to come here to a fallen world."

"A world of spiritual poverty to be surrounded by those who not only didn't understand who He was, but also those who hated Him and would kill Him, because of who He was. Why did He do it? Did He want more glory? No. He gave all the glory to God. Did He need more power? No. He had power over life and death. He had power to create this earth. His father had given Him all power. Then why did He come here? He came for two reasons: The first, because His Father asked Him to come. 'God so loved the world that He gave His Only Begotten Son, that whosoever believeth in him should not perish, but have everlasting life. For God sent not his Son into the world to condemn the world; but that the world through him might be saved.' The second reason Jesus came here was because He loved His Father and wanted to please Him, and because He loved us and wanted to save us."

"His only motive to come here was pure love. He endured the agony of Gethsemane and what followed: the verbal abuse, the ridicule, the humiliation, and mocking, from the spitting in his face, to the beating, the whipping, and the final brutal death by crucifixion. He did it all for love. What did His Atonement accomplish? It accomplished everything that we need to succeed in this mortal life."

"If you turn to the Revised Version of the First Epistle of John, you find these words: 'We love because He first loved us.' The scripture did not say, 'We love Him because He first loved us.' Instead it says, 'We love because He first loved us.' Because He loved us, we now have the power to love. As you love Him, you become like Him. Our hearts are slowly changed. Contemplate the love of Christ, and you will be empowered to love. You will experience a 'mighty change of heart.'"

"Why is this possible? I recently read "The Greatest Thing in the World" by Henry Drummond, where he teaches that it's possible because love begets love. It's a process of induction. Put a piece of iron in the presence of an electrified body, a powerful magnet, and the piece of iron for a time becomes electrified. It is changed into a temporary magnet in the presence of a permanent magnet. As long as you leave the two side by side, they are both magnets alike. If we remain side by side with Him who loves us, and gave himself for us, we too will become a permanent source of love. That is the inevitable effect of Love. There is no other way to get it. There is no mystery about it. We love others, we love our enemies, and we love everyone, because He first loved us."

"To give a practical application of this, let me tell you a story about my brother Jim. He's sitting in the back because I asked him to come today. Jim is my older brother by three years. In his youth, he was a 6'5" Marine. Today he is an ex-Marine that was sitting in my office a while ago when a small bird hit the window and fell to the earth. I watched as Jim went outside and gently picked the dying little bird up in his hands. This beautiful little creation of God had a breast of bright yellow feathers so Jim gave him a name, 'Little Yellow.' He then knelt down in the dirt by the window, and dug a grave to bury him, and took a Popsicle stick that was lying there and wrote on it 'Little Yellow', and placed it on the grave as a proper marker. He did this with a reverence and respect for this little fallen creation of God. Brother Jim, I believe that you must be one of the kindest ex-Marines alive on the earth today. Thank you, for your stunning example of love for even the smallest creations of God."

"About a year ago, Jim's wife of 26 years contracted cancer. She decided to move to Utah to be with her children and try to regain her health. Shortly after the divorce was final, word came down from Utah that her family used four words to describe Jim. They said he was weird, bizarre, quirky, and eccentric. When Jim heard this, he called a family friend, our nephew Brent, who lives in Utah. He said, 'Brent, her family all think that I'm weird, bizarre, quirky, and eccentric.' Brent answered without hesitation. 'Jimba (Jim's nickname), they are right. You are all of those things, that's why we love you.' Jimba has a crazy sense of humor and answered, 'Nevertheless, Brent, it's so much to live up to.'"

"This experience hit me right in the heart. As I pondered it, I learned a very important lesson from this. I know the Lord's admonition to us is 'Be Ye therefore perfect, even as your Father in

Heaven is perfect.' I know that the Lord would not tell us to do something that was not possible. To become perfect is possible, and we are on our way, but we are not there yet, so I have come to a renewed appreciation for imperfections. I used to just accept the imperfections in others, but now, I actually value them. I'm not placing value on bad behavior, but on the natural imperfections that we all have."

"Listen to these words of a man singing to his sweetheart: 'Cause all of me, loves all of you…all your perfect imperfection; Give your all to me; I'll give my all to you.' He labeled them 'perfect imperfections'. What a beautiful way for a husband and a wife to value the faults of each other as 'perfect imperfections.'"

"I've come to believe that those imperfections are what bring us together. They are what make us different from each other and enable us to relate better to each other, because we all have them."

"Think about the members of your family that are a bubble-off. We all have the uncles, the aunts, the cousins, the brothers or sisters with the quirks, the weirdness, or flaws that we overlook, and love them anyway, because they are family. What if we extended that unconditional love to everyone as Christ did? What would this world then be like?"

"How is it that a mother can so love a Down syndrome child that the world might see as having little value? How can a father so love the Prodigal son that forsakes the family values for sin or even crime and refuses to repent? That level of love is only possible because of the Atonement of Christ. Jesus looks at us with all our faults, our failings, and foolishness and loves us, in spite of them all. Because of Him, we have the power to do the same thing. Christ said, 'I am the way, the truth, and the life.'"

"Christ came to give us a more abundant life, a life abundant in love and therefore abundant in salvation for us. To love abundantly is to live abundantly, and to love forever is to live forever. Eternal life is bound up with love. There is no other reason why we should live on, than that we love and are beloved. It is when a man has no one to love him or that he no longer loves others, or himself, that he commits suicide."

"On the last analysis then, love is life. The Lord gave to the Relief Society sisters, the profound truth that everything else can fail but Charity (the pure love of Christ) Never Faileth, so life never faileth, so long as there is love. Eternal life also is to know God, and God is love."

"In conclusion I want to turn to the experience of Melvin J. Ballard, a modern Apostle of the Lord who recorded this:

......that night I received a wonderful manifestation and impression that has never left me. ......I was led into a room where I was informed I was to meet someone. As I entered the room I saw, seated on a raised platform, the most glorious being I have ever conceived of, and was taken forward to be introduced to Him. As I approached He smiled, called me by name and stretched out His hands towards me. If I live to be a million years old I shall never forget that smile. He put His arms around me and kissed me, as He took me into His bosom, and He blessed me until my whole being was thrilled. As He finished, I fell at His feet, and there saw the marks of the nails; and as I kissed them, with deep joy swelling through my whole being, I felt that I was in heaven in deed. The feeling that came to my heart then was: Oh! If I could live worthy, though it would require four-score years, so that in the end when I have finished I could go into His presence and receive the feeling that I then had in His presence, I would give everything that I am or ever hope to be!"

"May I leave you my testimony that Jesus Christ lives. I, like Brother Ballard, have been close enough to the pure source of love to draw on the power of His Atonement. For Nanci, my children, my grandchildren, my brother Jim, my extended family, this 30th ward family, my friends, and beyond, I feel a love that I didn't know was even possible. For that I am so grateful."

"To return to the topic given: 'How to strengthen the relationships between a husband, a wife and their children thru the Atonement of Jesus Christ is possible thru His perfect love.' I say this in the name of Jesus Christ. Amen."

Imperfect

John and Michael met in Booth One for yet another discussion and a hamburger.

"Look at this hamburger." John asked, "Can you believe how amazing these things are? You know, I have to thank you for coming to my ward to hear me give my sacrament talk. You were sitting next to my brother, Jimba and it meant a lot to me. He doesn't come to church that often and I'm sure that having him sit with you was helpful to him. Having my daughter, Tricia and my granddaughter, Emily, sitting on your other side was perfect."

Michael said, "I like Jimba; he has a great sense of humor. I really felt that your talk touched your brother. I sensed that something changed in him, if only for a while. Jimba is not one to sing hymns, but I could hear him softly singing along with each one. So I put the hymn book in front of him, so we both could share it. He willingly held the other half of the hymn book and sang every hymn with me. I think that Jimba really enjoyed your talk, and the part that got to him was when you were talking about the value of being imperfect."

"That part got to me as well. Let me tell you a little bit about how I grew up. My mother was a very loving and accepting person. She loved my brother and me, in spite of our imperfections, as all mothers love their children. She seemed to love everyone, no matter who they were or where they came from. My father loved me too, but he was always telling me that I had to strive to be perfect. Imperfection wasn't an option."

Michael continued, "My father was an entrepreneur and had his own business. He sold his bakery when I was 3 or 4 years old and started a company selling restaurant equipment. He traveled in four states, Monday through Friday, most of the weeks of the year. He wasn't at home much, because he was out sacrificing for his family. Being at home with only my mother's influence on my brother and me, allowed us to be our own imperfect selves. Valuing imperfections is a better way to be prepared for the realities of life."

Michael smiled and said, "My father had a strong work ethic and put me to work early on. Take a look at this picture, I was only 2 1/2 years old and he already put me to work in his bakery!"

Michael Morton "Working" In His Family's Bakery

John laughed and said, "Weren't there any child labor laws back then?"

"On a more serious note, your dad was not a perfect father. None of us are. I believe he understood something very important."

"You don't have to be perfect to sacrifice and serve. It brings to mind a hymn named 'Praise To The Man', which was a tribute to Joseph Smith. In the hymn are the words, 'Sacrifice brings forth the blessings of heaven.' I think your dad understood this principle."

Michael replied, "I think you're right. As I reflect back on my life, it hasn't been all bad. When I would get beat up and spit upon for my religious choices, there were always those around me that would lift me up and value those differences. That was a blessing to me. I didn't understand the concept that we choose the life that we will live here on earth. I understand now, that my father may have chosen a hard life and sacrificed family time together. He wanted to be an example to me and others of how to triumph over adversity and succeed. I wouldn't find out until many years later, at my patriarchal blessing, that I too had chosen a difficult life as well. Since joining the Church, I understand that sacrifice really does bring forth the blessings of heaven."

John nodded in agreement, "Michael, we are taught to sacrifice and strive for perfection like your father was trying to teach you. This is the same example that has been set for us by our older brother Jesus Christ. It is certainly a worthy goal, but the perfection part isn't a goal that we can achieve in this mortal life. As we serve others we sacrifice and as we continually improve we move towards perfection."

I Love You, Man

As Michael and John finished their meal, Michael said, "I want to tell you about a situation that has concerned me from the beginning of my journey into the Church. I have many friends in my ward, and I value their friendship very much. The thing that bothers me a little is when another brother says to me, "I love you."

"I find it a little disconcerting because I don't know what to say back. There is a man in my ward whose name is Eric. He is a friend of mine with a wife and family. He has said, 'I love you, brother' to me as we shake hands at Church sometimes. I know he means well, but it feels weird to say 'I love you' to another man who is not a family member or an old friend. I'm not used to talking to other men that way. Don't get me wrong, I have always said 'I love you' to my father, uncles, family relatives and sometimes old friends. It just doesn't seem natural to say it to men that I have only known a short while."

John said, "Michael your concerns remind me of another Michael from years ago. My cousin Mike followed me to BYU my sophomore year to pursue his education. He eventually graduated with an MBA in business and went on to become a successful real-estate developer in Southern California."

"While attending BYU, he went with me to church. He always felt uncomfortable when anyone speaking in church would say that they loved those they were addressing in the congregation. He would remark, 'They shouldn't say that they love us. They don't love all of us; they don't even know most of us. Why do they say stuff like that anyway?'"

John continued, "That was a stumbling block for Mike who had joined the church while attending BYU, but has been an inactive member ever since he left the wholesome environment of what I like to think of as the Lord's University. The answer to Mike's concern and yours as well, lies in Joseph Smith's remark concerning what happens to us as we grow closer to God."

"Joseph taught; 'A man filled with the love of God is not content with blessing his family alone, but ranges through the whole world, anxious to bless the whole human race.' John then said, "I believe those who were speaking of their love for you were demonstrating that reality."

John concluded, "Michael, the scriptures say, 'God is love,' so it only makes sense that the closer that you get to God, the more you will experience the 'pure love' of God. When I think of the more loving people that I know, they are the ones that are striving to emulate Him and the result is that they become more loving to all of God's creations and more likely to express that love. It's something that you just have to get used to because it wasn't the way of the world that we both grew up in. The longer you follow Christ, the more this feeling of universal love makes sense."

Chapter 33
Temple Baptistery
(Michael)

On my birthday, April 8, 2015, I turned 59 years old. The most exciting thing was that I would be starting on my birthday as a volunteer in the baptistery of the Mesa Arizona Temple. I was told to show up early, so that I could have a blessing by one of the members of the temple presidency and be set apart to serve in the temple.

John had said, "This will be very special to have a Jew serving in God's Holy house. I'm sure that your ancient ancestors would be very pleased with what you are about to do. This reminds me that Joseph Smith was chosen to become the leader for the restoration of the gospel and was 'set apart' from the rest of the world. He was visited by God the Father, who introduced his Beloved Son, Jesus. Jesus told Joseph not to join any other church. Never again could Joseph return to his previous way of life. Joseph was forever set apart and had a new and higher perspective of life. A calling gives you the opportunity to change and serve God as your spiritual responsibility."

I thought, *"In a sense, I, too, was about to be 'set apart' from the concerns of the world while working in the temple."*

John and Nanci joined me in the President's office with one of the members of the temple presidency, to be set apart. He explained that working in the temple would be a great blessing to me and my family. He asked me about how I came to the church, and I gave him a brief explanation.

He then had me sit in a chair so that he could set me apart and give me a blessing.

He placed his hands on my head and started, "By the authority of the Melchizedek Priesthood".........

During a part of the blessing, the President said, "Jesus changed the old Mosaic laws in an instant, when he showed us the true meaning of service, by kneeling and washing the feet of the apostles. He was an example of the highest authority serving the common man. Michael, as you continue to serve, everything in your life will fall into place, and the unimportant things will fall away." I could feel the power of that blessing running through me, as I had with the other blessings that I had received before. I was so grateful that I had been promised that my life would fall into place by serving a higher purpose.

The President then gave me a name tag and shook my hand. I felt fortunate that John and Nanci had attended my induction into service in the temple. I went down the hallway to the baptistery and reported for duty. Greg, the brother who was the coordinator in the baptistery for the third shift on Wednesday night took me around and showed me the different areas that I would be working in. He explained to me that Wednesday night was usually the busiest night in the temple baptistery. It was only 4 p.m., but young people were already coming in to do baptisms for the dead.

I have heard people say, "The Mormons made up the idea of baptisms for the dead." That simply isn't true; the Mormons didn't make up baptisms for the dead. It is recorded in the New Testament in 1 Corinthians:

29 Else what shall they do which are baptized for the dead, if the dead rise not at all? Why are they then baptized for the dead?   1 Corinthians 15:29

What this verse points out is that following the time of Christ, the members of that original church were practicing baptisms for the dead. The question is, why were they doing it then, and why are we doing it now? To be baptized, you need a physical body. When an individual dies, their spirit goes on into the spirit world and is taught the Gospel of Jesus Christ. If they accept it, they need to be baptized. That ordinance is accomplished in the temple by a proxy. These young people that are coming into the baptistery understand that they are providing this very important ordinance for spirits unable to accomplish it for themselves. This is a pure act of service by the youth of the LDS Church.

Greg, the baptistery coordinator said, "Michael, would you mind putting on a white jumpsuit and start baptizing people by proxy for the dead?"

I replied, "Sure, give me a suit, I'm ready." I thought, *"I am ready for this! What a great honor to be serving Heavenly Father by performing this ancient essential ordinance."*

Everyone attending the temple, including the temple workers, is dressed in white. The white clothing stands for purity and signifies that everyone is the same in God's eyes. I went and changed into the jumpsuit and entered the baptistery room.

As I said before, the Mesa Arizona Temple was dedicated on October 23, 1927. So the whole inside of the building has a rich, old world elegance feel to it. That was especially true for the baptistery. The ceiling seems to be about 30 feet high with huge murals painted on two of the walls. The murals have been beautifully restored. They depict the restoration of this ordinance to the earth. The tile work on the floors and the sides of the baptismal font consisted of tiny one inch tiles. These tiles were prevalent in bathhouses and bathrooms of that era and have a blue-green color to them.

The baptistery includes some very important symbolism. You can look down the side of the font and see that the font is resting on the backs of twelve oxen. The twelve oxen are representative of the Twelve Tribes of Israel. In most temples, the position of the baptismal font is generally located directly below the Celestial Room. This positioning reminds us that baptism is symbolic of the death and burial of the natural man. The coming forth or rebirth of an individual committed to following the commandments of God. Baptism is the first ordinance needed to gain entrance into the highest degree of Heaven, the Celestial Kingdom.

On a platform next to the font and overlooking the font, sits a desk and three chairs. This is staffed by three endowed priesthood holders. One sits behind the desk, records each baptism, and essentially runs the baptistery. The other two chairs are for two witnesses to make sure that the person being baptized is completely immersed underwater each time.

This reminds me of being immersed in a mikveh to become an Orthodox Jew. There are three witnesses who make sure that you are fully immersed, and they must be holy men. At mine, it was two Rabbis and a Cantor that witnessed my immersion.

I entered the baptismal font and proceeded to baptize members, acting in proxy for forty names. I was thrilled, as it was the first time that I had actually baptized anyone. There was a lull in people coming in, so I changed back into my all white outfit, complete with a white shirt and tie. We got ready for the influx of people coming to the temple on Wednesday night. Wednesday night is usually Mutual night for the different wards in the area. Young men and young women have a regularly scheduled activity night, called Mutual, because of the shared experiences in which there will be mutual respect and support for one another. Mutual is usually held once a week, on any day or evening, other than Sunday or Monday.

At about 5:30 p.m., the groups of young women and young men started coming into the chapel next to the baptistery. The thing that was most impressive to me was that their faces were glowing with the anticipation of performing this sacred ordinance. Their bright faces and desire to be there to do baptisms for deceased members of their families was inspiring. If they didn't come with their own ancestors names, then the temple would provide names of people to be baptized from over 100 years ago.

7:30 p.m. came, and the chapel next to the baptistery had filled and emptied twice with over 100 people each time. Since we were supposed to close at 8:30, most of the baptistery workers were let go. After they were sent home, we realized that there were a few young women who had been waiting in the lobby to do baptisms that we didn't know about. They did not come with any priesthood holders, and there were only four of us left. You really need six priesthood holders and a baptizer to properly perform confirmations and baptisms. We were a couple of men short.

The four of us that were left stood in the hallway and conversed for a moment. The comment was made that we didn't have enough priesthood holders to conduct the ordinances that were required. We could have turned them away, hoping that they would return again soon. At that moment, the Spirit spoke to me and said, Do not turn them away.

It was my first night and I didn't have any say so as to what went on in the baptistery. I blurted out, "I'll be happy to get into a jumpsuit again and baptize them."

Greg said, "We can all do double duty and not have to turn them away." I had spoken out of turn, but everyone agreed and we started the process. While we were confirming these four young sisters, three more young sisters walked in. We all looked at each other and said, "The more the merrier."

What a great feeling I had that first night working in the baptistery, as I had actively participated in several hundred baptisms for the dead. As I left the temple later that evening, I felt like I was walking on a cloud. I was so excited to have participated in those sacred ordinances.

After I got home, I got down on my knees and prayed to Heavenly Father. "Heavenly Father, I am grateful for the many blessings that you have brought into my life, including the wonderful people that have surrounded and supported me during this great time of change. I appreciate you letting me serve in your Holy Temple tonight, and I look forward to serving many more nights in the baptistery. I am grateful for everything that you have given me, even the small things. I open my heart to you and want to live according to your eternal plan. Please guide me in how to use my time and talents to help build your kingdom here on earth. I say these things in the name of Jesus Christ. Amen."

Chapter 34
We Believe
(John's Office)

Michael met John at his office for an early morning discussion before they started working on the book.

John said, "Michael, have a seat. I want to tell you the story of how the Articles of Faith for the Church were created."

"I believe that Joseph Smith was divinely inspired when he wrote a letter in 1842 to John Wentworth, the editor of the Chicago Democrat. In the letter Joseph gives an account of the first vision, Moroni's visit and the coming forth of the Book of Mormon. The Prophet then describes the golden plates, along with the ministry of apostles and prophets."

"He also recounts the organizing of the Church, the persecution that Mormons suffered and the founding of Nauvoo, Illinois. we also learn about thirteen doctrinal statements known as the Articles of Faith."

"Let me read you the Articles of Faith. They describe guidelines for members of the LDS Church."

The 13 Articles of Faith

1. We believe in God, the Eternal Father, and in His Son, Jesus Christ, and in the Holy Ghost.
2. We believe that men will be punished for their own sins, and not for Adam's transgression.
3. We believe that through the Atonement of Christ, all mankind may be saved, by obedience to the laws and ordinances of the Gospel.
4. We believe that the first principles and ordinances of the Gospel are: first, Faith in the Lord Jesus Christ; second, Repentance; third, Baptism by immersion for the remission of

sins; fourth, Laying on of hands for the gift of the Holy Ghost.

5. We believe that a man must be called of God, by prophecy, and by the laying on hands by those who are in authority, to preach the Gospel and administer in the ordinances thereof.

6. We believe in the same organization that existed in the Primitive Church, namely, apostles, prophets, pastors, teachers, evangelists, and so forth.

7. We believe in the gift of tongues, prophecy, revelation, visions, healing, interpretation of tongues, and so forth.

8. We believe the Bible to be the word of God as far as it is translated correctly; we also believe the Book of Mormon to be the word of God.

9. We believe all that God has revealed, all that He does now reveal, and we believe that He will yet reveal many great and important things pertaining to the Kingdom of God.

10. We believe in the literal gathering of Israel and in the restoration of the Ten Tribes; that Zion (the New Jerusalem) will be built upon the American continent; that Christ will reign personally upon the earth; and, that the earth will be renewed and receive its paradisiacal glory.

11. We claim the privilege of worshiping Almighty God according to the dictates of our own conscience, and allow all men the same privilege, let them worship how, where, or what they may.

12. We believe in being subject to kings, presidents, rulers, and magistrates, in obeying, honoring, and sustaining the law.

13. We believe in being honest, true, chaste, benevolent, virtuous, and in doing good to all men; indeed, we may say that we follow the admonition of Paul—We believe all things, we hope all things, we have endured many things, and hope to be able to endure all things. If there is anything virtuous, lovely, or of good report or praiseworthy, we seek after these things.

Joseph Smith

Michael responded, "So, The Articles of Faith, describe what every Mormon should believe."

"You are right Michael. Joseph Smith gave all of the members of the Church a definite set of articles to live by and follow."

Michael stated, "Now, let's look at what Jews believe."

"Judaism maintains that the righteous of all nations have a place in the world to come. Judaism generally recognizes that Christians worship the same God that Jews do and those who faithfully follow the tenets of their own religions can be considered righteous in the eyes of God."

"No religion should be arrogant enough to think that they are going to be the only ones allowed in heaven. God wants all of his children to return and live with him."

"Contrary to popular belief, Judaism does not maintain that Jews are better than other people. Although we refer to ourselves as God's chosen people, Jews do not believe that God chose them because of any type of genetic superiority. God offered the Torah (first 5 Books of the Bible) to all the nations of the earth, and the Jews were the only ones who accepted it. The Jews were also the first to believe in monotheism (worshiping one God)."

"In Judaism, your actions are as important as your beliefs, particularly towards your fellow man and woman."

"There is a widely accepted list of Jewish beliefs, named Maimonides's Thirteen Principles of Faith. These principles, are thought to be the minimum requirements of Jewish belief."

"Maimonides or Rambam (acronym for Rabbi Moshe Ben Maimon) became one of the most prolific and influential Jewish philosophers, Torah scholars and physicians of the Middle Ages. A sculpture of Maimonides hangs in the U.S. House of Representatives. He created these principles for all Jews and here are summaries of each one:"

13 Principles of Faith

1. The existence of God.
2. God is one and unique.
3. God is spiritual and incorporeal.
4. God is eternal.
5. Prayer is to be directed to God alone and to no other.
6. The words and revelations of God's prophets are true.
7. Moses' prophecies are true, and Moses was the greatest of the prophets.
8. The Torah (first 5 books of the Bible) that we have today is the one dictated to Moses by God.
9. The Torah given by Moses will not be replaced and that nothing may be added or removed from it.
10. God's awareness of all human actions and thoughts.
11. God will reward the good and punish the wicked.
12. The coming of the Jewish Messiah.
13. The resurrection of the dead.

Michael continued, "In this list, we see that these principles are very basic. Even though these principles are easy to understand, the necessity of believing each one of these has been disputed at one time or another."

"My uncles used to tell me a joke. It goes, 'If two Jews have a discussion, you will end up with three opinions!'"

John laughed and said, "That's a good one."

Michael concluded, "Jews have always considered the nature and relationships between God, man, the universe, life and the afterlife at great length. The only thing that is missing is a official and definitive belief on any of these subjects. The joke my uncles told contains a large amount of truth in it. In Judaism, there has always been substantial room for personal opinion on all of these matters, because Judaism is more concerned with actions than beliefs."

"That is why I have often said that the LDS faith is the icing on the cake (base) of Judaism. I would not give up either. The addition of a living prophet in the LDS faith giving clear, concise principles and values to live by is essential in this Last Dispensation."

John replied, "Well said Michael. I agree, both religions have their place, not only in history, but in this Last Dispensation."

Chapter 35
Thank You King Follett
(Michael and John in Booth One)

Michael asked, "John, you have always said that the truth was very important to you. Is there a specific truth that you were talking about?"

John answered, "In the beginning, at age 14, I felt the need to get the full truth as to the purpose of life. I understood that the truth can make us free, but I wasn't sure even what that truth was. I just knew that I needed some very important knowledge that I was missing. This was necessary to move forward and make the best decisions for the challenges that life would present to me. This important knowledge was best expressed in a funeral sermon that Joseph Smith gave in Nauvoo for his friend King Follett. The passing of this good brother in an unfortunate accident provided the catalyst for one of the greatest sermons ever given. This sermon was given April 7, 1844, just two months before Joseph would be martyred. Some 20,000 people, mostly church members, were assembled to hear this amazing sermon."

"I felt like Joseph was talking to me when he said: 'There are very few beings in the world who understand rightly the character of God. The great majority of mankind do not comprehend anything, either that which is past, or that which is to come, as it respects their relationship to God.'"

"In this sermon Joseph Smith asked the following question; 'I want to ask this congregation, every man, woman and child, to answer the question in their own hearts, what kind of a being God is? Ask yourselves; turn your thoughts into your hearts, and say if any of you have seen, heard, or communed with Him? This is a question that may occupy your attention for a long time. I again repeat the question; what kind of being is God? The scriptures inform us that

'This is life eternal, that they might know thee the only true God, and Jesus Christ, whom thou hast sent.'" (John 17:3)

"Joseph continued, 'If any man does not know God, and inquires what kind of a being He is--if he will search diligently his own heart—if the declaration of Jesus and the apostles be true, he will realize that he has not eternal life; for there can be eternal life on no other principle.'"

John remarked, "Joseph was now addressing the heart of my own concern. He was about to reveal to all that were assembled the answer to the all-important questions that had troubled me for years. 'Who is God? What sort of being was He in the beginning? What is He like now and where did He come from?'"

"Joseph said, 'God Himself was once as we are now, and is an exalted man, and sits enthroned in yonder heavens! That is the great secret. If the veil were rent today, and the great God who holds this world in its orbit, and who upholds all worlds and all things by His power, was to make Himself visible—I say, if you were to see Him today, you would see Him like a man in form—like yourselves in all the person, image, and very form as a man; for Adam was created in the very fashion, image and likeness of God, and received instruction from, and walked, talked and conversed with Him, as one man talks and communes with another.'"

"Joseph continued, 'In order to understand the subject of the dead, for consolation of those who mourn for the loss of their friends, it is necessary we should understand the character and being of God and how He came to be so; for I am going to tell you how God came to be God. We have imagined and suppose that God was God from all eternity. I will refute that idea, and take away the veil, so that you may see. These ideas are incomprehensible to some, but they are simple. It is the first principle of the gospel to know for a certainty the character of God, and to know that we may converse with Him as one man converses with another, and that He was once a man like us; yea, that God Himself, the Father of us all, dwelt on an earth, the same as Jesus Christ Himself did; and I will show it from the Bible.'"

"Joseph then said, 'Here, then, is eternal life---to know the only wise and true God; and you have got to learn how to be Gods yourselves, and to be kings and priests to God, the same as all Gods have done before you, namely, by going from one small capacity to a great one; from grace to grace, from exaltation to exaltation, until you attain to the resurrection of the dead, and are able to dwell in everlasting burnings, and to sit in glory, as do those who sit enthroned in everlasting power. And I want you to know that God, in the last days, while certain individuals are proclaiming His name, is not trifling with you or me.'"

Pausing, John explained, "Finally, this was the truth for which I was searching. To me this is the most empowering truth ever given. To know absolutely that I am a son of God and that I can grow up and become just like my Father in Heaven. To me, that is the truth that has made me free. Free to grow to my full potential and free from doubt as to what that potential is."

"Joseph Smith taught: 'It is the first principle of the gospel to know for a certainty the character of God. I want you all to know Him and to be familiar with Him. We must have a correct idea of his perfections, and attributes."

John continued, "What our Heavenly parents really are is exactly as Joseph Smith described them: A loving father and mother who reside in heaven; a glorified man and woman who has provided the way for us to become like He and She is, exalted and perfected. This great secret as to who God really is has been hidden for thousands of years and is now restored. It came with a price. Joseph Smith was killed for speaking this truth. The restored church was brutally persecuted and many great souls suffered to bring this knowledge to us and we now have the full truth."

"How grateful I am to live in a period of history when this revealed truth pushes back the darkness of the centuries with its pure light. A modern prophet of God, Lorenzo Snow, said it simply, 'As man is, God once was and as God is, man may become.'"

Chapter 36
The Scattering and Gathering of Israel
(John's Home)

John and Nanci's new home backed up to the beautifully-groomed 7th Tee on a golf course in Mesa, Arizona. John and Michael were on the back patio relaxing and sipping a refreshing drink by the pool.

Michael and John on John's Back Patio
Photo by Rebekah Baird

John remarked, "Michael, I can't thank you enough for helping Nanci and I purchase this home. Your skill as a real estate broker made it happen. You have remarkable insight for negotiating business deals."

Michael looked around and replied, "Thanks, John, I think that this is a beautiful and uniquely designed home. I'm glad that I could help you get it.

Michael said, "I wanted to talk to you about something. Maybe it's because I'm new to the Church, but sometimes I get overwhelmed with so much new information."

John replied, "I know what you mean. It can be overwhelming for someone who hasn't been exposed to our doctrine, to receive it as quickly as you have. It really takes a seasoned member to help a new convert to assimilate into this restored gospel culture. Let me explain it to you this way. Just like your Jewish faith, we believe prophets are God's way of speaking to His people. It is through the words of these prophets that we receive the word of God. This is a wonderful and yet intense method of restoring the truth. Prophets have always been necessary to correct the false doctrine that continues to fill the earth."

Michael said, "Ok, that makes perfect sense. With that in mind, explain the scattering and gathering of Israel through the words of the modern LDS Prophets, and I'll see if I can keep up?"

John replied, "Sure. The scattering of Israel begins with the Abrahamic covenant. God promised that all nations will be blessed by the descendants of Abraham. To accomplish this, there had to be a scattering of those descendants of Jacob/Israel to all the nations of the world."

"The scattering of Israel began in 721 B.C., when the Assyrians carried the Ten Tribes away into captivity. The scattering continued in 587 B.C., when the Babylonians carried Judah away into captivity. After the death of Jesus, the remaining Jews were scattered by the Romans among all of the Gentile nations from 66 - 70 A.D."

Michael remarked, "I know that God promised in the last days that He would gather Israel back again. From an LDS point of view, why is it important for Him to gather them?"

John answered, "You're right, God did promise that He would gather His children again. I think that Joseph Smith best explains the importance of God's promise. In March of 1844, just three months before his martyrdom, he spoke on this vital subject:"

"What was the object of gathering the …people of God in any age of the world? ….The main object was to build unto the Lord a house (Temple) whereby He could reveal unto His people the ordinances of His house and the glories of His kingdom, and teach the people the way of salvation; for there are certain ordinances and principles that, when they are taught and practiced, must be done in a place or house built for that purpose."   Joseph Smith

John continued, "In 1836 the members of the LDS Church completed the first Latter-day Temple in Kirtland, Ohio. God uses His temples to reveal the ordinances and teach the way to salvation. Joseph received several visions in the Kirtland Temple. One such manifestation was the appearance of Moses. Moses gave Joseph Smith the keys of the gathering of Israel from the four corners of the earth. Those symbolic keys gave Joseph Smith the priesthood authority to begin the gathering of Israel."

> 11 After this vision closed, the heavens were again opened unto us; and Moses appeared before us, and committed unto us the keys of the gathering of Israel from the four parts of the earth, and the leading of the ten tribes from the land of the north.
> D. & C. 110:11

"Michael, as you know, I have been an ordinance worker in the Mesa Arizona LDS Temple for over 9 years. During that time I have participated in hundreds of sacred ordinances. This has been a privilege and a blessing that words cannot describe. The sacredness and importance of these ordinances are very real."

"For me personally, I feel gathered when I attend the temple. In the temple we learn the things of eternity and receive ordinances of salvation for ourselves and our ancestors. The purpose of gathering is to be able to enter the holy temples, where we receive the sacred ordinances and make the associated covenants. By faithfully living those sacred covenants, we are endowed with the priesthood power to stand in the presence of, and become joint heirs with God."

"Let's take a look at modern revelation for a minute. Turn to section 84 in the Doctrine and Covenants, go to verse 20-22 and read those verses for me."

> Michael read:
> "20 Therefore, in the ordinances thereof, the power of godliness is manifest.
> 21 And without the ordinances thereof, and the authority of the priesthood, the power of godliness is not manifest unto men in the flesh;
> 22 For without this no man can see the face of God, even the Father, and live."   D. & C. 84:20-22

"That's the key to eternal joy," John explained. "The power of the priesthood is found in the ordinances including the sealing of families. For example, how joyful would I be in heaven without being sealed to my eternal companion? No matter how glorious heaven will be, if Nanci is not my wife forever, it will not be heaven to me. As God gathers His people back to him there must be temples for them to perform these ordinances. Now the LDS Church has over 150 temples. Let's continue on with Joseph's explanation:"

"…Ordinances instituted in the heavens before the foundation of the world, in the priesthood, for the salvation of men, are not to be altered or changed. All must be saved on the same principles."

"It is for the same purpose that God gathers together His people in the last days, to build unto the Lord a house to prepare them for the ordinances and endowments, washings and anointing......."

"..........Why gather the people together in this place? For the same purpose that Jesus wanted to gather the Jews—to receive the ordinances, the blessings, and the glories that God has in store for His Saints."   Joseph Smith

Western Wall of the Ancient Hebrew Temple in Jerusalem
Photo Courtesy of shwebook

Michael said, "The Jews have always loved God's Holy Temple in Jerusalem. Even today, they gather there to worship at the ancient wall of the Temple Mount. When Rome destroyed the Second Temple in 70 A.D., only one outer wall, the Western Wall, remained standing. No one knows why they didn't destroy that one remaining wall. The Western Wall isn't part of the original Temple, it is just part of the outer wall surrounding the Temple Mount."

"Even though it is an outer wall, this remnant of what was the most sacred building in the Jewish world quickly became the holiest spot in Jewish life. Throughout the centuries Jews from all over the world made the difficult pilgrimage to Palestine, and immediately headed for the the Western Wall to pray to God. The prayers offered at the wall were so heartfelt that gentiles began calling the site the "Wailing Wall." This undignified name never won a wide following among traditional Jews; the term "Wailing Wall" is not used in the Hebrew language."

"The Western Wall has been subjected to far worse than semantic indignities. During the more than one thousand years Jerusalem was under Muslim rule, the Arabs often used the Wall as a garbage dump, so as to humiliate the Jews who visited it."

"When the Wall was under Jordanian rule from 1948 to 1967, the Jordanian government signed an armistice agreement in 1949 allowing Jews the right to visit the Wall. The Jordanians never honored that agreement. This was yet another example of the persecution that Jews have endured."

"One of the first people to reach the Wall in the 1967 Six-Day War was Israeli Defense Minister Moshe Dayan. He revived a traditional Jewish custom by inserting a written petition into the cracks of the Wall. Later, it was revealed that Dayan's prayer was that a lasting peace 'descend upon the House of Israel.' The age old custom of inserting written prayers into the Wall's cracks was established once again."

John replied, "That is an incredible historical perspective of the Great Temple in Jerusalem."

"Yes," agreed Michael, we know that the Jews have been literally gathered to their homeland in Israel. When do you think the Jews will be spiritually gathered?"

"I don't know the exact time," John answered, "but Brigham Young, who was the second prophet of the Restored Church said it best:"

"By and by the Jews will be gathered to the land of their fathers, and the ten tribes, who wandered into the north, will be gathered home, and the blood of Ephraim, the second son of Joseph, who was sold into Egypt, which is to be found in every kingdom and nation under heaven, will be gathered from among the Gentiles, and the Gentiles who will receive and adhere to the principles of the Gospel will be adopted and initiated into the family of Father Abraham, and Jesus will reign over his own and Satan will reign over his own"

Brigham Young, Discourses of Brigham Young, 121–22

John continued, "I just love the way that Brigham Young says things so clearly. Let's see if I can be as clear with this thought. Lucifer's whole mission in life is to destroy marriages, families and

God's kingdom here on earth. The LDS Church has the antidote to Satan's poison. It's available in the Lord's Temples."

"Around the world, Mormons are universally known for emphasizing........STRONG FAMILIES! When active members of the Church attend the temple regularly, they draw on the power of the ordinances and personal revelation. These sacred ordinances and the spirit of revelation are preserved in purity in the Lord's holy houses. This in turn, helps the members preserve their marriages and families, which are the most valuable relationships in this life."

Michael agreed, "John, that sounds clear to me. I too believe in the importance of families. Let's bring this all up to date in modern times. What do you think a person would have to do to be gathered today?"

"Well, you and I know what it took for us to be gathered," John pointed out. "Let's consider how a modern day prophet would explain it;"

"Now, the gathering of Israel consists of joining the true church and their coming to a knowledge of the true God. ...Any person, therefore, who has accepted the restored gospel, and who now seek to worship the Lord in his own tongue and with the Saints in the nations where he lives, has complied with the law of the gathering of Israel and is heir to all the blessing promised the Saints in these last days."   The Teachings of Spencer W. Kimball, 438-39

John continued his explanation, "In the beginning of this modern day gathering, the saints were told to first come to Kirtland, Ohio to build a temple, then to Missouri, then to Nauvoo, Illinois and finally to the top of the mountains in Salt Lake City, Utah. As they tried to build a temple at each location, persecution forced them to move to a different place. Now, the saints are not being gathered to any one particular location to build a temple. Listen to this modern apostle and how he describes where and why the faithful saints will gather."

"With the creation of stakes and the construction of temples in most nations with sizable populations of the faithful, the current commandment is not to gather to one place but to gather in stakes in our own homelands. There the faithful can enjoy the full blessings of eternity in a house of the Lord. There, in their own homelands, they can obey the Lord's command to enlarge the borders of His people and strengthen her stakes. In this way the stakes of Zion are 'for defense, and for a refuge from the storm, and from wrath when it shall be poured out without mixture upon the whole earth.'" (D&C 115:6)

Elder Dallin H. Oaks - General Conference April 2004

After a brief pause, John asked, "So Michael, have you been able to keep up?"

"I believe so, John. I have always seen many similarities between the two religions. I'll need to read those quotes again to get the full meaning of what was said."

Chapter 37
Heavenly Recipe
(Michael and John in Booth One)

Michael and John met a couple of days later for lunch in Booth One.

"After thinking about the scattering of the Israelites," Michael reflected, "I feel like we may be missing something important. Let's go back to why the Twelve Tribes of Israel were scattered."

John replied, "There were basically two reasons why they were scattered. One is that they were wicked, not keeping their covenants, and were refusing to live the truth that was given to them. God then allowed their enemies to scatter them. The second, and I think the better reason, was that it was necessary for them to be scattered among all the nations like seedlings in the wind."

Suddenly John paused and said, "Seriously, Michael, focus all of your attention on this next thought. The Israelites had been so completely dispersed among all the nations that it gave them a place of great importance in the rise and development of almost every nation. It is the mixing of the tribes of Israel among the Gentiles by which the promises and great blessings that the Lord gave to Abraham are fulfilled. This could be likened to the leavening of the bread or the salt that gives the savor."

9 For, lo, I will command, and I will sift the house of Israel among all nations, like as *corn* is sifted in a sieve, yet shall not the least grain fall upon the earth.   Amos 9:9

Michael restated, "The tribes were scattered among all of the nations. I know from the Bible that Abraham was promised blessings through his seed being spread over the whole earth. When the tribes weren't faithful, Heavenly Father scattered the tribes because they didn't keep their covenants. Since the tribes were scattered, Satan must have thought that this was his opportunity to turn men's hearts against the Israelites and promote their persecution. Since the Israelites were divided, he wanted to conquer and exterminate them once and for all. Satan thought that he had foiled God's plan to save His children. I think that God was one step ahead of Satan in His protection of scattered Israel. He said to Father Abraham:"

> 3 And I will bless them that bless thee, and curse him that curseth thee: and in thee shall all families of the earth be blessed.
>
> Genesis 12:3

Continuing, Michael said, "We know that God also promised the following:

> 17 But Israel shall be saved in the LORD with an everlasting salvation: ye shall not be ashamed nor confounded world without end." Isaiah 45:17

"God protected Israel so that the spreading of Abraham's seed was a way to spread the concept of worshiping one God (monotheism) to influence every nation. Heavenly Father knew that His chosen people were a strong people and would survive under any circumstances. It is such an important concept that God trusted Israel to bring the understanding of worshiping one God to all nations. The Israelites became His secret ingredient in His recipe for the ultimate salvation of all of the people on earth!"

"Yes, a heavenly recipe!" John laughed. "Spoken like a baker's son!"

Michael suddenly realized part of the cause for Jewish persecution and said, "I now understand the reasoning for the persecution of the Jewish people. I always thought that the world was blaming the Jews for the death of Jesus, but that's not accurate. When Jesus, who was a Jew, walked the earth, his followers were

Jews and the Jewish people loved Him. The political climate of the time caused the Jewish leaders to conspire with the Romans to kill him."

Michael continued, "We know from scripture that the adversary, Satan, was an evil spirit being from the beginning."

8 He that committeth sin is of the devil; for the devil sinneth from the beginning. For this purpose the Son of God was manifested, that he might destroy the works of the devil.

1 John 3:8

Michael concluded, "He has always been an enemy to God and against everything that God wants to accomplish. Since the children of Israel are the secret ingredient in God's plan, then Satan will do everything in his power to destroy Israel. The real cause of the Jewish people being persecuted is now clear to me. If the world understood this truth, then perhaps the persecution of the Jews would end. This means that anyone bent on the destruction of the Jews and Israel is under the influence of Satan."

"Amen to that!," John interjected. "Michael, you have also just discovered why the Mormons were marked for extermination by an executive order of the Governor of Missouri. On October 27, 1838, Extermination Order #44 was issued against Mormons. This was an order given by our own government sanctioning mass removal or death! The term "extermination" is often associated with genocide. The Mormons however were able to flee to the safety of the Rocky Mountains to escape their extermination."

Michael replied, "Similar events happened to the Jews during World War II, when the holocaust was brought on by the Nazis in Germany. Unfortunately they had no way to flee, so over 6 million Jews were exterminated."

John stated, "Everyone should pause and ask themselves, **'Why were both the Jews and the Mormons marked for extermination**

by the leaders of their own governments?' There is an answer to this question. In your mind Michael, what is that answer?"

"I believe the answer is Satan," Michael responded. "Satan will do anything to stop God and His covenant people from doing their work."

"God's work in His own words are," John recited:

"39 For behold, this is my work and my glory---to bring to pass the immortality and eternal life of man."

Moses 1:39 Pearl of Great Price

"Satan is trying desperately to stop God's work, but he will fail in the end," John explained. "Satan tries continually to convince this world that he doesn't exist. He does exist and is the destroyer of all that is good. He is acting like he is the ruler of this world, which explains why the Bible warns that due to his evil influence, every nation will turn against Israel in the last days to destroy it."

Michael replied, "This explains why the world is in such a mess. Let's not forget that for the faithful, Satan is close, but God is closer."

"Satan's days are numbered," John smiled. It's all going to change when the Savior returns. Remember, when Satan tries to remind you of your past, you just remind him of his future..........he doesn't have one!"

Chapter 38
I Am Home
(John's Office)

Michael and John met at John's office. They had finally gotten to one of their last discussions of the final chapters. They followed the same routine that they had always followed when meeting at John's office.

Their routine consisted of meeting early in the morning, before John's business opened, go into John's office and close the door. They would then get down on their knees to pray. They each took a turn giving a prayer, one after the other. As each man took his turn, he first prayed how grateful he was for all that Heavenly Father had given him. Then, he prayed for guidance from the Spirit to put the right words on paper that would be pleasing to God and inspiring to their fellow man.

Then they would sit on John's Italian leather couch. Michael would be on the laptop editing, and John would be reading the different chapters out loud from copies that had been printed.

That day, Michael said, "John, I have something to tell you."

"Lay it on me, baby." (John often said that)

Michael explained, "I want to tell you something that I've never told anyone. It's about the writing on the canyon wall that I saw when I was here on the business trip back in November of 2012. I saw the words, 'I AM HOME', written on the face of the canyon wall. I have thought and prayed about it many times. I have asked God, 'What did it mean? Could it mean more than just a message from God saying that I was supposed to move to Mesa? I think that 'I AM HOME' means much more than what I first thought it meant."

"What does it mean, Michael?"

Michael answered, "When I saw it written on the canyon wall, I didn't fully understand the concept that we are all spiritual beings that have left a heavenly home to have an earthly experience. What we are meant to learn from this experience in mortality is how to return home to our Heavenly parents to live with them once again. From what I have learned, I now know that Heavenly Father was showing me a much deeper concept in the written words, 'I AM HOME'. He was showing me how important it was to learn how to come home to my Heavenly Mother and Father and all those who knew me as a spirit being. 'I AM HOME' was his way of telling me that being with God is home."

"It doesn't matter whether you are in New York, L.A., Mesa or Jerusalem. Wherever you are in the world, we can become more like God by bringing His love to all of our fellow men. I think that 'I AM HOME' was His way of telling me that He is where home is for each one of us. On this magnificent journey that we are on, we must develop within each of us the character of God, so that when we meet our Heavenly parents again, we will be like them."

John didn't say anything for a moment. "Michael that is one of the most profound things that I have ever heard you say."

Michael and John sat there for a few minutes, thinking about what Michael had just revealed.

I AM (John's Office)

After a few minutes of silence, John reflected, "It is amazing that you would say that. It was just a few months ago that I was questioning the very words, 'I AM'. Did you know that 'THE GREAT I AM' is referring to Jesus Christ?"

Michael had a stunned look on his face. He then said, "John, I always thought that 'THE GREAT I AM' was Heavenly Father."

John explained, "That is the same misunderstanding that I grew up with. We both didn't understand this concept from what we were taught when we were young. I was a Protestant and you were a Jew and we didn't know that 'THE GREAT I AM' was Jesus Christ."

"Christ is a Greek word and Messiah is a Hebrew word. Together they mean 'the anointed.' Jesus Christ is the Firstborn of the Father in the spirit. He is the Only Begotten of the Father in the flesh. He is Jehovah, the God of the Old Testament, 'THE GREAT I AM,' and was foreordained to his great calling before the creation of the world."

"Under the direction of the Father, Jesus created the earth and everything on it. He was born to Mary at Bethlehem, lived a sinless life, and made a perfect atonement for the sins of all mankind by shedding of his blood and giving his life on the cross. He rose from the dead, thus assuring the eventual resurrection of all mankind. Through Jesus' atonement and resurrection, those who repent of their sins and obey God's commandments, can live eternally and experience a fullness of joy."

"When Moses asked God in Exodus 3:13-14, "Behold, when I come unto the children of Israel, and shall say unto them, 'The God of your fathers hath sent me unto you'; and they shall say to me, what is His name? What Shall I say unto them? And God said unto Moses, 'I AM THAT I AM': and He said, Thus shalt thou say unto the children of Israel, 'I AM hath sent me unto you'.""

John continued, "I always wondered why the Lord referred to Himself as 'I AM'. After I read that passage in Exodus, I prayed about it and asked why. I was impressed to look up all the name-titles given to Him. After doing this, I knew why He is THE GREAT I AM. Those two words, I AM, is an all-inclusive name to describe all that He is. Michael, I suggest that you read these name-titles for Jesus Christ and add 'I AM' in front of each one. Imagine that Christ is introducing Himself to you. As you do this, I believe your heart will fill with a deep feeling of reverential respect and gratitude for this sinless, perfect God. He came to earth to save all that would believe in Him and He called Himself, I AM. Ponder the following titles:"

I AM:
Emmanuel;
The prophet;
Wonderful, Counselor, the mighty God;

The Everlasting Father;
The Prince of Peace;
The Stem of Jesse;
The Mighty One of Jacob;
The Messenger of the Covenant;
The Redeemer;
The Holy One;
The Holy One of Israel;
Blessed of God;
The son of David;
The son of Abraham;
The Son of Mary;
Joseph's son;
The carpenter's son;
Jesus of Galilee;
Jesus of Nazareth;
The beloved Son of God;
The Son of the living God;
The Son of the Most High;
Son of the Highest;
God's only son;
God's Holy Child;
One with the Father;
The Christ of God;
The chosen of God;
God's anointed;
The Lamb of God;
A teacher come from God;
The anointed one;
The Messiah;
The firstborn of the Father in the spirit;
The Only Begotten of the Father in the flesh;
Jehovah of the Old Testament;
The greatest being ever to be born on earth;

The perfect example;
The Lord of Lords;
The King of Kings;
The Creator;
The God of the whole earth;
The Captain of our Salvation;
The Bright and morning Star;
In all things, above all things, through all things, round about all things;
Alpha and Omega;
The First and the Last;
The only name by which we can be saved;
The name that is above all other names;
The Truth;
The Life;
The Light;
The Way;
King of the Jews;
Living water;
The Governor that shall rule Israel;
King of Israel;
Savior of Israel;
Savior of the world;
The Lord;
Lord of the Sabbath;
A Rabbi;
The light;
The Bread of Life;
The Good Shepherd;
The Resurrection and the life;
The way, the truth, the life;
The true vine;
The Holy One;
The Just One;

The Prince of Life;
The Judge of quick and dead;
A righteous man (by the Centurion);
Lord of both the dead and living;
The wisdom of God;
The Advocate with the Father;
The Lion of the tribe of Judah;
The word of God;
The Almighty.

"Michael, to this amazing list you have added one more name title that means everything to both of us: 'I AM HOME'. When you saw those words on the canyon wall, when you first arrived in Arizona, you thought that God was telling you that Arizona would be your new home. As time went on, you came to understand that those words have a deeper meaning. You discovered that Jesus Christ, 'THE GREAT I AM', is the only way back home. You came to know that home is where our earthly and heavenly parents wait to greet us. A celestial home awaits us and it's filled with family, friends and eternal joy."

"Don't we all want to go home? We do, and now we both have discovered the way."

Michael asked, "Do you think the Lord would mind if we added this new name-title to this long list?"

"I don't think He would mind," answered John. "I AM HOME is such a beautiful and meaningful name-title. He has shown us the way home. We are on the path homeward bound. To be honest, in this troubled world, I've always been a little homesick. I think you have been as well, because when things went sideways, you didn't think that you had a specific purpose in life. In fact, you almost tried to send yourself home the wrong way."

Photo by Rebekah Baird

Michael concluded, "We now know how to return home the right way, and that truth has made us free to accomplish that goal. So before that time comes, we are free to live this life to its fullest. We are free to overcome sin, because we now know what it is, and the consequences it brings. We can now recognize sin, stripped from its many disguises. We are free to recognize all evil sooner and flee from it quicker. We are free to reach our full potential as sons of God. We have been given the truth and the truth has made us free."

"One of the amazing modern LDS Prophets, Wilford Woodruff came to the same conclusion about returning home to God and stated it simply:

'I HAVE FOUND THE KINGDOM OF GOD, AND IN IT I WILL LIVE, AND IN IT I WILL DIE.'"

Chapter 39
Friendship
(John's Office)

"Who finds a friend, finds a treasure."

Jewish Proverb

"Friends who share a common commitment, share a common destiny."

John and Michael Proverb

Michael

I first met John a couple of months after I moved to Mesa, Arizona. We bonded instantly because we had a similar sense of humor. At first, I was impressed by his business acumen. He had struggled in his business for many years before success came, never giving up and always moving forward. By the time that I met him, he was a successful business man. This was impressive to me, as I had always measured people by their material wealth.

As my heart started to change with the knowledge of the truth about eternal life and the Church, my paradigm shifted. I was no longer impressed by material things and money. I was drawn to people that held a deeper reverence for the real purpose of life. Suddenly, I realized that my new found friend had an inner strength of spiritual purpose like I had never seen before. We had originally bonded over a similar sense of humor. As time went on, that original bonding turned into deeper and more spiritual discussions.

I often felt that the information that I was receiving was coming to me so fast and furious that it was like drinking from a fire hose. John's knowledge of scripture would always help me to put my thoughts and personal revelations into context. Even though I was going through a time of extreme growth and change, I could always count on John for the right explanation and an understanding of what I was going through.

John never criticized me and always had an open mind. He took an incredible amount of time from his busy schedule to counsel with me through my amazing journey of discovery. How many of us are lucky enough to have a true best friend? I know that I am a very lucky person. John, I will be forever grateful.

John

From the first time I met Michael, I sensed that this was a unique individual and someone that I needed to get to know better. As our friendship grew and we decided to co-write this book, something remarkable transpired.

As we spent dozens of hours over several months together working on this book, we both sensed that we were in the presence of the Spirit of God. It was the Spirit that would direct our progress, bring beautiful insights to our experiences and always leave us with the most uplifting and wonderful feelings. This happened every time we met to write and was so real that we always looked forward to our next meeting.

In the end, what did I take away from this amazing experience? First and foremost, was a deep respect for Michael. During this entire effort, Michael always expressed the deepest respect for his Jewish heritage. He has never diminished the teaching or traditions of his Jewish forbearers, but instead has honored it all and joyfully added to it. He has had the wisdom to appreciate what he was given in his youth and then show the courage to move forward and embrace the new truth that God was giving him. He is a sterling example of following the principle that it's never too late to change your direction in life. He has faithfully followed in the footsteps of his ancient ancestor Abraham. A quote from the Book of Abraham comes to mind:

2 And, finding there was greater happiness and peace and rest for me, I sought for the blessings of the fathers, and the right whereunto I should be ordained to administer the same; having been myself a follower of righteousness, desiring also to be one that possessed great knowledge and to be a greater follower of righteousness, and to possess a greater knowledge…"

Pearl of Great Price: Book of Abraham 1:2

My Will Is God's Will Forever

"Michael, you have followed the example of Abraham and are a forerunner to what Jesus said about the children of Israel receiving the truth of personal salvation first and then they will receive that same truth last:

16 So the last shall be first, and the first last: for many be called, but few chosen."   Matthew 20:16

John continued, "You have proved to be a pioneer in your own right. I thought of you when I read excerpts from President Monson's message."

"To be a Latter-day Saint is to be a pioneer, for the definition of a pioneer is "one who goes before to prepare or open up the way for others to follow." And to be a pioneer is to become acquainted with sacrifice. Although members of the Church are no longer asked to leave their homes to make the journey to Zion, they often must leave behind old habits, longtime customs, and cherished friends. Some make the agonizing decision to leave behind family members who oppose their Church membership. Latter-day Saints move forward, however, praying that precious ones will yet understand and accept."

"The path of a pioneer is not easy, but we follow in the footsteps of the ultimate Pioneer—even the Savior—who went before, showing us the way to follow."

"Come, follow me," He invited.

"I am the way, the truth, and the life," He declared.

"Come unto me," He called.

"The way can be trying. Some find it difficult to withstand the mocking and unsavory remarks of foolish ones who ridicule chastity, honesty, and obedience to God's commands. The world has ever belittled adherence to principle. When Noah was instructed to build an ark, the foolish populace looked at the cloudless sky and then scoffed and jeered—until the rain came."

President Thomas S. Monson
'True To The Faith Of Our Forefathers'
Ensign July 2016

Michael continued, "We named this book, **'Gathering Israel'** because our stories are about us being personally gathered. We are part of the latter-day gathering of Israel that is foretold in the Old Testament, New Testament and the Book of Mormon. We have a Heavenly Father that is a perfect loving parent. He loves all of His children the same, no matter who they are. Our patriarchal blessings revealed that we are each of different tribes of Israel, Ephraim and Judah, but both of us are sons of the same God."

John agreed, "You are exactly right, we are all sons and daughters of Heavenly Father. God's prophets have predicted this gathering all through the centuries. For me, being gathered is following Christ, keeping the Lord's commandments, and having a daily relentless desire for righteousness. I can't think of a better way to live my life. I thank God that I have been gathered."

Michael concluded, "I agree. I know now that my will is God's will forever."

About The Authors

    Michael Morton is a convert to the Church of Jesus Christ of Latter-day Saints. Converting from Judaism, he was baptized on his birthday in April of 2013. His journey to the Church began on a business trip to Mesa, Arizona from his home in Denver, Colorado in November 2012. While visiting the Gilbert Temple construction site, he was given a copy of the Book of Mormon. As he held the sacred book in his hands, the Spirit spoke to him and told him, "The book is true."

    Michael then received and followed specific promptings from the Holy Spirit to immediately leave his home and move to Mesa, Arizona. Sacrificing everything, he moved in just 60 days and started his journey of conversion.

    Since April 2013, Michael has given his unwavering testimony at many firesides and family home evenings. He brings a unique perspective to each and every talk he gives on the similarities between Judaism and the LDS Church. Michael has published a book with coauthor John Wudel about their unique experiences on their compelling journeys to the Mormon faith.

    Michael is the father of two children and currently resides in Mesa, Arizona.

John Wudel joined the LDS Church at age 19 while attending Brigham Young University. John spent 10 years in the Church Education System (CES), teaching seminary full time in six different high schools. He also taught and directed institutes of religion in three different colleges and universities.

A food chemist by trade, John not only holds a chemistry degree, but also taught qualitative analysis at the university level. His expertise at engineering food formulas has resulted in specialty formulations throughout the United States and globally. His company, Wudel International, won the Excellence in Exporting Award in 2015. The "E Award" is the highest award the United States government gives to its top exporters. Wudel International won this award for its outstanding exporting to 92 countries.

John's love for the truth, both in science and religion, has led him to this written testimony of deep gratitude for the gift of the Gospel that he has received. He has published a book with coauthor Michael Morton about their unique experiences on their compelling journeys to the Mormon faith.

John is the father of four children and the grandfather of sixteen grandchildren. He currently resides with his eternal companion, Nanci, in Mesa, Arizona.

Submit Your Own Special Conversion Story

We are looking for stories that represent each of the Twelve Tribes of Israel from converts that have been gathered to the Church of Jesus Christ of Latter-day Saints.

Feel free to send us a summary of your personal story of the miracle of how you were gathered to the Gospel of Jesus Christ. If you so choose, you may include your lineage.

We will treat each story with the reverence and confidentiality that it deserves. If we decide to include your story in a future book, we will be in contact with you to gain your permission and work out the details. We are thrilled to be offering this opportunity to share these stories with the world. All Twelve Tribes of Israel need to be represented and we anxiously await your submission.

Some of the most important work going on in the world today is the effort being put forth for the gathering of Israel. The Lord's work is most exemplified in the miracle of conversion. We believe in these miracles and think the world should have a chance to hear them.

The Twelve Tribes of Israel: Reuben, Simeon, Judah, Issachar, Zebulun, Benjamin, Dan, Naphtali, Gad, Asher, Ephraim and Manasseh.

Respectfully,
Michael Morton and John Wudel

Submit Your Own Special Conversion Story
at www.GatheringIsrael.com/Submit-Your-Story/